Gender Stories

Negotiating Identity in a Binary World

Sonja K. Foss

Mary E. Domenico

Karen A. Foss

WAVELAND
PRESS, INC.

Long Grove, Illinois

For information about this book, contact:
  Waveland Press, Inc.
  4180 IL Route 83, Suite 101
  Long Grove, IL 60047-9580
  (847) 634-0081
  info@waveland.com
  www.waveland.com

CONTENTS

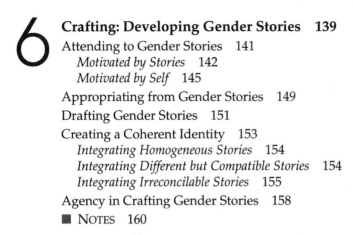

The Next Chapter: Constructing Gendered Worlds   235

ACKNOWLEDGMENTS

This book is the confluence of many stories from different people. The immediate project benefited greatly from the assistance of a number of colleagues and friends, including Gordana Lazić, who provided valuable general research assistance. Daniel Aid, Rebecca Gilbert, Gavin Leach, Jennifer Cunningham Logan, Brian L. Ott, David Proper, and Alexis Pulos identified artifacts and provided insightful analyses.

Kristen L. Cole, Laura K. Hahn, Stacey Overholt, Catherine Egley Waggoner, and e. j. Yoder distributed surveys about gender to their university classes. These surveys were invaluable in helping us understand the contemporary gender landscape. Thanks, too, to all the students across the United States who took the time to complete these surveys. Your frank and thoughtful words provide texture and depth to the book. We also wish to thank the students in Sonja's Gender and Communication class at the University of Colorado Denver in spring 2007, where she tested some of the ideas that became central to our conceptualization of gender.

We are especially grateful to Katherine Aid, Jane Caputi, Victoria Chen, and Sarah Nicolazzo for reading earlier drafts of the manuscript. Your comments made this a better book, and your encouragement affirmed our direction. We also appreciate the assistance of Kristen L. Cole, Alexis Pulos, M. Rosie Russo, and Casey Wopat with the instructor's manual. The pedagogical creativity you displayed will be useful to everyone who uses this book to teach courses on gender.

As always, we are indebted to our publishers, Neil Rowe and Carol Rowe, for their patience and unwavering trust in our vision. Finally, our heartfelt thanks to Anthony J. Radich, Howard M. Haenel, and Stephen W. Littlejohn for showing us how varied and creative gender stories can be and for sustaining us through our work with food, laughter, and love.

one

GENDER STORIES
AN INTRODUCTION

We are all storytellers, and we are the stories we tell.
Dan P. McAdams, Ruthellen Josselson, & Amia Lieblich, *Identity and Story*

Once upon a time, the story of gender seemed to have a predictable and universal plot line. The story began with the physical union of a woman and a man, the sharing of warmth and fluids, and the fateful meeting of an egg and a sperm. Chromosomes paired up—XX or XY—and nine months later, a girl or a boy was born. Girl infants, swaddled in pink blankets, were taken home to pink rooms with ruffled curtains and mobiles of unicorns and rainbows. Boys, swaddled in blue, were taken home to blue rooms with plaid curtains and mobiles of dinosaurs and spaceships. Girls played with dolls, miniature dish sets, and pretend makeup. Boys played with action figures, miniature cars, and pretend power tools. Prom night was a foreshadowing of the marriage to come—the young woman lovely in her floor-length gown, the young man handsome in his tux. If years of parental attention and socialization went as planned, girls and boys became young women and young men poised for the future mating of more eggs and more sperm.

Today, in addition to the classic story—which was never as uniform as it seemed—gender has developed multiple and intriguing plot lines. Parents buy dolls for boys and trucks for girls. Not only do girls play soccer and boys wear earrings, but young women also take other young women

1

to the prom and young men marry each other. Men are giving birth to babies, as Thomas Beatie, a transgender man, did in 2008. Beatie, who was born female, had his breasts surgically removed, underwent hormone therapy, legally changed his name, and married a woman. When the couple wanted a baby, Beatie was impregnated with donated sperm.[1] Some babies now have no gender. In 2011, the parents of a baby born on New Year's Day in Toronto, Canada, decided to keep the infant's gender a secret because they don't want their child to be restricted by conventional categories of gender.[2] Males and females switching roles, a father bearing a child, and a genderless baby are stories that make this a dynamic, exciting, and sometimes bewildering time in which to study gender.

You have probably seen Lady Gaga's video *Born This Way* or episodes of *Glee, South Park,* and *Family Guy* with gender-bending themes, but you don't need the media to appreciate the contemporary gender landscape. As a college student, you are surrounded by a multitude of different gender presentations—jocks and fashionistas, men with long hair and flowing scarves, and women with tattoos who ride Harleys. You can't make assumptions about people's sexuality from how they look. The most femme woman you know—she wears high heels, a push-up bra, and red lipstick—may identify as lesbian. The forward on your lacrosse team—a tall, muscular, hairy, and aggressive man—may have a boyfriend or a girlfriend. Regardless of what you think about gender and gender roles, your own experience shows you that there are many gender stories with many different plot lines being lived all around you.

As you listen to your classmates tell their gender stories, you will hear even more versions of life as a gendered person. You will hear the ways that people enjoy and appreciate their gendered selves as well as the tensions that arise personally and socially from feeling pressured to conform to certain norms of gender identity and expression. In contrast to the simplified dominant system of female/feminine and male/masculine, you will hear a rich and illuminating variety of personal stories about how people manage the lifelong process of negotiating their genders. These stories portray how various people have adopted, modified, or even rejected the dominant system of gender.

This book is designed to engage you in an extended conversation about such gender stories. Stories might feel like a strange way to embark on a field of study because the common understanding of *story* is that of a fiction—an invented narrative. We have based this book on stories because we believe that engaging with stories provides a unique opportunity for understanding gendered life. Stories are a primary means by which people understand one another's belief systems and ways of living. While theories can be dismissed as illogical, unscientific, or immoral, personal stories cannot be discounted so easily, even when they tell stories about people and relationships that are unfamiliar, uncomfortable, or confusing. Listening to one another's stories requires a different kind of engagement than listening to other kinds of information. Hearing the details of someone's life story not only introduces you to new ideas and possibilities but allows you a glimpse into someone else's reality. Stories have the power to make you experience a "vividly felt insight" into the lives of other people.[3]

From your earliest encounters with nursery stories, you have become accustomed to listening to and trying to comprehend the different meanings people make of their lives. When you read *Harry Potter,* see *The Phantom of the Opera,* or watch a movie like *Dark Shadows,* you enter other people's worlds and are able to appreciate their experiences. In the same way, engaging with different gender stories can help you see and appreciate different perspectives on gender. We believe this kind of insight can lead to a better understanding of yourself and others and, by enhancing your knowledge about gender, can allow you to make more informed choices in your life.

In the rest of this chapter, we explain how we are using the terms *gender, story, identity, binary,* and *agency*—key terms that will help you understand some of the complexities and challenges involved in discussing gender stories. We share our perspective on this book and explain how our approach to teaching gender differs from other approaches. We also suggest ways for you to approach the rest of the book.

GENDER

Before taking a gender studies course, you may not have had the opportunity to analyze your own beliefs and feelings about gender, and you may be unaware of some of your own assumptions and biases. When you read the following debates about and ways of conceptualizing gender, try to determine which attitudes and definitions ground your own perspectives. We believe that becoming conscious of your own perspectives is a fruitful way for you to begin your engagement with this book. As you engage further, you will have the opportunity to reflect on your current understanding of gender, express your own views about gendered life, and learn from the perspectives of others.

CHALLENGES

Discussions about gender can be challenging for a number of reasons. The most basic reason is the nature of symbols and their relationship to human communication. Humans communicate by using symbols to create and convey meanings. Words and images such as advertising slogans and the logos that represent products might be the first kinds of symbols that come to mind, but virtually everything can function as a symbol that conveys meanings. Some symbols have commonly accepted meanings—a foot-high purple Mohawk signals "punk," for example, and a suit and tie signal "executive"—but other symbols, like *gender*, are often more ambiguous. *Gender* can refer to any of the ways humans are differentiated into categories. *Male* and *female, gay* and *straight*, and *masculine* and *feminine* are among the categories commonly associated with gender. Think about all of the meanings associated with these pairs of words—the variety makes misunderstandings likely.

Discussions about gender are also complicated by whether people understand the concept as static or evolving. People who stress the constant nature of gender point out that, despite variations across cultures and throughout historical time, there have been consistent trends of social attitudes and behaviors regarding gender. Men have predominately occupied the social roles of civic and religious leaders, have been primary wage earners, and have been considered the heads of their families. Women have assumed primary domestic roles as wives, mothers, and caretakers. People who view gender as enduring often do not believe that gender categories and roles and how they are valued can or should change.

Other people emphasize the opposite idea about gender. Across cultures and throughout history, they assert, notions of gender have changed dramatically. People who view gender as evolving point to how women in the twenty-first century are quarterbacks and CEOs, and men are househusbands and flight attendants. Another point made by people who view gender as a changeable concept is that genders that were recognized in the past—like spinster and invert—have mostly disappeared, while genders that have not been historically recognized—like transgender and queer—are now part of social discourse. People who see gender as evolving welcome multiple gender categories as intriguing possibilities and may even see no need for gender categories at all.

A third complicating factor in discussions about gender is that each perspective on gender contains assumptions about human life and attempts to prescribe how gendered life *should* be lived. In other words, beliefs about gender have political, social, and moral ramifications. Some people see gender as a secular issue of equal rights; others view gender as under the authority of religious beliefs. This conflict surfaces, for example, in discussions about gay marriage. Religious people who believe that intimate relationships should involve a man and a woman may have difficulty communicating with people who believe gay men and lesbian women should have the same legal rights to marriage as straight people. When people hold strong views that are seemingly irreconcilable, productive conversation is often impossible.

Consider the following perspective:

> I'm what's called a transsexual person. This means I was assigned one gender at birth, and I now live my life as something else. I was born male and raised as a boy. I went through both boyhood and adult manhood, went through a gender change, and "became a woman." A few years later, I stopped being a woman and settled into being neither. . . . I think what I've found is a pretty interesting hole in the theory that there's actually such a thing as a real man or a real woman.[4]

This view is offered by Kate Bornstein in *My Gender Workbook*. Bornstein is a performance artist and gender theorist who hosts an online blog for lesbian, gay, bisexual, transgender, and queer (LGBTQ) teenagers. Bornstein's blog addresses the condemnation and violence that LGBTQ teens receive from other people and offers hope and alternatives to young people who are considering suicide.

Joseph Nicolosi offers a different perspective:

> We cannot go along with people who . . . say that each of us can "be whatever we want to be," in terms of gender identity or sexual orientation. They speak as if being gay or lesbian did not have the deepest consequences for us as individuals, for our culture, and for the human race. They speak as if our anatomy were in no way our destiny. They imply that when we help our children to grow more fully into the maleness or femaleness that is their created destiny, we are merely perpetuating outdated gender stereotypes. But the human race was designed male and female; there is no third gender.[5]

Nicolosi is a psychologist and president of the National Association of Research & Therapy of Homosexuality. He provides therapy to parents who are concerned about the development of their child's gender and to men who want to diminish unwanted homosexuality and develop heterosexual potential instead.

In these passages, Bornstein and Nicolosi express conflicting views of gender. Bornstein says there is no such thing as a real man or a real woman and that people can be male, female, another gender, or no gender. Nicolosi says there are only real men and real women because the human race was designed with two distinct genders. These views are irreconcilable, but they make sense to two real people because of their different experiences with gender. Such vastly different perspectives can make any conversation about gender very difficult.

The ambiguity and multiple meanings of the term *gender*, different views on the static or changing nature of gender, prescriptions for gender, and life experiences can make conversations about gender confrontational and challenging. While public and academic discourses often take the position that someone must be right and someone wrong, we approach the challenge of different ideas with the assumption that each person has an experience of and a position on gender that are worth listening to and worthy of respect. We believe that each individual voice has the potential to make an important contribution to a larger, ongoing conversation about gender. Listening to a multitude of voices provides a basis for understanding how actual people experience themselves and make meaning of their lives.

CONCEPTUALIZATIONS OF GENDER

Because gender is such a complicated and potentially confusing concept, we begin by reviewing different ways that *gender* has been conceptualized so that you understand how we are using the term. Gender scholars have adopted conceptualizations that treat (1) gender as equivalent to sex; (2) gender as separate from sex; and (3) gender as the assignment of meaning to bodies.

GENDER AS EQUIVALENT TO SEX

One conceptualization of the term *gender* is grounded in biology and the physiological characteristics a person possesses. This view makes no distinction between *gender* and *sex* and often draws on examples from the animal kingdom as models for human sexuality and gender roles.[6] Because this perspective rests on the assumption that there are two biological sexes—female and male—there are also two genders—feminine and masculine. This means that who you are and who you can become are determined by the anatomy and physiology of your body. A view of gender as sex also assumes that the only valid expression of sexuality—desire for another person and intimate acts—takes place between a man and a woman.

Because gender is rooted in biological characteristics in this perspective, femaleness and maleness are seen as essences that are constant and unchanging across cultures, geographical locations, and historical time periods. In women and in men, inborn drives and physiology are said to explain desires and behaviors. A woman wants children and has the primary role in caring for them because she has a maternal instinct and a vagina, ovaries, breasts, and certain hormones such as estrogen. A man is stronger than a woman, more competitive, and dominant socially because he is innately aggressive and has a penis, testicles, and certain hormones such as testosterone. The view of gender as equivalent to sex is evoked in statements like, "Women are naturally nurturing" and "Men can't help being aggressive."

GENDER AS SEPARATE FROM SEX

Another way of conceptualizing gender and sex contrasts the two terms. In this perspective, *sex* is your body, including your physical attributes, hormonal characteristics, and reproductive functioning. *Gender* is defined as the roles, behaviors, and personality traits you acquire as a result of socialization. *Sex* is what you are born with, and *gender* is what you become through interacting with other people.[7] For most of you, this means you were either born with a penis, testicles, and XY chromosomes, or you were born with a vagina, uterus, ovaries, and XX chromosomes. Subsequently, you were assigned a gender based on your sex. In other words, you were born and have remained one of two sexes—female or male—and you have become a gender—feminine or masculine—as the result of how you were raised and the influences of your family, the media, schools, churches, and other social institutions. While *sex* is determined by your body, *gender* develops according to your unique social interactions in your culture.

When gender is conceptualized as separate from sex, there are many ways to become feminine or masculine because there is no precise correlation among sex, sexual orientation or preference, and gender. A person can be born female or male and acquire feminine, masculine, or a combination of gender characteristics. Separating sex from gender provides a way to explain that femininity includes a wide range of appearances, behaviors, and social positions—from a Catholic nun to a roller-derby queen to the white-gowned woman on the cover of *Bride* magazine. Likewise, masculinity can account for a male ballet dancer, a business executive, and a football player. People can be male or female and express their sexuality in a number of ways—as gay, straight, lesbian, bisexual, asexual, queer, and/or some combination. Separating sex from gender also provides a way to describe transgender persons as people whose sex—male female—does not align with their gender—masculine, feminine, androgynous, or genderqueer.

GENDER AS THE ASSIGNMENT OF MEANING TO BODIES

A third way to conceptualize gender—and the one we adopt in this book—considers gender as the assignment of meaning to bodies. This view considers *gender* to be socially constructed and to include what, in the two former perspectives, is called *sex*. We elaborate on social construction in chapter 2, but, for now, the simple explanation is that socially constructed behavior is not an inborn part of a person. Socially constructed gender means that the system of categorizing your anatomy and designating you as either female or male is not biologically determined. Rather, the naming of your body as one type or another is only possible and made meaningful due to culture. That culture can guide or shape the meaning of a penis or vagina may seem counterintuitive to you, but, in fact, politics, religion, and other cultural factors have always given meaning to these basic terms. To say that gender and sex are socially constructed means that bodies, in and of themselves, do not determine what is meant by sexual difference or sameness. Culture, through human interaction, determines what is meant not only by *boy, girl, man*, and *woman* but by words like *penis, vagina, testosterone*, and *estrogen*.

When we say that gender is the assignment of meaning to bodies, we are addressing the process by which people categorize and label—socially construct—people as gendered individuals. This definition includes various terms that people use to identify themselves and others (for example, *male, female, queer, androgynous, lesbian, gay*, and *straight*). There are no definitive correlations among bodies, sexual orientations, and social roles; they are all socially constructed. You can be male and have any kind of body; you can be female and have any kind of body. You can be male and have any kind of gender; you can be female and have any kind of gender. Likewise, any kind of body can experience sexual desire for any other body.

Like the conceptualization of gender as sex above, our conceptualization does not separate the concepts of sex and gender, but our rationale is very different. In the above conceptualization, to see gender as equivalent to sex means that your anatomy determines both sex and gender. We see sex not as the label (*male* or *female*) given to a body but as the sexual act— "doing it, any way ya do it," alone or with other people.[8] Sex, then, may include masturbation and the sexual activities in which you engage with other people, but sex is only one of many aspects of gender. Sex does not mean the designation of a category that defines you.

Our conceptualization treats gender as the entire person—biological, psychological, sexual, emotional, and interactional. *Gender* takes into account not only your body and sexual orientation but also your race, class, nationality, education, religious beliefs, and personality traits. These additional attributes cannot be separated from how you self-identify as a gendered person or present your gender to other people. Anthropologist Marianne Gullestad uses the term *partcultures* to describe how, in contemporary life, most people belong to multiple identity groups.[9] The various ways you describe yourself—Catholic, heterosexual, and middle class, for example—derive from different partcultures or subcultures with different sets of behaviors and social practices. These flow into each other, contributing to complex meanings for your genders. Someone who is upper middle class, is Latino, has a penis, is gay, and is a college professor embodies a different gender—a different sense of self, social roles, and social position—from someone who is poor, white, has a penis, is gay, lacks a college education, and is homeless. For similar reasons, Sarah Palin embodies a different gender from Angelina Jolie, and Ryan Gosling embodies a different gender from Kanye West.

Our conceptualization of gender does not treat gender as a stable aspect of a person. From your own experience, you can probably appreciate how, at different times in life—as a toddler, as a teenager, when starting a family—people experience their own genders differently, and their genders are seen differently by other people. Throughout the human life cycle, various dimensions of gender become more or less significant. The ways a five-year-old expresses gender is different from the ways a twelve-year-old expresses gender. What matters to an eighteen-year-old in terms of gender is likely very different from what is salient for a sixty-year-old. Your sense of what appearances and actions your gender involves and how you feel about your gendered self have most likely shifted over time and will continue to do so.

You also change your gender several times a day as you respond to and interact within different social contexts. Bornstein describes these shifts in this way: "In response to each interaction we have with a new or different person, we subtly shift the *kind* of man or woman, boy or girl, or whatever gender we're being at the moment. We're usually not the same *kind* of man or woman with our lover as we are with our boss or a parent. When we're introduced for the first time to someone we find attractive, we shift into being a different *kind* of man or woman than we are with our childhood friends."[10] Even when you simply change out of a suit and into jeans or sweats, you make a subtle alteration to your gender. You may also adjust your gender due to social pressures to look and act certain ways, as when you cover your tattoos for a job interview. In both kinds of encounters, your moods, attitudes, and the ways you express yourself differ. As your internal state and outward actions change, so does your gendered self. This means that you enact gender differently in different contexts, and the result is that you always embody multiple genders.

STORY

"Who am I?" is a question that you would likely answer by sharing details about your life. Psychologist Roger Frie suggests that when you answer this question, you organize details about yourself into a story that makes sense of your life by giving meaning to your past and pointing to your future.[11] "I grew up in a small town in Texas, and I moved to Colorado to go to a big university. Someday, I hope to practice law in New York City" is an example of such a narrative. The form and content of your stories reveal who you think you are—your social and cultural identities, your beliefs and feelings, your desires and how you plan to attain them.[12] Your personal stories—how you describe the experiences that have shaped your development—then, are the way you arrive at an understanding of yourself as a person.

Your life constitutes a story starring you in the lead role. If you think back over your life until now, you can probably identify numerous plot twists and different genres (comedy, drama, or tragedy). You have accomplished things that made you feel successful, and you have suffered disappointments. You have been close to people and, at times, have felt alone. Perhaps you have had a profound experience like a serious illness or the loss of someone important to you. All of these experiences constitute chapters in your own unique story. This uniqueness—no one has lived or ever will live a life exactly like yours—means that your life is being told in your own distinctive style and from your own particular point of view.

Your life story features a constantly changing cast of characters with whom you interact at home, work, school, and in other social settings. In turn, you are a character in the stories of other people. One way to imagine this dynamic is to think of the narrative development of a movie or a play. The plot usually depends on the entrance of new characters who introduce new relationships, dilemmas, and potentialities. In the same way, whenever a new person—a friend, a teacher, or even a casual acquaintance—enters your life, that person has the potential to have an impact on or even to alter your life story. When other people become part of your story, you are offered new possibilities, and you, in turn, have the potential to shape other people's stories as you interact with them. Your story, then, is the result of a complex set of interactions between you and the world.

According to communication scholar Walter Fisher, all forms of communication should be considered narratives, a view that allows for a more complete, richer perspective on being human. Fisher points out that whatever the purpose of a particular form of communication—persuasion, argumentation, or explanation, for example—storytelling is always involved.[13] This means that all communication, whether conversations, nonverbal behaviors, movies, songs, or theories, tells a story. This book is a story: our story about how we envision gender and communication. If all forms of communication are storytelling, then the world itself is a set of stories with which you interact.

Among the stories you hear and tell are gender stories. From the moment you were born—and even before—those around you were constructing gender stories for you and about you and sharing them with you. Parents and other caregivers are often highly invested in having their children learn only certain gender stories, and they may work hard to filter or screen out narratives that contradict their preferred stories. Your parents may have selected the kinds of schools you attended, made sure you were active in a certain church, and permitted you to watch only certain television shows and movies. But, of course, due to the pervasiveness of gender stories in US culture, you probably didn't have much difficulty discovering gender stories different from those told to you by your parents. You learn gender stories at school and work, and you are also exposed to more generalized cultural narratives about gender in the music you hear, the cartoons you watch, the ads you see, the websites you surf, and in virtually everything else around you.

All of the various gender stories you encounter assign different meanings to bodies. Each story presents you with a different perspective on gender that contains a particular ideology—a set of beliefs about appropriate gender behavior. Keith learned the following gender story from his father:

> My father believes that women are strong, independent, and equal to men. They certainly don't need to be taken care of! My father sees marriage as a partnership between two equally capable humans who bring different opinions, ways of doing things, and skills to a relation-

ship. So I grew up seeing two very strong individuals work out a creative and effective partnership.

Nikki also learned about gender from her family:

> I grew up in a religious home with a history in Ukrainian Catholicism, where men and women have strict roles. Men were deacons and altar boys; women were not allowed on the altar. I learned that, at church and at home, women are supposed to be helpful and take care of other church members, while the men made decisions about church business.

As a result of exposure to widely varied gender stories, you may feel pulled in many directions. Psychoanalyst Lynne Layton explains, "In a complex culture such as ours, in which a multiplicity of positions are visible in cultural products, on the nightly news, on the streets, and within our own families, we engage in and take in multiple versions of gendered subjectivity."[14] In other words, you have internalized multiple gender stories, which increase your options for enacting gender but may cause tensions and conflicts as you construct the gender stories that become your gender identity.

IDENTITY

Your identity is your sense of self or how you define yourself. Identities—"I'm a Muslim," "I'm a physical therapist," or "I'm Italian-American," for example—assemble different aspects of the self into an arrangement that has unity over time. Identity is more, however, than a set of labels that you give yourself. Identity formation involves the ongoing process of how you structure yourself into a being that makes sense to you. As you interact with other people, you construct and reconstruct your identity. Over the course of a lifetime, you construct multiple versions of your identity, giving new meanings to yourself as a person.[15]

Identity is a social phenomenon, which means that your sense of self, like your gender story, has developed as a result of your interactions with other people and with social institutions. This process began in your family. Starting when you were an infant interacting with the people around you, you began to discover how the world worked and who you were in relation to the world. As a child, you began to identity the groups and categories to which you belonged—"I'm a Ruiz, I'm German, we like spaghetti"—and how to act as a member of these groups. Perhaps your family said grace before meals or attended religious services on Saturday or Sunday. These behaviors may have become part of your identity—"I'm a religious person." Perhaps your family was actively political, demonstrating against war and canvassing for local elections. In this case, being politically active might be a part of your identity.

In addition to learning how people of your race, ethnicity, religion, and political commitment looked and acted, you began as a child to distinguish how to be male or female and how to express masculinity or femininity. You learned how to act and how you should feel about yourself as a man or a woman. Depending on how those around you performed gender, you may have learned messages such as: "women do the cooking," "men mow the lawn," "girls should be soft spoken," and "big boys don't cry." Of course, you may also have learned that "men do the cooking," "women mow the lawn," "boys should speak softly," and "big girls don't cry." Regardless of which messages you learned, this information became part of your identity through a process of internalization.

There are a number of theories about how the process of identity formation occurs. Social learning theory says you learned to be who you are by observing others, imitating them, and being rewarded or punished for certain behaviors. Gender definitions start at birth when a baby is named, put in a pink or blue blanket, given a distinctive hair style and particular kinds of clothing, and provided with certain types of toys and playmates. This difference in treatment sets up a system of being rewarded for certain behaviors and discouraged from others. For example, girls tend to be rewarded for being obedient, gentle, loving, and quiet, and boys are rewarded for the opposite qualities.

Cognitive development theory says that children develop a sense of identity in stages. Very young children may confuse gender roles and identities and say, "Mommy is a boy," but by the age of five or six, children typically have developed a more consistent awareness of their own gender identities and the gender identities of other people.[16] By this age, children begin to actively choose models from which to learn identity, seeking those models that will result in success in social situations. When children are rewarded for acting certain ways—for acting like a girl or a boy, for example—they adopt those patterns of behavior as part of their identities. Children also begin to punish their peers for acting outside of the gender models they have adopted.

The theory of symbolic interaction says that identity develops through communication with other people. In this model, you learn who you are by discovering how others view you and responding to their evaluations. People such as your parents told you who you were when they delivered messages such as "what a smart girl you are" or "what a handsome boy you are." By comparing yourself to other people and evaluating their expectations, you internalized some expectations as your own. These expectations and corresponding behaviors became part of your identity. All of these theories point to how personal identity is shaped by social forces.

We have been discussing the identity-formation process that occurs in childhood, but you continue to develop your identity throughout your life. Adolescence and young adulthood are particularly critical times for identity development. Psychologist Erik Erikson described these as the periods of time when people in modern societies are specifically challenged to answer the questions, "Who am I?" and "How do I fit in the adult world?"[17] These are the stages when you begin to make decisions about who you will be for the rest of your life. You begin to assemble a life narrative that becomes, quite literally, not only the story you live by but also who you are as a person. This life narrative is the foundation of your identity.

We have been talking about identity as if you have only one, but people actually have multiple and shifting identities that have a variety of meanings.[18] Communication theorist Michael Hecht explains that identity includes several layers or frames—personal, enacted, relational, and communal. The personal frame is your internal self-concept, such as "I am a student." The enacted frame is your performance of that self-concept—you attend classes and participate in study groups. The relational frame consists of the identities interacted in certain relationships—the identity *child* requires *parent,* for example, and *lover* requires *loved one.* The communal frame is the identity you share with other members of groups to which you belong, such as *student, Jew,* or *Navy Seal.* In addition, the identity frames interact with one another. In terms of gender identity, this means that your view of yourself as gendered (personal frame) is juxtaposed with how others see you as gendered (relational frame) as well as how your communities (communal identity) define gender positions.[19] If someone asked you right now to explain your identity, a natural response would be, "I have many identities—which one should I share?"[20] Although we highlight only one of your identities throughout this book—gender identity—keep in mind that you have multiple identities that stem from the different ways you engage with the world.

The title of this textbook is *Gender Stories: Negotiating Identity in a Binary World.* As implied by the word *negotiating,* we believe gender identity does not always unfold in an uncomplicated way. You may be most familiar with the concept of negotiation in the business world, where negotiating means to bring about something—perhaps a contract or a loan—through discussions among concerned parties. Negotiating often occurs when people do not initially agree on the terms of a contract or business deal. Through interaction with others, an agreement is reached about how a contract or deal will be arranged and conducted. But even when an agreement is reached, unresolved issues can remain. Those involved don't get precisely what they want; people sometimes compromise and adjust their behaviors to go along with the group. Likewise, to say that gender identities are *negotiated* means that gender identities are created within circumstances where there can be expectations and disagreements about the forms that they take.

You may not be used to thinking about gender in terms of negotiation, but you are probably aware of expectations and tensions that are experienced around developing gender identities. You may have adopted certain aspects of your gender because of the expectations of and pressure from other people. Perhaps your family has strict ideas about what it means to be a man or a woman, and you don't agree with those definitions. Perhaps your religion puts restrictions on how gender should be performed, and you have to work hard to meet those restrictions given the different environments in which you find yourself. Your friends might accept only certain performances for how to be male or female, and you are more comfortable expressing yourself as a combination of genders. In all of these circumstances, you might find yourself needing or wanting to negotiate changes in your gender identity.

Engaging with the world around you as a gendered person can be complicated by the expectations of other people. As with all negotiations, when you negotiate your gender identity, you may find yourself adjusting to expectations by compromising, or you may find yourself resisting the efforts of other people to change you. Depending on your social interactions with other people—the norms governing those interactions and how supportive you feel the people around you are about your gender—your gender identity might be quite easy to negotiate, or you may have ongoing, unresolved issues.

BINARY

Most Western countries, including the United States, organize gender according to a male-female binary. These two realms—feminine and masculine—are set up as opposites so that whatever is feminine is not masculine, and whatever is masculine is not feminine. In chapter 3, we discuss at length what this binary system is and how it functions in your life. We summarize this concept briefly here to introduce you to one of the main themes of this book. Although every person actually is made up of feminine and masculine characteristics, in Western cultures, the binary division is considered natural and inevitable.

Every person is supposed to fit clearly into one of the two categories. The deciding factor is your body: If you have a penis and testicles, you are assumed to be masculine and a boy or a man; if you have a vagina and a uterus, you are assumed to be feminine and a girl or a woman. Further, the binary system dictates that having one set of physical apparatuses translates into a certain sexual orientation, certain ways of thinking and behaving, and certain life roles. The normative position is to be heterosexual, to pursue interests and careers that fit being male or female, and to think and act like either a female or a male. This system ignores the many intersexed people who have ambiguous genitals—who don't clearly have a penis or vagina, for example—and marginalizes anyone whose body doesn't "match up" with their feelings and desires—such as people who identify as gay, queer, or bisexual. The binary system does not, therefore, encompass the variety of genders, sexualities, and activities that actual people live.

The gender binary is an extremely influential backdrop to your entire life. As you will discover, the binary system pervades all aspects of your development as a person. From childhood onward, you are trained to develop a certain identity and a particular type of narrative of self that reflects your understanding of how you fit into the binary system. Although you can and do script a unique personal gender story, the culture in which you live constantly works to confine your identity according to its rules—to persuade you to live within the masculine and feminine realms of the binary.

AGENCY

Agency is the capacity to act or make a difference; to have agency means to feel or to believe that you can change things that matter to you. The essential characteristic of agency is the idea that you have some degree of control over the events in your life. Life doesn't just happen to you—it is something you can have a role in constructing. You can make decisions and take actions that have a substantial effect on your immediate world. Because you are partially constructing the reality you share with other people, you can change not only yourself but also the world that you share with others when you enact agency.

One simple way to think about agency is to think about the choices—both small and large—that you make each day. You eat a banana, cereal, or toast for breakfast. You drive your car, take the light rail, or bike to school. You do or do not respond to a friend's text. You read assigned chapters regularly throughout the semester or put off reading until the night before the exam. You are always making choices, and those choices have an impact not only on your life but also on the lives of people around you. In terms of gender, you are always making choices—how to dress, relate to people of the same and different genders, initiate and maintain intimate relationships, organize living arrangements, and form your own family. On many levels, you are continually making choices about how to construct and share your gender stories.

Some people consciously and deliberately construct a gender story with which they are comfortable and that works for them in the world. Particularly when people are trying to negotiate their gender identities, they consciously consider what they want and how to enact their desires. Most people, however, construct and perform many gender stories without conscious thought. Many aspects of your gendered self are probably constructed and performed almost automatically because you have accepted some gender stories as true and necessary or because you haven't yet been exposed to alternate stories that appeal to you.

When you become a conscious agent, you become more mindful of your choices and more strategic about how to enact the choices that will lead to the outcomes you want in your life. You realize that you have options and the power to rearrange different aspects of situations; you do not have to accept things the way they are. Sometimes, the aspect of the situation you choose to alter is internal—you change your view of yourself and decide to alter the identity or stories you present to the world. At other times, the aspect of the situation you choose to alter is external—you do something to cause a change in the circumstances around you. The point is that, in all situations, you have the power to create some kind of change.

OBSTACLES TO ENACTING AGENCY

One of the biggest obstacles to the conscious construction and performance of your gender stories is that different genders are expected to enact agency in different ways. People are expected to follow two sets of rules within the gender binary. The kinds of agency that are permitted for

people designated *female* differ from the kinds of agency that are permitted for people designated *male*. These rules shrink the possibilities for
enacting agency by placing limitations on what agency looks like for different genders. In most Western cultures, no matter what genders a person constructs and performs, almost everyone knows how male-
designated and female-designated people are supposed to act to create
change. You can probably tell easily which of the following ways of enacting agency are seen as male or female:

- Being independent and able to solve problems on your own
- Connecting with other people and changing things with their
  agreement and assistance
- Forcefully stating your views and trying to get others to go along
  with your plans
- Giving up some of your decision-making authority when you com-
  mit to a relationship[21]

Even though no one person always uses the same tactics to cause
change, you were probably able to identify the first and third ways of
enacting agency as traditionally male and the second and fourth ways as
traditionally female. There can be negative social consequences when you
do not enact agency in ways that meet expectations. If people identify you
as female and you are too independent or forceful, you may be called a
bitch. If people identify you as male and you are not independent or forceful enough, people may call you a *sissy*. In these cases, the same behaviors
are labeled differently because cultural norms about gender impose different frameworks of interpretation on agency.

In different contexts, there also may be structures or rules, for example, that inhibit your ability as a gendered person to make changes in
your life and your world. The rules that govern how people with normative, accepted genders enact agency often differ from the rules for people
with nonnormative genders. In Philadelphia, if you buy a multi-ride pass
to take public transportation, transit employees are allowed to deny transportation to you if your perceived gender does not match the "male" or
"female" sticker on the pass. This policy means that those of you whose
gender performances are not clearly identifiable by others as female or
male are subjected to a different set of rules from people who are clearly
identified as one of the two genders sanctioned by the binary. Such rules
pose potential obstacles to exercising agency.

Another obstacle to exercising agency is that there may be circumstances or situations in your life where you simply do not believe you can

exercise agency or cause change. This feeling may arise in situations where you do not feel accepted, are being harassed, or are threatened. Some gay teenagers whose families and communities are not supportive, for example, feel so powerless to change their situations that they think their only option is suicide. Some women who are in abusive relationships feel powerless to leave their abusers. Some men feel so pressured to conform to social norms of being strong, unemotional, and driven to make money that they feel powerless to adopt different ways of performing their gender. Other men feel that being aggressive and even violent is an integral part of their gender and the primary way in which they attempt to exercise control over their worlds.

This is not to say that change is easy—sometimes it is very, very hard. Although you might have a hard time identifying them, even in the most difficult circumstances, you always have some options. A despairing gay teenager could seek out a supportive adult or an online peer community, a battered woman could decide to break her silence and tell her sister or a friend that she is being abused, a man who feels stuck in his job could meet with a career counselor to get ideas about how his skills and expertise could be used in another field, and an abusive man could acknowledge that he needs to deal with his violent temper. The more conscious you become of always having choices and of the different strategies for enacting agency, the more you will be able to explore the full range of your options in any situation.

STRATEGIES FOR ENACTING AGENCY

You will be able to enact agency more successfully in all kinds of situations if you become familiar with potential strategies. There are three primary ways of exercising personal agency. You can (1) do it yourself; (2) influence others who can/will make changes; and (3) reframe a situation that is not the way you would like it to be.

DOING IT YOURSELF

Sometimes agency means that you assess conditions around you and see that you can change something by taking a particular action. Doing it yourself can be as simple as deciding that you do not like your current hairstyle and taking steps to change it. The next time you have your hair cut, you ask the stylist to cut it a different way. Or perhaps you decide that your current job isn't getting you where you want to be, so you exert your agency by updating your resume and beginning a job search. Perhaps you are bothered by the word *bitch*, and you ask your friends not to use the word. You decide to start an organization, to have a baby, to go to school, to stop going to church. No matter the situation, your agency assumes the form of taking some active step that addresses something in your life that you would like to be different.

INFLUENCING OTHERS

In other cases, you might choose to enact agency by influencing others to take action. You realize that you cannot change some condition or solve a problem by yourself. Maybe you don't have direct access to the people who have the ability to make the change, you don't have the necessary knowledge or expertise, or you do not have the time and money you need to accomplish the change. In these cases, you turn to people who have at least some of what is required—access and resources, for example—and encourage them to do what is necessary for the change you desire to happen. Asking others to make the changes you think are necessary is a very common way of enacting agency. You probably used it when you were a child and wanted something—a pink princess costume for Halloween or to get your ears pierced, for example. You undoubtedly had a whole arsenal of persuasive tools you used to influence your parents to make these kinds of changes happen.

You are still doing the same thing now, but you have a larger number of people around you whom you can try to influence to change conditions, whether that means fixing something you don't like or improving a condition or situation in some way. You might try to influence people who have the capacity to pass laws and implement policies. So, for example, you might ask your legislator to vote yes on a constitutional amendment banning gay marriage or to support reproductive freedom. In this form of agency, you try to persuade people to take action on a condition where you desire a certain outcome. Other people are, in essence, serving as mediators of change for you.

Influencing others can also involve asking others for help. Asking your mother to help you design a prom dress or show you how to use a condom are examples of this kind of agency. If you are religious, you might choose to enact agency by praying and seeking to enlist God's help in making your marital relationship more harmonious. If you are gay but have not told other people and want to, you might go to the LGBTQ resource center on campus for advice and support. Whether you try to persuade someone to take an action on your behalf or ask for help to change something, you are exercising agency by engaging others.

REFRAMING

Both the strategies of doing it yourself and working with others to make change take some resources on your part. If you are going to take direct action to solve some problem, you have to be able to articulate the problem, figure out a way to address it, and have the self-confidence to move ahead with your plan. If you are going to influence or ask others for help, you have to gain access to those people, have them pay attention to you, and be perceived as somewhat credible. But, of course, there are times when you do not have the required resources. You cannot figure out by yourself what to do to solve the problem, you do not know how to gain access to those who can make change, and you do not have sufficient credibility to convince your audience even if you gain access. There is still one form of enacting agency available to you.

You have the option of selecting a different interpretation for what you are experiencing or observing.[22] This process is called *reframing*. Reframing means shifting perspectives so that you view a situation from a different vantage point. Using this strategy, you symbolically draw a different frame around the same set of circumstances. Because the labels you put on a situation serve as a structuring principle and focus your attention on certain aspects of a situation—often the frustrating or painful aspects—reframing involves intentionally renaming what is happening to you. Reframing is especially useful when you are feeling stuck in a situation that seems impossible to change.

A common situation that involves reframing is when a relationship ends badly, and you end up feeling abandoned. Particularly if your love interest said hurtful things about you before leaving, your usual reaction is probably to interpret the story as a tragedy and yourself as a victim. You are miserable focusing on the pain of being alone, the injustice of what was said, and fears of never having another intimate relationship. As long as you stay in this mind-set, you can't see other possibilities. Reframing opens up new options—it constructs new interpretations—that you couldn't see when you were looking at a situation from only one viewpoint.

If you reframe the breakup, you have many options for interpretation. You can choose to see the other person as not right for you and be pleased that you both figured this out relatively early in the relationship. You can choose to see the other person as a wonderful person who deserves to be with someone she loves and respects, even though she no longer perceives you as that person. You can focus on the fact that a wonderful person loved you as evidence that other wonderful people will love you in the future—that you are lovable and wonderful. You can look forward to the opportunity to meet new people and to participate in new activities and new relationships. You can decide that being alone is just fine. You get the idea: Reframing often involves focusing on your strengths and abilities as a person and how, regardless of the external situation, you can make your life better. You realize you cannot make someone love and want to be with you, but you do have many other options for dealing with the breakup.

Raya, a liberal Muslim woman, provides another example of reframing. In her religion, shaking hands with men is considered wrong, and she has been judged harshly by other Muslim women for doing it. When she was looking at the situation only from within the structure of her religious community, these judgments made her feel ashamed and anxious. Reframing allowed Raya to find a new perspective on the situation and to expand her view of herself. She observed and appreciated how she was now a member of both her religious community and her college community, each of which entails different responsibilities and possibilities for behavior. She realized that to be who she wants to be as a student in a Western culture meant modifying some traditional behaviors, so she decided to shake hands with Western men who offer their hands in greeting.

Bret's experience was similar. He decided he wanted to be openly gay—to change the way he looked and to signal his preferred sexuality—at school and at his job. As he began to alter his appearance to express his preferred sense of gender by wearing brighter colors and earrings, he experienced taunts and harassment from some of his peers. For a while, when he was focused on the negative external reactions he was receiving, Bret was tempted to go back to hiding his gender identity. But then, as he puts it, "I decided to focus instead on how great I felt with my new look. I cut my hair into a style that I love and bleached it blonde. I realized that how I was altering my appearance would make it more possible for me to meet other gay men and maybe attract a boyfriend." He knew he couldn't change some of his peers, but he could seek out new friends.

Of course, reframing is influenced by the context in which it is attempted. The ways institutions and other people interact can actively hinder or help an individual's efforts to reframe. For example, if a woman is sexually assaulted on campus and receives messages from the police or campus security personnel that she deserved the assault because of how she was dressed and because she was walking alone at night, reframing her experience in ways that make her feel strong and empowered may be difficult. On the other hand, she will have an easier time reframing if the police direct her to the campus women's center or a supportive medical clinic where others confirm her ability to make good decisions for herself regardless of what has occurred.

Reframing is a very powerful strategy that can move you from a position of feeling utterly powerless to revealing possibilities you could not have imagined before. There is yet another step beyond reframing called *enactment*—acting as if the change you want has already occurred. Instead of remaining focused on the problem, on your frustration or anger, or on possible solutions for the external situation, you put your energy into behaving in ways that correspond with the change you desire. Behaving as if the undesirable condition no longer exists can, in certain circumstances, be a very powerful way to exert agency. This was the strategy Indian liberation leader Mahatma Gandhi was advocating when he said, "We must be the change we want to see."[23] This idea is echoed by feminist theorist Sonia Johnson in her statement, "Live today as you want the world to be."[24] When you behave as if a condition has already changed, you refuse to give an undesirable condition absolute power over you.

Drew felt she was being discriminated against at her job because of her gender. Not only did she think that she had been passed over for advancement, but she observed that her boss rarely asked for her opinion on business decisions, although he routinely asked male employees for their input. She became increasingly resentful and even thought about leaving her position, even though she had gone to school for years and engaged in a lengthy search to find a job she thought was a good fit. As long as Drew interpreted her situation only as sex discrimination in the workplace, the only options she could think of for herself were to file a grievance or a lawsuit or to quit. While filing a grievance is at times a legitimate option, Drew found another way to deal with the situation through reframing. She began to act as if her boss valued her as an employee. In meetings, Drew began to offer her views before being asked. She stopped treating her boss as an enemy, began appreciating his vision for the current project, and began to get to know him better and to share details about her life and interests. To her surprise, her boss responded positively and began to treat her as part of the working team. In this case, the external environment changed because Drew enacted agency by behaving as though the change she desired had already happened.

Acting as if an undesirable situation has already changed sometimes results in an internal change. When Josh proposed to his girlfriend Maisha, he knew he had a more traditional sense of marriage than she did, but their different views did not become a major problem until after the wedding. When Josh and Maisha set up house together, he believed she should do all of the shopping, cooking, and cleaning. He also wanted her to curtail her studying time so that she would be available to do things with him. For months, the couple fought over dirty dishes and laundry and what he perceived to be her overly committed life as a student. At some point, Josh realized something had to change or the marriage wouldn't last. Instead of continuing to fight with his wife, Josh reframed how he saw his marriage. Rather than complaining about how his wife wasn't meeting her obligations in the home, he began to focus on how interesting his wife was as a person (which had been what had attracted him in the first place) and how glad he was that she was going to school because he really wanted her to be able to pursue her life interests. Josh essentially reframed the situation from "she is a bad wife" to "I support her choices."

Constructing human stories involves agency. When your stories do not produce the outcomes you desire, you can make choices. We hope this book helps you to become more deliberate about your decisions and strategies. Your agency is always practiced in a context that involves others, so we also emphasize the importance of considering how you negotiate the agency of others.

ALLOWING AGENCY TO OTHERS

An important part of being a consciously agentic person also involves not restricting other people's choices. You want to take actions and choose options concerning gender that are right for you because you are the person who knows the most about you, your life, and how you want to live it. The same goes for other people; they want to be able to construct their gender identities as they choose. While being open to other people's decisions sounds easy in theory, letting other people make choices is sometimes very difficult. You might not be able to stop your mental judgments or evaluations of other people's choices, but you always have a choice about whether to act on those thoughts in ways that hurt or restrict other people. Trying to influence other people's life choices disallows the agency of others; it is an activity that should be engaged in only after thorough self-questioning and self-reflection. When people make choices that seem self-destructive, lacking in foresight, or morally wrong, you might feel justified in intervening and trying to influence their life choices. In fact, when someone is in a dangerous situation, intervening can be a responsible course of action.

Agency, then, is the power to make desired changes. Various strategies are always available to you to change yourself or the external environment in ways that align more with how you want yourself and the world to be. In terms of your gender stories, becoming conscious of these strategies increases the likelihood that you will be able to negotiate the gender stories you really want to have. Being aware that you have the authority to create and enact your own preferred gender stories can help you appreciate that other people have the right to negotiate their own preferred gender stories as well.

OUR PERSPECTIVE

For the past year, whenever one of us told someone we were writing a book about gender and communication, the reaction was almost always a knowing smile accompanied by, "Thank goodness—we need one!" The implication was that the deep and universal problems that males and females have when trying to communicate are the only possible focus of a book like this. But what is most interesting for us about gendered communication is not the male-female conundrum that receives so much attention. We propose a new and different conversation about the subject—one that we believe is more enriching and productive. Because we understand that you, our reader, may also be expecting the customary approach to gender and communication, we want to explain the perspectives that guide this book.

- Although we appreciate multiplicity and recognize that it can be realized only by adopting a global perspective, we focus on a Western cultural perspective and, in particular, on gender culture in the United States. We believe that an in-depth analysis of the construction, operation, maintenance, and capacity for change in one gender system is valuable and can be transferred into other cultural contexts. While we attempt to acknowledge the rich variety of racial, ethnic, religious, class, and educational subcultures that intersect with gender in the United States, we are aware that we leave out multiple standpoints that enrich and challenge Western understandings of gender.

- We take the social construction of gender seriously and see it operating at individual, interpersonal, and societal levels. This means that we treat gender as a culturally dependent and socially constructed system of categories, norms, labels, and expectations that are created through communication. We do not reinforce and reinscribe the binary as the natural, inevitable order of human life.

Instead, we explain the binary division of culture as a historical dynamic that is fluid and evolving.

- Many communication textbooks on gender focus on verbal and nonverbal differences between women and men. Consequently, these textbooks inadvertently essentialize male-female differences and reinforce the gender binary that divides women and men into two separate and often alien categories. Building on current research that shows that there are far more communication differences *within* groups of men and *within* groups of women than *between* men and women, we do not limit the communicative options available to any person on the basis of perceived gender. We focus instead on the individual variations that result from contextual factors such as motivations, relationships, cultural norms, and power dynamics.

- Because we want everyone to be involved in the conversation we are initiating, we do not insist that any ideological perspective about gender is right and true. In our experience, when an ideology is imposed on classrooms, the result is alienation, hostility, resistance, and silencing of those who do not agree. While we acknowledge the value of the critical cultural perspective from which gender is commonly taught—and our approach does not contradict that perspective—our goal is for you to grapple with the diverse and conflicting views that reflect the complex gender world in which you live. Instead of trying to change you, we want you to become more conscious of what you believe and to understand how the belief systems of others make sense to those individuals.

- We want you to understand how you can enact agency in becoming the gendered person you want to be—sharing your gender stories with others and responding to others' stories. We are aware that agency is a contested concept in terms of who has it and who doesn't and under what circumstances agency can and cannot be exercised; we will not resolve these debates in this book. Instead, we take an interpersonal approach, focusing on agency in the minute interactions of daily life (how individuals look, speak, and act) because we want you to appreciate the degree to which you affect yourself, other people, and the world through your personal communication practices.

- One of our objectives for the book is to discuss gender in ways that are applicable to your life. To learn about students' experiences with gender, we surveyed students from colleges and universities around the country, asking them to share their experiences with gender. They told us that their worlds—in the media, at school, and in their churches and families—are filled with people who express gender in a rich variety of ways. Students also said that they live in a world where understandings of gender are in flux, contradictory, and confusing. We want to provide a textbook that not only mirrors your actual experiences but provides you with tools for reflecting on, constructing, and negotiating gender in this context.

Our perspectives guide and inform the four sections of this book. The first section consists of this introduction and a chapter on the social construction of reality. In this introductory chapter, we have familiarized you with the key concepts of gender, story, identity, binary, and agency. In chapter 2, we explain the concept of social construction and demonstrate how it applies to gender in terms of cultural variations, shifting conceptions of bodies, and expanded options for expressing and changing gender roles. The second section consists of three chapters that explain how the Western gender binary functions. Its chapters explore the gender ideals that the binary imposes throughout the life cycle; scientific research that perpetuates differences between men and women; and popular culture in which gender stories reinforce, revise, or rewrite the gender binary. The third section outlines the process by which gender stories are crafted from fragments of other stories, the considerations that go into performing gender, and the various ways people respond to gender performances. The last section asks you to reflect more deeply on the consequences of your own gender stories and performances for the gender binary and the world you share with others.

OUR GOALS FOR YOU

Just as we have intentions of our own for this book, we have a number of goals for you. One of our primary goals is for you to participate in a spirited conversation about gender. Instead of treating you as a passive recipient of knowledge, we view you as the cocreator of a shared and ever-evolving understanding of gendered life. We believe that your story—how you came to be gendered, what you value, how you experience the world, and what you hope for the future—will help make this conversation deep and rewarding. Comprehensive understanding of any issue emerges only from a conversation that includes many voices. When people freely contribute their unique interpretations, the result is increased understanding and wisdom for everyone, so we urge you to add your own perspectives and to listen carefully to those of others. We do not anticipate that the conversations you will have as you make your way through this book will resolve all existing contradictions and conflicts, but we do anticipate that you will grow as a person and develop a greater understanding of gender.

A second goal we have is for you to become more conscious about how you construct and perform your gender stories. This is not to say that you have always been unconscious of these processes. Most people *do* think about how they present themselves to the world as a gendered person—at least in some situations. Whatever your level of consciousness about your gender is now, we hope that engagement with this book will increase your awareness so that you can more consciously enact your individual agency in terms of gender. Aside from that, we have no agenda about the particular gender stories that you select and perform. If you like your current gender stories just the way they are, you can continue to perform them. If you develop greater clarity about the options you have in terms of your own gender stories and want to make some changes, we encourage you to make them. We applaud whatever gender stories you choose, especially if you have consciously and deliberately chosen them.

Our third goal is for you to gain a better understanding of and respect for all of the gender stories that other people present to you. This means staying open to a diversity of opinions about and approaches to gender. When you encounter people who have different perspectives from your own or who behave in ways contrary to what you find appropriate, how do you react? We suggest that you stay open to difference and embrace challenges to your usual thinking rather than trying to persuade people to be different. We would like you to seek out diversity, even if contact with difference causes discomfort or confusion. We believe that encountering difference respectfully can be an exciting foray into new ways of thinking and being.

You are about to enter a conversation about gender that has been going on for centuries. We want you to appreciate that you are a unique person who has a valuable contribution to make to this ongoing discussion. Honor your own perspective because what you have to offer this conversation is unique. Honor the perspectives of others because they can teach you things you cannot learn on your own. Let the conversation begin.

▮ NOTES

1. Russell Goldman and Kate Thomson, "'Pregnant Man' Gives Birth to Girl," *abcNEWS/ Health*, July 3, 2008, http://abcnews.go.com/Health/story?id=5302756&page=1

2. Kathy Witterick, "Baby Storm's Mother Speaks on Gender, Parenting, and Media," *Postmedia News*, http://www.edmontonjournal.com/news/Baby+Storm+mother+ speaks+gender+ parenting+media/4857577/story.html

3. Trinh T. Minh-ha, *Woman Native Other: Writing Postcoloniality and Feminism* (Bloomington: Indiana University Press, 1989), 123.

4. Kate Bornstein, *My Gender Workbook* (New York: Routledge, 1998), 7.

5. Joseph Nicolosi and Linda Nicolosi, *A Parent's Guide to Preventing Homosexuality* (Westmont, IL: Intervarsity, 2002), 12.

6. Roberta Satow, *Gender and Social Life* (Boston: Allyn & Bacon, 2001), xi.

7. Roberta Fiske-Rusciano, *Experiencing Race, Class and Gender in the United States*, 5th ed. (New York: McGraw-Hill, 2009), 59.

8. Bornstein, *My Gender Workbook*, 27.

9. Marianne Gullestad, quoted in Paul John Eakin, *How We Create Identity in Narrative* (Ithaca, NY: Cornell University Press, 2008), 16. See also Marianne Gullestad, *The Art of Social Relations* (Oslo: Scandinavian University Press, 1992), 20.

10. Bornstein, *My Gender Workbook*, 8.

11. Roger Frie, "Identity, Narrative, and Lived Experience after Postmodernity: Between Multiplicity and Continuity," *Journal of Phenomenological Psychology* 42 (2011): 49.

12. Deborah Schiffrin, "Narratives as Self-Portrait: Sociolinguistic Construction of Identity," *Language in Society* 25 (1996): 194.

13. Walter R. Fisher, *Human Communication as Narration: Toward a Philosophy of Reason, Value, and Action* (Columbia: University of South Carolina Press, 1987).

14. Lynne Layton, *Who's That Girl? Who's That Boy? Clinical Practice Meets Postmodern Gender Theory* (Northvale, NJ: Jason Aronson, 1998), 56.

15. Dan P. McAdams, Ruthellen Josselson, and Amia Lieblich, *Identity and Story: Creating Self in Narrative* (Washington, DC: American Psychological Association, 2006), 7–8.

16. Teri K. Gamble and Michael W. Gamble, *The Gender Communication Connection* (Boston: Houghton Mifflin, 2003), 38–42.

17. McAdams, Josselson, and Lieblich, *Identity and Story*, 4.

18. Michael L. Hecht, "Communication Theory of Identity," in *Encyclopedia of Communication Theory*, vol. 1, ed. Stephen W. Littlejohn and Karen A. Foss (Thousand Oaks, CA: Sage, 2009), 139–41.

19. Hecht, "Communication Theory of Identity," 140.

20. Peter Raggatt, "Multiplicity and Conflict in the Dialogical Self: A Life Narrative Approach," in *Identity and Story: Creating Self in Narrative*, ed. Dan P. McAdams, Ruthellen Josselson, and Amia Lieblich (Washington DC: American Psychological Association, 2006), 15.

21. Layton, *Who's That Girl? Who's That Boy?*, 41–50.

22. Sonja K. Foss and Karen A. Foss, "Constricted and Constructed Potentiality: An Inquiry into Paradigms of Change," *Western Journal of Communication* 75 (2011): 214–15.

23. Mahatma Gandhi, *Mahatma Gandhi: Inspiring Thoughts*, M. Johri, comp. (Delhi: Rajpal, 2009), 98.

24. Sonia Johnson, *Wildfire: Igniting the She/volution* (Albuquerque: Wildfire, 1989), 251.

two

DRAMATIC FICTION
THE SOCIAL CONSTRUCTION OF REALITY

The life you thought inevitable, unalterable, and fixed
in some foundational reality is smoke, a mental construction,
fabrication. So, you can reason, if it's all made up,
you can compose it anew and differently.

Gloria Anzaldúa, "Now Let Us Shift the Path of Conocimiento"

From your third-row seat in the theatre, you lean forward, captivated by Juliet's face as she searches the moonlit garden for Romeo. You know that what is happening on the stage—their love, their feuding families, and their effort to be together—isn't real. You know that the Verona you are seeing onstage with its balcony and roses is a fabrication, but you willingly grant the scene substance and become immersed in it. As you enter the world of the play and start to care about the fates of the star-crossed lovers, you become not only an observer but a participant in creating the dramatic fiction. While you may not have thought about it before, the imagined reality of the play is cocreated by everyone involved in the theatrical production—not only Shakespeare but the director, actors, set designers, lighting technicians, and audience. The reality of the play is a human construction created through the communication of everyone involved.

Just as you participate in constructing a world as you watch a play in the theatre, you create the reality of your everyday life outside of the theatre. This process is called the *social construction of reality*, and it is the way in which people create reality together through communication. Our goal in this chapter is to introduce you to the idea that gender is not fixed and stable but is created, as all realities are, through communication. We do this by describing (1) the social construction of reality; and (2) the social construction of gender.

SOCIAL CONSTRUCTION OF REALITY

A common understanding of reality is that it is an objective realm that exists apart from human beings. In this view, individuals come to know reality by observing it, discovering what is out there, and then communicating about their observations. From the perspective of social construction, however, the process is just the opposite. Reality isn't something that exists prior to communicating about it; reality comes into existence through communication. In other words, reality depends on communication in order to become "real."

The fact that reality is created through communication does not mean that a material or physical world doesn't exist and that physical objects are simply figments of individuals' imaginations. There are physical objects in the world—the big piles of dirt and rocks that some people know as *mountains*, for example. What the social construction perspective says is that the pile of dirt and rocks cannot be conceptualized as a mountain until someone gives it that label. This perspective does not deny the existence of a mountain but points out that the way in which individuals understand a mountain is governed by the categories and labels they have learned or created for it. Even the simplest observation of a mountain "involves some form of categorization; it is not just seeing what is before the eyes but seeing it *as something*."[1] The label of *mountain* allows you to distinguish a pile of dirt and rocks from other natural outcroppings like cliffs, hills, and trees, and it also gives that pile a certain meaning. Communication about a mountain can make it, according to the perspective of the person doing the naming, into a barrier, a pleasant place for a hike, a challenge to conquer, or a place of refuge from the city. The huge pile of dirt and rocks takes on various meanings because of how human beings approach it through their symbol use.

The same construction process applies to nonphysical objects such as events, academic disciplines, religions, wars, rights, and political systems.

These are not objective realities, either. Rather, they are all social realities that have been constructed and created by humans through their communication. Individuals perceive and interpret both material and abstract stimuli in the world—often unconsciously but sometimes consciously. The labels they use or the descriptions they create to describe what they encounter construct the version of the world they inhabit. As communication theorist Kenneth Burke explains, communication allows humans to invent everything that is a part of their reality:

> But can we bring ourselves to realize . . . just how overwhelmingly much of what we mean by "reality" has been built up for us through nothing but our symbol systems? Take away our books, and what little do we know about history, biography, even something so "down to earth" as the relative position of seas and continents? What is our "reality" for today . . . but all this clutter of symbols about the past combined with whatever things we know mainly through maps, magazines, newspapers, and the like . . . about the present?[2]

The process by which communication creates reality begins with each person's perceptions and interpretations. Individuals are constantly interpreting and assigning meaning to the stimuli they encounter, whether physical objects or abstract ideas. The particular labels and meanings individuals give to the elements of the world arise from a number of sources. In many cases, of course, they come from the language individuals learn as children. As children acquire the names for things—especially physical phenomena in their worlds—they echo those labels as they encounter and interpret phenomena. This process continues throughout life as people learn new concepts and technical vocabularies, for example. The labels used for naming also come from the realities of everyday lives. People interpret things in certain ways because of their personal experiences, so their interpretations reflect their interests, expectations, biases, and habitual patterns of perceiving. Individual interpretations also may be the result of deliberate choices. Individuals can choose to use a particular frame for interpreting a phenomenon and use a particular symbol for naming it that reflects the vantage point of that frame. You can choose to label a move to a new city, for example, as a *misfortune* or an *adventure*, suggesting two different frames for your communicative choices.

Symbols not only create a particular reality, but they create orientations or attitudes that generate various motives for actions. The labels that are assigned to phenomena in the world suggest ways to act toward those phenomena. When you name an event an *adventure* rather than a *misfortune*, you experience it as a different reality and thus are primed to act according to your interpretation. Similarly, if a father defines his young child as *gifted*, he will accept the child's interruptions and tantrums as signs of the child's intelligence. If, however, he labels and interprets the child's behavior as *misbehavior*, he will read those same behaviors as signs of rudeness and a lack of respect. Depending on the label assigned, he will respond very differently—either encouraging or tolerating the behaviors or disciplining the child.

People do not create the interpretations and meanings that constitute their realities in a vacuum. Everyone is creating interpretations and meanings and thus individual realities. As individuals interact with one another, however, some discover that they share interpretations and meanings for some things, resulting in a collective reality. When individuals share a common sense about reality, their realities are said to be *intersubjective*, which means that more than one person sees reality in the same way. This shared reality results from many types of communication or symbol use. People share their interpretations and communicate using symbols of all kinds: verbal discourse, written words, visual images, the manipulation of space, appearance, and bodily movements, to name a few. All of these mechanisms allow people to share some meanings. When they do, they collectively construct a common reality based on their similar interpretations.

Communication makes the sharing of meanings possible by detaching the interpretations of individuals from their original contexts. The experiences of individuals "thus become readily transmittable"[3] to a larger group; communication enables those experiences and particular interpretations to be available to everyone within a community. Only some members of US culture, for example, have had the experience of surviving a roadside bomb while fighting in Iraq or Afghanistan. But, as the soldiers who had this experience talk and write about it, as journalists cover such events, and as movies are made about wars that involve roadside bombs, the experience is transmitted to others in the culture through communication. As a result, as sociologists Peter Berger and Thomas Luckmann explain, the experience is transformed into "a generally available object of knowledge"[4] and "becomes accessible and, perhaps, strongly relevant to individuals who have never gone through it."[5]

Examples from a variety of contexts illustrate the process by which individual interpretations become intersubjective. A family often has its own reality because family members develop and use the same labels for phenomena. Through their participation in family stories, practices, and rituals, certain interpretations and meanings for phenomena and values that are important to the family are developed, transmitted, and reinforced. The parents and children might have a similar perspective, for example, on the importance of religion, the need to revere the mother, the value of the family relationship over any others, and the importance of education. The family's shared reality is the result of communication among family members that encourages the adoption of similar meanings for various phenomena of relevance to all or most of the family members.

A corporation such as Apple also has its own reality, created by the communication of its CEO, technology designers, marketing specialists, and customers. The members of the Apple community share similar interpretations of, for example, the value of the Apple brand, the need for an aesthetic sensibility in the design of technology, and the genius of Steve Jobs. Their shared interpretations, communicated regularly with one another, create and maintain Apple's culture. Their communication also attracts others whose worldviews are similar to those in the Apple community and whose own communication patterns help maintain and reinforce that culture. As participants' communication becomes habitualized and ritualized, the communication continues to be reproduced for participants in the group as well as displayed to outsiders.

Groups of people who share common realities as a result of similar interpretations have the capacity to use their communication to create all sorts of complex and sophisticated structures in their worlds, including laws, organizations, institutions, governments, political and economic systems, moral codes, obligations, and religions. Shared meanings about simple phenomena in the world expand to create much more complex phenomena. All of the structures around you seem to exist independently of human symbol use, but they, too, were (and are) socially constructed.

Despite the fact that all of the elements of the world are socially constructed, most things in the world are likely to seem very solid and real to you. Many of the inventions of groups of people—things like institutions, for example—are perceived as independent of the people who created them. The process by which phenomena are viewed as solid and immutable is also a communication process. When an institution is created by a community of people, its original creators see it as tenuous, easily changeable, and certainly not a fixed and objective reality. As a result, the institution "remains fairly accessible to deliberate intervention" by its creators.[6] Since they themselves shaped the reality, it is "fully transparent to them." They not only "understand the world that they themselves have made,"[7] but they know that they have the capacity to redo it and to reconstruct it. Those responsible for having constructed the institution are capable of changing or even abolishing it if they choose.

The history of the university at which Sonja teaches provides an example of how the communication process creates an institution. She teaches at the University of Colorado Denver, which began as a satellite campus of the University of Colorado at Boulder about forty years ago. When the campus began, there were only a few professors teaching at the campus, and they all knew each other, saw each other regularly, and worked together to create a new university. As they did, they clearly had the sense that they were creating an institution and that, at any time they chose, they could create a different institution or revise aspects of it simply by changing their minds and their communication. Because these professors were the ones who had used communication processes to create the institution, they viewed the university as something constructed and pliable.

As the creators of an institution pass it along to others through communication, the institution acquires the quality of an object and is experienced by newcomers as something that exists apart from them; they tend not to see it as something that is the product of human communication. Because the newcomers "had no part in shaping it, it confronts them as a given reality."[8] The world of the University of Colorado Denver as a system of codes and practices is not transparent to these newcomers, and the mechanisms that might be used to change the institution are not obvious to them. They did not create the institution through their communication, so they can easily forget that the objectivity and permanence they sense about the institution is a humanly produced, constructed reality.

Forty years after its construction, the University of Colorado Denver no longer feels like something that was created through communication and that can be recreated through communication. Most of the original creators have retired, and the professors who teach there now know nothing about its origins or the multiple and supple ways in which it was initially conceptualized. To a professor new to the campus, the university feels like something that is well established, entrenched, and solidly real that would require considerable effort to change in even small ways. As Berger and Luckmann explain, the institution now seems to possess a reality of its own, "a reality that confronts the individual as an external and coercive fact."[9]

But the university only seems solid, and the habitualized communication practices that are holding it in place can be changed. When a new core curriculum is implemented at the university, change happens through the talk of administrators and professors with one another, in dialogues with other educators, in exchanges with legislators in Colorado, and perhaps even in conversations with business executives who hope that the university will produce students with skills they can employ in their businesses. Students also can create change in the university, as University of New Mexico doctoral student Lissa Knudsen demonstrated when her advocacy efforts led to the passage of a law requiring employers to provide nursing mothers with a clean, private space to breast pump and with flexible break times to accommodate their pumping. University of New Mexico employees now have spaces in which women who are breast feeding their babies can pump milk when they are at the university.[10]

There may be instances in which the creators of something like an institution work very hard to make it seem real and inalterable to others. They may be particularly diligent in their efforts to legitimize, justify, and reinforce it through communication for any number of reasons. They may deliberately try to reify their creation because they benefit in some way from the perception that it is something solid and real. Groups that have a vested interest in keeping the social order as it is so that they retain their power and status may work particularly hard to insure that what they have created is seen as invulnerable. When segregation existed in the South, for example, a number of socially created structures kept blacks from being constructed as equal to whites—secret membership organizations such as the Ku Klux Klan, laws that made voting difficult for blacks, and separate schools and restrooms for blacks and whites, to name a few. This was an instance in which a particular social construction of race was maintained by whites in order to preserve their power.

In other instances, people may vigorously try to maintain an institution they have created in order to develop and reinforce an in-group/out-group distinction. The blood-quantum laws of Native American tribes or nations are an example. *Blood quantum* refers to the degree of ancestry required for an individual to be counted as a member of a Native American tribe or nation. A blood-quantum requirement of 1/2, for example, means that tribe members must have one parent from the tribe or nation; a requirement of 1/8 means that they must have one great grandparent who was a member. Blood-quantum laws were developed by the US government to determine who could be awarded "annuities in the form of money, goods, or medical care." Such laws also were designed with the idea that, as a result of intermarriage and intermixing, over time, fewer Native Americans would qualify, and the government would no longer need to honor its treaties with them. Some tribes now use such laws to restrict the number of individuals in a tribe or a nation and thus lessen the number eligible for financial and other benefits—profits from casinos or the settlement of land claims, for example.[11] In each case, a particular construction of membership happens through communication that makes the in-group's creation more and more inaccessible to outsiders, strengthening the group and making it more cohesive.[12]

A group's desire to see something it has created continue, however, may not be motivated by any malicious intent or a desire to exclude others. Perhaps they are pleased with their creation and believe that it serves a good purpose. Once people invent and manifest something into reality—an organization or a law, for example—they want to see it survive. A group of people who founded an art center in a community might want it to continue to exist because they believe in the mission of the center to provide people with the opportunity to participate in a wide variety of art forms. A community that has adopted laws to protect endangered species of birds might want those laws to endure because they believe the world benefits from maintaining natural diversity. In these cases, communication is used to maintain and preserve the creation by making the organization or law appear solid and necessary.

Everyone lives in a dramatic fiction—a socially constructed reality. Individuals interpret experiences in the world and share their interpretations with others through the use of symbols. As people discover that they have overlapping interpretations of some phenomena, they form communities based on those interpretations; they now experience a reality they have collectively created. Over time, communities create more complex and sophisticated structures in their worlds. Although these seem to be solid, immutable structures, they were created through communication. As entrenched and solid as such structures might seem, what built them—communication—also can change them.

SOCIAL CONSTRUCTION OF GENDER

The social construction perspective says that what people "know" to be real is always a product of "human definition and collective agreement."[13] This is true of gender as well. You might not have thought about gender as a social construction because gender appears to be so rooted in physical things like biology, bodies, and genitals. If anything might be thought of as natural and not socially constructed, it might be gender. But, like everything else, gender is an invention. Gender distinctions are human creations and do not exist independently of cultural ideas about them. A gender system "is not writ in the stars, the primordial soup, the collective unconscious, or our genes."[14] It is "an artifice, a delusion, an ideology—a social construction."[15]

The social construction of gender begins, as all such constructions do, with individual interpretations. Individuals create a sense of what gender is and the kinds of meanings that may be assigned to gendered bodies. In many instances, these individual constructions are largely informed and dictated by existing categories for gender that train people to see and interpret gender in certain ways. Your individual interpretations related to gender are influenced by cultural norms that impose a particular system of definitions of gender on what you are observing. Whether you are perceiving a mountain or a woman, for example, what you know about the concept and how you experience it are always filtered through your culture. As French philosopher Monique Wittig explains, when particular types of people are seen as women, "they *are* women. But before being *seen* that way, they first had to be made that way."[16] The cultural norms that result from social construction help make women into different kinds of people in different cultures.

Groups of people with similar ways of perceiving and interpreting gender form a community in which their understanding of gender is similar. Something known and understood as *gender* comes into existence. Its common meaning may derive from existing cultural definitions or from sources such as religion or various subcultures that channel perceptions of gender in some directions rather than others. Over time, a common understanding of gender develops, and all or most of the participants in this particular community conceptualize gender in a similar way.

There are a number of consequences that result from members of a group or a culture sharing similar interpretations of gender. When groups and cultures divide gender into two realms of female and male, that conception of gender seems concrete and fixed, and the division of people into two genders is something that is taken for granted. In Western culture, for example, societal institutions, structures, and practices are built on this gender system. A dual system of restrooms exists, survey respondents are asked to select one of two genders when they provide demographic information, toy stores are divided into boys' and girls' aisles, and household items and clothing are delineated according to gender, for example. Gender is also used to separate women and men in various ways and can be the basis for unequal or special treatment. Thus, the construction of gender through communication has profound significance. You will learn more about this system of practices in the next chapter.

In the section below, we provide four illustrations of the social construction of gender. Each example shows how something that appears to be fixed and stable in terms of gender actually has been socially constructed. The examples show great variation in how gender is conceptualized in different cultures and through different historical periods; thus, gender is not as "real" as you may be used to thinking that it is. The four illustrations we use to show gender as a social construction are: (1) arbitrary differences; (2) cultural differences; (3) categorical differences; and (4) historical differences.

ARBITRARY DIFFERENCES

One way to see that gender is socially constructed is to look at the key elements of the gender system of most Western cultures. Gender scholars Suzanne Kessler and Wendy McKenna have assembled a list of the beliefs about gender that characterize this system:

- Genitals are the essential signs of gender.
- There are two and only two genders.
- Everyone must be classified as a member of one gender or another.
- The male/female dichotomy is the natural one.[17]

As you read this list, you might find that you agree with all or most of these statements because you actively participate in the system of beliefs, values, and norms that defines gender in these ways. No one told you that this system is arbitrary and, in fact, it may seem like the natural or even the only way to conceptualize gender. But this system is based on one attribute—genitals. If Western cultural beliefs about gender included the idea that genitals do *not* determine gender and that gender is based on something else, a very different kind of gender system would result.

The arbitrariness of the Western gender system is made apparent when you see how a gender system could be organized around something other than genitals. To illustrate how such a system could look, neuroscientist Cordelia Fine imagines a gender system organized around handedness:

> Imagine, for a moment, that we could tell at birth (or even before) whether a child was left-handed or right-handed. By convention, the parents of left-handed babies dress them in pink clothes, wrap them in pink blankets, and decorate their rooms with pink hues. The left-handed baby's bottle, bibs, and pacifiers—and later, cups, plates, and utensils, lunch box and backpack—are often pink or purple with motifs such as butterflies, flowers, and fairies. Parents tend to let the hair of left-handers grow long, and while it is still short in babyhood a barrette or bow (often pink) serves as a stand-in. Right-handed babies, by contrast, are never dressed in pink; nor do they ever have

pink accessories or toys. Although blue is a popular color for right-handed babies, as they get older any color, excluding pink or purple, is acceptable. Clothing and other items for right-handed babies and children commonly portray vehicles, sporting equipment, and space rockets; never butterflies, flowers, or fairies. The hair of right-handers is usually kept short and is never prettified with accessories.[18]

With her parody, Fine highlights the arbitrary nature of the current Western gender system and illustrates how its social construction is just one possible system out of an infinite variety for conceptualizing and organizing gender. Certainly, a focus on genitals as a source of gender division has a logical explanation behind it. As sociologist Risto Heiskala notes, a division based on genitals is "related to the biological reproduction of the human species" and thus to the survival of the species: "It is possible to see equally well with green, blue, grey, and brown eyes, but only men produce sperm and only women have a womb and breasts capable [of] producing milk."[19] Notice that this way of categorizing people addresses only the human reproductive function and leaves out all of the other human capabilities that are crucial for survival of the species—intellect, creativity, resilience, and productivity, for example. Although assignment of meaning to the body on the basis of genitals makes some sense, other activities or attributes could be privileged as the means for dividing people into categories. There is nothing real, magical, or preordained about any system of gender categorization.

Just because a certain category system is arbitrary, however, does not mean it is inconsequential. "Political, legal, economic, scientific, and religious institutions" all engage in social construction to create differences, to "determine that some differences are more important than others, and to assign particular meanings to those differences."[20] The categories that are invented by certain communities can significantly influence people's lives because they are "used to organize experiences, to form social relations, to evaluate others, and to determine social rankings and access to important resources."[21] This is certainly the case with gender divisions and categories, as you will have the opportunity to explore in the next chapter.

CULTURAL DIFFERENCES

Other cultures provide a second example of how gender is socially constructed. You may be accustomed to looking at the world through a lens of only two genders, but in many other cultures, there are individuals who embody genders in addition to male and female. These additional gender categories are known as *third sex* or *third gender*. Two-spirits in native North American cultures, *hijras* in Indian culture, and sworn virgins in the Balkan culture are examples of third genders. Gender categories outside of the binary also exist in Western cultures, of course, but individuals are not accustomed to seeing or acknowledging them—they tend to be dismissed as unnatural or are assumed to be variations on the two reigning categories of female and male. For this reason, to look at cross-cultural examples can be useful as a way to see not only the specific ways in which other cultures understand gender but also the often-hidden variety in the Western gender system. The fact that many cultures have more than two genders again points to the constructedness of any gender system.

TWO-SPIRITS IN NATIVE NORTH AMERICAN CULTURES

A third-gender category historically called *berdache* exists in over 150 native North American tribes.[22] A more contemporary label is *two-spirit*, meaning an individual of mixed gender who embodies both male and female spirits. Today, the term *two-spirit* is used by native peoples to refer to both the historic two-spirit and to those who identify as lesbian, gay, and transgender.[23] According to native beliefs, each person has both an inner and an outer form, and sometimes these forms have different genders, which create two-spirits who fluctuate between them to become a third gender. Some individuals become two-spirits based on dreams or visions, but most are identified by their families because of their preferences for activities associated with a gender other than the one they were assigned at birth.

The attributes and roles of two-spirits vary across cultures, but some common features distinguish two-spirits as members of a distinct gender that is neither male nor female. They cross or mix typical gender roles in their clothing and occupations, wearing the clothing and performing the work associated with both women and men—domestic work, hunting, weaving, and making pottery, for example.[24] Two-spirits are also believed to have sacred powers and typically play special roles in community rituals; they are often healers, conveyors of oral traditions and songs, foretellers of the future, and matchmakers. Although male two-spirits generally engage in sexual relations with men and female two-spirits with women, these patterns are not consistent, and two-spirits may have sexual relationships with individuals of any gender.

HIJRAS IN INDIAN CULTURE

In India, about half a million people identify as a third gender called *hijra* that has been widely recognized for over a thousand years. *Hijras* are recognized as physiological males who have a feminine gender identity and who are seen as neither men nor women. They may be men who choose to relinquish their lives as men; intersex men with ambiguous genitals; or men who undergo castration to remove the penis, testicles, and scrotum. *Hijras* take female names, refer to themselves with feminine pronouns, and wear women's clothing, but they are not considered women because they do not bear children. Neither are they considered men because they do not typically engage in traditional male-female sexual relationships.[25] Like two-spirits, *hijras* are considered to have special spiritual powers and perform special ritual functions. In their traditional ritual role, they danced at weddings and at the birth of male children to bring good luck and fertility, but they also now dance at college functions and bachelor parties.[26]

SWORN VIRGINS IN THE BALKANS

A Balkan third gender recognized since the early 1800s is comprised of persons with female-designated anatomy and physiology who take a vow to abstain from matrimony and motherhood. They wear men's clothing, perform men's jobs, and are publicly recognized as men. They participate in male rituals, vote in public elections, and go to war as soldiers. Women become sworn virgins under a variety of circumstances. One situation that sometimes prompts the transformation of a woman into a man is when there are no male children in a family, so a daughter is raised as a son from infancy or early childhood in order to provide the family with a male heir. Another situation is when someone designated female at birth lives as a woman for many years and then reconstructs herself as a man to escape women's restrictive roles and to enjoy the social status of men.[27]

Seventy-eight-year-old Pashe Keqi is an example of a sworn virgin who became a man at the age of twenty after her father's death. Keqi's four brothers had been imprisoned or killed during military campaigns in Albania, leaving her the only child. To provide a male heir for the family, Keqi cut off her long black hair, dressed in her dead father's clothing, and began living as a man. "Back then, it was better to be a man because . . . a woman and an animal were considered the same thing," Keqi explains. "Now Albanian women have equal rights with men and are even more powerful. I think today it would be fun to be a woman."[28]

Some cultures have devised gender systems that include more than the two categories of male and female that characterize the Western gender system. Gender may appear to be a naturally occurring phenomenon, but it is not an objective biological reality. It is invented through particular interpretations and interactions that construct different conceptualizations of gender from one culture to another. The examples of two-spirits, *hijras*, and sworn virgins illustrate the variety of culturally constructed gender systems.

CATEGORICAL DIFFERENCES

A third example that reveals the social construction of gender is the different terminology that has been used to construct bodies and sexuality over the centuries. You might view your body as either female or male and associate certain terms with your sexuality, and these perceptions might seem very natural to you. But human bodies were not constructed and conceptualized as two opposite forms (male and female) with two sexual orientations (heterosexual and homosexual) until the nineteenth century. The various meanings that were adopted for bodies and sexual orientations from the mid-1700s to the early 1900s were quite different from current meanings and illustrate how prevailing cultural beliefs have a profound impact on categories of gender.

In the mid-eighteenth century, public dissections of cadavers were a primary means of gaining anatomical knowledge. People bought tickets to observe physicians as they explored and classified previously unseen internal organs in public theaters. You may think that the dissection of some bodies with testes and penises and other bodies with ovaries and vaginas would produce precise knowledge of different types of bodies, but what actually happened was the creation of a one-sex model of human anatomy and physiology—a male model. According to historian Thomas Lacquer, the more anatomists dissected, explored, and made drawings of female anatomy, the more they were convinced that the female body was simply an inferior version of the male body.[29]

Anatomical drawings from the period show that the female body was understood to be that of a man "turned outside in,"[30] with the vagina seen as an internal, inverted penis. There was no separate vocabulary for female anatomy. Ovaries were labeled *testes*, fallopian tubes were labeled *spermatic ducts*, and the uterus was understood to be an *internal scrotum*. Although female structures and organs were eventually given names such as *vagina, uterus, clitoris, labia,* and *fallopian tubes,* anatomists did not begin to draw two distinctly different kinds of bodies—one male, the other female—until the late eighteenth and early nineteenth centuries. The reason anatomists were so late in recognizing the physical differences between bodies was that the social construction of their worlds allowed them to give only male labels and meanings to body parts.

Variations in the application of the terms *heterosexual* and *homosexual* provide another example of the social construction of gender. Although a division of sexuality into heterosexual and homosexual orientations may seem like the only logical way to categorize types of sexual activity, many societies have divided sexuality in very different ways. In classical Greece, for example, sexual practices were not distinguished by the object of attraction or sexual activity. Instead, what mattered was "the intensity of that practice" or "the degree of activity" as "shown by the number and frequency of acts."[31] A Greek man's sexual partner could have been "a woman, a free man, or a slave."[32] The kind of partner he had was not what was important. The only offenses that could be committed were "quantitative in nature"[33] and pertained to an excess of sexual activity. What distinguished moral from immoral sexual practice, in other words, was whether a man was moderate or excessive in the amount of sexual activity in which he engaged.

The meanings of the terms *heterosexual* and *homosexual* also have changed over time and provide another example of variation in the construction of gender. The earliest known use of both terms in the United States was by physician James Kiernan in an article published in a medical journal in 1892. Kiernan's definitions of the terms *heterosexual* and *homosexual* were very different from how they are used today. *Heterosexual* referred to people who display "inclinations to both sexes" and who employ "abnormal methods of gratification."[34] In other words, heterosexuals were "essentially bisexuals who masturbated, in modern parlance."[35] Heterosexuals were seen as perverse because they experienced erotic deviance—they were attracted to both genders and also sought sexual pleasure not linked to the reproduction of the species. The "hetero in these heterosexuals referred not to their interest in a *different* sex, but to their desire for *two different sexes*."[36] The term *homosexual* was used to define someone whose "general mental state is that of the opposite sex."[37] For Kiernan, both *heterosexual* and *homosexual* referred to perverted or abnormal sex because they described sexual desires and practices unrelated to procreation. Not until the twentieth century and the influence of psychologists like Sigmund Freud did the terms *homosexuality* and *heterosexuality* acquire their current meanings.

The social construction of concepts and terms to categorize different bodies and sexual orientations continues today. Gender scholar Judith Halberstam, who studies women who feel that they are more masculine than feminine, invented the term *female masculinity* to describe these individuals. She uses the term to indicate that a person can be female and not only *have* masculine characteristics but *be* masculine.[38] Halberstam reasons that women who embody masculinity—and presumably men who embody femininity—should have labels and social meanings that accurately define their gender positions. Biologist Anne Fausto-Sterling has also addressed the need to develop a greater variety of gender terms, focusing on the limitations of a two-gender system for labeling people born with ambiguous genitals. To include intersexed people, Fausto-Sterling proposed a five-gender system—*male, female, herm* (true hermaphrodite), *ferm* (a female pseudo hermaphrodite who has an ovary but male secondary sex characteristics), and *merm* (a male pseudo hermaphrodite who has a testis but female secondary sex characteristics). More recently, Fausto-Sterling has noted that five gender labels are still insufficient to describe the variations in body types that actually exist.[39] As you interact with the gender stories of others, you might recognize a variety of different genders beyond female and male. These examples of the evolution of constructed meanings for bodies and sexualities illustrate again that gender is socially constructed.

HISTORICAL DIFFERENCES

The evolution of women's social roles is another example that points to the social construction of gender. If radically different kinds of behaviors are expected at different times from people with the same kinds of bodies, those behavioral expectations must be constructed rather than stable and biologically real. The gender-role expectations for both men and women have changed significantly over the last few centuries in the United States, but the changes have been particularly wide ranging for women. These changes separate gender roles from biology and, in doing so, make visible the social construction of gender.

In the nineteenth century, women in the United States were constructed as physically inferior to men based on their generally smaller bodies, the belief that they had less physical stamina than men, and the perception that they were physically incapacitated every month by menstruation. In addition, women's nervous systems were seen to be finer, more irritable, and more prone to overstimulation and fatigue than those of men. Women were constructed to be intellectually inferior because they were believed to have smaller brains, and their brains were considered more primitive than those of men.

Because their bodies were perceived to be physically weak, middle-class white women during this century were restricted to the private domestic sphere and were not allowed to participate in the public sphere of work and politics. (Many immigrant women, lower-class women, and women of color, of course, were allowed to and usually had to work.) The public sphere was presented as a rough world of temptation and violence, where a man did what was required in order to succeed. A woman who ventured into such a world could easily be taken advantage of because she was such a weak and delicate creature. A doctrine of separate spheres dictated that women take on only low-pressure activities away from the public sphere such as running a household and raising children. They could not own property, vote, attend college, serve as jurors, or run for political office. True womanhood was constructed as adherence to four virtues: purity (sexual purity), piety (devotion to religion), submissiveness (to fate, duty, God, and men), and domesticity (making the home a refuge for men).

The gender roles of women in the nineteenth century began to change when women who later would be called *feminists* began to challenge their assigned social roles. Women writers such as Mary Wollstonecraft in England and Elizabeth Cady Stanton in the United States advocated for the rights of women and protested the lack of opportunities for women to be educated, employed, and participants in public life. Efforts to change how women's gender roles were constructed gradually became focused on securing the right to vote for women. In the women's suffrage movement of the late 1800s and early 1900s, which is now known as the *first wave* of feminism, suffragists advocated for a change in gender roles—being able to vote would require that women enter the public sphere. The suffragists also violated conventional gender roles themselves—they spoke in public, held demonstrations, and were jailed for their activities—all of which were considered unthinkable for women at the time. On August 26, 1920, the Nineteenth Amendment to the Constitution was passed, granting women the vote. The construction of women as able to contribute to the decisions and policies that affected their lives changed their gender roles on several fronts. They began to enroll in institutions of higher education and to enter professions such as medicine and law that earlier had been closed to them.

Women's gender roles were radically altered again in the 1960s. Women had worked outside the home during World War II, when their work was needed in factories to support the war effort. But they had been sent back to the domestic sphere after the war through a massive propaganda campaign designed to remove women from factory jobs so that their positions could be given to war veterans. As a result, the construction of women in the 1950s and 1960s changed again. For some women, this meant that the only proper life goal was to get married and to be a stay-at-home wife and mother. Prestige lay in having a husband who was successful enough to keep his wife out of the workplace. Of course, many women did work and had to work. Although some middle-class women worked outside of the home, the career options open to them were limited—they could be teachers, nurses, or secretaries. Their limited career options were reflected in newspapers of the time, which divided the classified ads into *Help Wanted—Men* and *Help Wanted— Women*. Medical schools and law schools had quotas to keep women out or to keep their numbers low. During this period, discrimination on the basis of sex was legal, and employers routinely paid women less than men for doing the same jobs. Men were constructed to be the money makers and managers, and women were left out of almost everything having to do with finances. Women could not get credit without male cosigners, for example, and credit cards were issued in their husbands' names. The agreed-upon proper clothing for middle-class women when they went out in public was dresses, hats, girdles, and nylons. Women did not wear pants in most public settings, and girls were not allowed to wear pants to school.

The publication of Betty Friedan's book *The Feminine Mystique* in 1963 challenged the set of gender roles that characterized women's lives in the middle of the twentieth century. Her book triggered a second wave of feminism that was focused on gaining equal rights for women in the public sphere. Passage of the Equal Rights Amendment (ERA) to the Constitution served as a defining event of the second wave, although the movement eventually included younger, college-aged women and women of color advocating a whole range of reforms. The Amendment read: "Equality of rights under the law shall not be denied or abridged by the United States or by any state on account of sex." Although the ERA never became law, many of the changes in women's roles that would have been required by the Amendment were implemented as states adjusted discriminatory laws under the assumption that the ERA would pass.

As a result of the second wave of the feminist movement, the construction of women and their appropriate roles changed considerably. Women routinely began attending college and holding professional jobs that were not limited to teaching, nursing, and secretarial work. An awareness of the impropriety of discrimination led to the passage of laws that could be used to challenge discriminatory practices. Birth control became widely available, providing women with greater freedom in terms of whether and when to have children. Strict dress codes for women disappeared, and women began to wear pants and a variety of styles of clothing both in public and in the home.

In the early twenty-first century, women's roles are different still. Many women—especially young women—believe that a universal definition of femininity does not exist and that all gender roles are open to them. Their identities are multiple, and women of all ethnicities, races, and cultures are constructing their own genders. Sometimes, this takes the form of combining, for example, choices such as career woman, lover, lesbian, mother, consumer, tomboy, and sex symbol. Women are no longer anomalies in professions that used to be for men only. What would have been unthinkable in earlier centuries has been accomplished—a woman running for president of the United States or sitting on the Supreme Court, for example. Many women are unapologetically sexual, and they express their sexuality in whatever ways they feel comfortable, including wearing sexy clothing. They express emotions that traditionally were constructed to be unfeminine such as anger, aggression, and competitiveness, and they use language and gestures that once would have been considered inappropriate for women.

Such changes in women's roles have been made possible in part by the third wave of feminism, which goes by such names as *grrl power, riot-grrl feminism, lipstick feminism, transfeminism,* and *cybergrrl feminism.*[40] The origin of the third wave in the early 1990s is sometimes traced to Rebecca Walker's article, "Becoming the Third Wave," in which she stated, "I am not a postfeminism feminist. I am the Third Wave."[41] As women's options expand and they create new kinds of gender identities, they are once again constructing substantially different gender roles for themselves.

In the United States in the last century, dramatic changes have occurred in the gender roles assigned to women. The fact that such variation can happen within one culture within a relatively short amount of time suggests great variation in the social construction of gender. At one moment in history, women are not allowed into the public sphere; in another, they are welcomed there. At one moment, women are seen to be natural caretakers of men and children; at another, the caretaking role is not seen as a central duty. As is suggested by a review of three periods in American history in which feminism caused changes in women's gender roles, gender is not essentially or inherently tied to bodies. It is constructed through communication to address the desires, motivations, and expectations of those who participate in that construction process.

CHANGEABLE NATURE OF REALITY

An objective reality that is true throughout time for all human beings does not exist. Instead, groups of people create their own realities based on their own interpretations and their sharing of those interpretations through communication. This same process applies to the construction of gender. Evidence for the socially constructed nature of gender can be seen in the arbitrariness of the Western gender system, in third genders in other cultures, varied gender labels for bodies and sexual orientations, and gender roles that evolve over time.

Because reality is less real and concrete than you might previously have thought, we encourage you to see that everything can be changed. Even those aspects of experience that appear to be fixed and immutable are changeable because they are constructed. Individuals have the capacity to change even entrenched social patterns and the most solid-appearing structures through communication. Because all individuals contribute to the social construction of reality, you are an agent in the making of your world, affecting what happens through your communication.[42] Your world is made and remade in each moment as you make and manage meanings through the process of communication. Whether through acts of support, apathy, or defiance, you create and recreate the structures under whose influence you live.

In the next chapter, you will have an opportunity to do some more exploring of and reflecting on the process of social construction. In particular, you'll see the social construction of gender in action as you learn about the gender system that characterizes life in the United States—the gender binary. Constructed and reinforced through various communicative practices, it infuses virtually all aspects of your life.

■ NOTES

[1] Jonathan Potter, *Representing Reality: Discourse, Rhetoric and Social Construction* (Thousand Oaks, CA: Sage, 1966), 22.

[2] Kenneth Burke, *Language as Symbolic Action: Essays on Life, Literature, and Method* (Berkeley: University of California Press, 1966), 5.

[3] Peter L. Berger and Thomas Luckmann, *The Social Construction of Reality: A Treatise in the Sociology of Knowledge* (Garden City, NY: Anchor/Doubleday, 1967), 68.

[4] Berger and Luckmann, *The Social Construction of Reality*, 69.

[5] Berger and Luckmann, *The Social Construction of Reality*, 68.

[6] Berger and Luckmann, *The Social Construction of Reality*, 58.

[7] Berger and Luckmann, *The Social Construction of Reality*, 59.

[8] Berger and Luckmann, *The Social Construction of Reality*, 59.

[9] Berger and Luckmann, *The Social Construction of Reality*, 58.

[10] Bryan Gibel, "Law Makes Work Easier for Breast-Feeding Moms," Daily Lobo.com, September 15, 2009, http://www.dailylobo.com/index.php/article/2007/03/law_makes_work_easier_for_breastfeeding_moms

[11] David Treuer, "How Do You Prove You're an Indian?" December 20, 2011, http://www.nytimes.com/2011/12/21/opinion/for-indian-tribes-blood-shouldnt-be-everything.html

[12] Berger and Luckmann, *The Social Construction of Reality,* 87.

[13] David M. Newman, *Identities and Inequalities: Exploring the Intersections of Race, Class, Gender, and Sexuality* (Boston: McGraw-Hill, 2007), 36.

[14] Shari L. Thurer, *The End of Gender: A Psychological Autopsy* (New York: Routledge, 2005), 13.

[15] Thurer, *The End of Gender,* 15.

[16] Monique Wittig, "One Is Not Born a Woman," in *Feminist Frameworks: Alternative Theoretical Accounts of the Relations between Women and Men,* ed. Alison M. Jaggar and Paula S. Rothenberg, 3rd ed. (Boston: McGraw-Hill, 1993), 179.

[17] Suzanne J. Kessler and Wendy McKenna, *Gender: An Ethnomethodological Approach* (Chicago: University of Chicago Press, 1978), 113–14.

[18] Cordelia Fine, *Delusions of Gender: How Our Minds, Society, and Neurosexism Create Difference* (New York: W. W. Norton, 2010), 209–10.

[19] Risto Heiskala, "Modernity and the Articulation of the Gender System: Order, Conflict, and Chaos," *Semiotica* 173 (2009): 219.

[20] Karen E. Rosenblum and Toni-Michelle C. Travis, "Constructing Categories of Difference: Framework Essay," in *The Meaning of Difference: American Constructions of Race, Sex and Gender, Social Class, and Sexual Orientation,* ed. Karen E. Rosenblum and Toni-Michelle C. Travis, 3rd ed. (Boston: McGraw-Hill, 2003), 3.

[21] Newman, *Identities and Inequalities,* 41–42.

[22] Will Roscoe, "Native Americans," in *glbtq: An Encyclopedia of Gay, Lesbian, Bisexual, Transgender, and Queer Culture,* ed. Claude J. Summers (Chicago: glbtq, 2004), http://www.glbtq.com/social-sciences/native_americans,3.html

[23] Roscoe, "Native Americans."

[24] Will Roscoe, "How to Become a Berdache: Toward a Unified Analysis of Gender Diversity," in *Third Sex, Third Gender: Beyond Sexual Dimorphism in Culture and History,* ed. Gilbert Herdt (New York: Zone, 1994), 329–72.

[25] Serena Nanda, "Hijras: An Alternate Sex and Gender Role in India," in *Third Sex, Third Gender: Beyond Sexual Dimorphism in Culture and History,* ed. Gilbert Herdt (New York: Zone, 1994), 373–418.

[26] Ruth M. Pettis, "Hijras," in *glbtq: An Encyclopedia of Gay, Lesbian, Bisexual, Transgender, and Queer Culture,* ed. Claude J. Summers (Chicago: glbtq, 2004), www.glbtq.com/social-sciences/hijras.html

[27] René Grémaux, "Woman Becomes Man in the Balkans," in *Third Sex, Third Gender: Beyond Sexual Dimorphism in Culture and History,* ed. Gilbert Herdt (New York: Zone, 1994), 267.

[28] Dan Bilefsky, "Albanian Custom Fades: Woman as Family Man," http://nytimes.com/2008/06/25/world/europe/25virgins.html

[29] Thomas Lacquer, *Making Sex: Body and Gender from the Greeks to Freud* (Cambridge, MA: Harvard University Press, 1990), 70.

[30] Lacquer, *Making Sex,* 81.

[31] Michel Foucault, *The Use of Pleasure: The History of Sexuality: Volume 2,* trans. Robert Hurley (New York: Pantheon, 1985), 44.

[32] Foucault, *The Use of Pleasure*, 47.

[33] Foucault, *The Use of Pleasure*, 45.

[34] Jonathan Ned Katz, "The Invention of Heterosexuality: The Debut of the Heterosexual," in *Sexualities & Communication in Everyday Life: A Reader*, ed. Karen E. Lovaas and Mercilee M. Jenkins (Thousand Oaks, CA: Sage, 2007), 21–22.

[35] Amin Ghaziani, "The Reinvention of Heterosexuality," *The Gay & Lesbian Review Worldwide* 17 (2010): 27.

[36] Katz, "The Invention of Heterosexuality," 22.

[37] Katz, "The Invention of Heterosexuality," 22.

[38] Judith Halberstam, *Female Masculinity* (Durham, NC: Duke University Press, 1998), 1–4.

[39] Anne Fausto-Sterling, "The Five Sexes, Revisited," in *The Social Construction of Difference and Inequality: Race, Class, Gender, and Sexuality*, ed. Tracy E. Ore, 4th ed. (Boston: McGraw-Hill, 2009), 119–26.

[40] Charlotte Kroløkke and Anne Scott Sorensen, *Gender Communication Theories and Analyses: From Silence to Performance* (Thousand Oaks, CA: Sage, 2006), 15.

[41] Rebecca Walker, "Becoming the Third Wave," *Ms.*, January–February, 1992, 41.

[42] W. Barnett Pearce, *Making Social Worlds: A Communication Perspective* (Malden, MA: Blackwell, 2007).

three

THE CLASSICS
THE GENDER BINARY

> *He is playing masculine. She is playing feminine.*
> *He is playing masculine because she is playing feminine.*
> *She is playing feminine because he is playing masculine. . . .*
> *If he were not playing masculine, he might well be*
> *more feminine than she is—except when she is playing*
> *very feminine. If she were not playing feminine,*
> *she might well be more masculine than he is—*
> *except when he is playing very masculine.*
> *So he plays harder. And she plays . . . softer. . . .*
> *How do we call off the game?*
>
> Betty Roszak and Theodore Roszak, *Masculine/Feminine*

The classics teach people what it means to be human in the context of a cultural tradition. Classics such as Mark Twain's book *The Adventures of Huckleberry Finn*, Michael's Curtiz's film *Casablanca*, and Mary Cassatt's painting *Mother and Child* teach people in Western culture how to answer big questions about life: What is a compassionate person? Is romantic love or loyalty to a cause more important? What is the essence of a mother-child relationship? As a student, you may have encountered these and other Western classics without thinking very much about why they endure or how they have taught you to think about yourself, other people, and the world. Part of the reason that some works continue to be contemplated by generation after generation is, of course, because they are elevated examples of certain art forms or genres, but classics also endure because they offer a shared cultural experience that helps create and maintain a community of people. Classics are foundational to culture because, by addressing major human questions through a particular cultural lens, they contribute to the social construction of a shared and stable reality.

Another type of enduring classic is the cultural master narrative.[1] Cultural master narratives are powerful stories that express "the social arrangements and values of a society" and instruct members of a culture to be certain types of people who live certain kinds of lives.[2] Master narratives socially construct reality by offering you ways to see yourself and the world and by encouraging you to think, feel, and behave in prescribed fashions. Unlike the plot of a single book or a movie, master narratives are not located in one source; rather, they play out through many cultural artifacts, systems, and institutions. A theme like democracy or freedom may be the basis for a movie plot and also play out in institutions such as Congress and the courts. Themes like equality and love are the subject of many books and works of art, and they play out in social systems like marriage and family. Master narratives strongly influence people in a culture by providing frameworks for living that are presented and reinforced through multiple sources.

The master narratives of a culture—whether they are portrayed in a book, a movie, a painting, or a system like a family—"naturalize the status quo" by defining certain types of people as ideal and certain behaviors as the norm.[3] Master narratives tell you what kind of person you should be and how you should act. In *The Adventures of Huckleberry Finn*, Huck Finn teaches you to be compassionate and loyal; *Casablanca* tells you to have moral courage and be true to your beliefs; and Cassatt's painting *Mother and Child* shows you the tender love a mother should feel toward her child. In these works, master narratives prescribe human behaviors by repeating ideas and values that reinforce cultural norms. By doing so, they contribute to the ongoing stability of a certain way of life.

Two of life's biggest questions in the Western world are: What does it mean to be a woman? What does it mean to be a man? These questions are addressed in a classic master narrative that teaches you to think about gender in prescribed ways and to adopt particular ways of being gendered. This master narrative establishes a status quo by defining normative social arrangements and values concerning gender. Like other master narratives, this one is reflected in a variety of cultural artifacts, systems, and institutions—in everything from gendered clothing to religious beliefs to marriage vows. The most striking characteristic of the Western master narrative about gender is the division of the world into two realms—masculine and feminine. Because of this division into two distinct parts, the narrative is often called the *gender binary*. In the following sections, we describe this binary, examine the ideals it reinforces, look at how it influences you throughout your life, and discuss how it functions as a matrix for gender.

BINARY GENDER SYSTEM

A binary is the division of something into two parts, and, in Western cultures, binaries are the default mode for organizing and structuring the world. Because of this perspective, to see things in opposites and as having two—and only two—possibilities seems natural. In almost every realm of Western thought—culture, economics, states of being, looks, and emotions, for example—meaning is constructed through binary frameworks. Some of these frameworks are: civilized/savage, East/West, rich/poor, dependent/independent, oppressed/liberated, pretty/ugly, and happy/sad. As a Westerner, you have been trained to perceive categories in these types of binary opposites instead of seeing life as more nuanced. For example, the Western perspective on life leads to seeing the answer to a question as right or wrong, a news story as true or false, and actions as good or bad. A binary, oppositional perspective masks more complex and realistic views—a question can be partially right, a news story can be somewhat true, and an action can have both good and bad consequences.

Binary systems also encourage you to value one part of an oppositional pair over the other. When a binary framework is in place, most people see one of the categories as better or more desirable than the other. If you grew up in Western society, you probably can identify which side of the above binaries is desirable or undesirable. Civilized, West, rich, independent, liberated, pretty, and happy are positively valued in Western culture. Their opposites—savage, East, poor, dependent, oppressed, ugly, and sad—are seen as negative or less desirable. Categorization into binary opposites, then, creates a hierarchy of more and less valued concepts.

The binary Western perspective on the world extends to gender; people are assigned one of two identities—male or female. When a baby is born, you ask "What did you have?" When you tell a story about someone, one of the first things you say is, "Last night, I met this guy . . ." or

"A woman in my communication class. . . ." You mention assigned categories because you have learned that whether a person is male or female is fundamentally significant. As is true of other binary opposites, the binary gender system implies that the distinction is natural and inevitable and that there are two—and only two—genders, one feminine and the other masculine.[4]

Because the categories of female and male seem natural, designating a person as female or male based on biological and physical characteristics—their genitals, hormones, and reproductive systems—seems straightforward and uncomplicated. When you see an adult with breasts, long hair, and feminine features, you label this person a *woman* according to the terms of the gender binary. When you meet someone with broad shoulders, facial hair, and an Adam's apple, you label this person a *man*. Yet, if you think about it, this automatic designation is usually based on assumptions because, in most social circumstances, you cannot tell the nature of someone's genitals, hormones, or reproductive system. Unless you are changing a baby's diaper, are on a nude beach, or are in an intimate relationship with someone, you do not, in fact, know that a person you are calling *female* or *male* belongs to either category based on physical characteristics.

So natural does the binary categorization of gender seem that it can be disconcerting not to know immediately if the person you are looking at is male or female. The importance of correctly signaling femaleness or maleness is what causes new parents to dress their infants in pink or blue clothing and surround them with Barbie dolls or Tonka trucks. During the 1960s, when boys and young men began to wear their hair long, some adults complained that they could no longer tell who was female and who was male. Today, some people intentionally obscure their genders by wearing ambiguous clothing that combines expected male and female gender presentations. Other people simply do not physically resemble what males and females are supposed to look like in the binary. When you encounter someone of ambiguous gender walking across campus, you might do a double take to try to figure out which gender applies because a person must be one or the other, according to the dictates of the binary.

Just as the answer to a question can be partially right or partially wrong, the binary's feminine/masculine distinction is inadequate to categorize all genders. While Western culture designates only female and male bodies, human bodies vary significantly in terms of biological appearance and functioning. There are many intersexed people whose genitals, hormones, and/or reproductive systems cannot clearly be classified as either male or female. Biologist Anne Fausto-Sterling estimates the percentage of babies born with a body that is neither male nor female as 1.7.[5] Because Western culture has socially constructed only two categories for gendered beings, there is no category for these babies. Because the female/male binary system serves as the normative standard into which everyone is expected to fit, the traditional response to intersexed babies is to alter them surgically to make them more closely resemble either the male or female biological category.

Just as actions are supposed to be good or bad in a binary—and not some combination—the oppositional nature of the gender binary sets up norms and expectations that females and males have distinct sets of emotions and behaviors. Which gender dreams about a wedding? Cries easily? Is insensitive to the feelings of others? Talks more? Because you live in the gender binary and are schooled in the classic master narrative that suggests that certain feelings and actions are associated with females and others with males, you probably respond without hesitation, choosing *either* men *or* women as the answer to each question. Yet, you have probably experienced both males and females talking about getting married someday, crying when they are upset, being insensitive, and dominating conversations. Likewise, in any group, all of the men are not taller, bigger, and stronger than all of the women. Conditioned by the binary, however, it seems reasonable to say, "men are stronger than women." All women are not shorter, smaller, and weaker than all men, yet many people accept the statement "women are the weaker sex" as natural. The classic gender master narrative, in other words, simplifies the range of behaviors that people exhibit into one of two different types—male or female.

The categorization of all people into male and female is not the only consequence of the gender binary. As in all binaries, one term is seen as better than the other. In the Western gender binary, the masculine typically is valued more than the feminine, and the feminine is considered less than, weaker than, or somehow deficient compared to the masculine. Even concepts that are not inherently gendered—peace and war, irrationality and rationality, for example—get gendered according to these valuations. Using violence as a means of settling disputes is considered male; making decisions on the basis of feelings is considered female.

Within the general categories of masculine and feminine, subcategories further refine the different valuing of gender categories. The masculine gender is valued more when it is combined with heterosexuality and whiteness. The Western master narrative considers not white and not straight not only different but also deviant from what is ideal.[6] Gender theorist Judith Butler refers to this consequence of the binary as *heterosex-*

ual hegemony to convey heterosexuality as a norm or standard.[7] According to Butler, the division of the world into masculine and feminine categories, combined with heteronormative expectations, is entrenched in every Western cultural social system and institution. This means that in all systems and institutions—family, religion, technology, the economy, and politics, for example—you are valued more if you are white, male, and heterosexual.

In the classic gender binary, those who meet idealized or normative gender expectations—people who are white, male, and heterosexual—are seen as more legitimate and more important than other people. They experience their identity as "normal, neutral, and universal."[8] Those who meet normative expectations have more access to resources, and their perspectives are given more weight and more status.[9] Historically, white, male, heterosexual people have had more political and social power than other people. They have had more say in and control over how social institutions—schools, churches, and governments, for example—are organized. In contrast, those who do not fit the ideals or norms of the gender binary are more likely to be marginalized, excluded, and underrepresented in the world. Consequently, people who aren't white, male, and heterosexual "have to adjust their lives according to the dominant perspective."[10] The hierarchy of values translates into very different life experiences for those who are valued most by the binary gender system from those who are not valued as much.

The classic Western master narrative about gender teaches people the meaning of male or female. The master narrative is fundamentally binary, which means it classifies each person as male or female based on genitals, divides human attributes and emotions into two realms, and values one category over the other. Like all classics, the gender binary teaches people to live in a particular culture—specifically, it teaches you how to be male or female and how to maintain existing social relations and institutions. We turn now to the ideals for femininity and masculinity that the binary prescribes.

BINARY IDEALS

Like all classics, the master narrative of the gender binary instructs members of Western culture in the right way to be a gendered person. It also reinforces normative roles in order to maintain a cultural community of certain systems and institutions. Similar to the messages you receive from looking at Cassatt's painting of a loving mother gazing at her child or a film like *Casablanca* that depicts a man who is principled and brave enough to stand up for what he believes, the binary gender system presents ideals that prescribe what you as a man or as a woman should value in life. The binary narrative instructs you how to be an ideal person in terms of appearance, personality, and behaviors. The gender ideals of the binary exert an influence that affects everything, including how you cut your hair, the clothes you wear, what makes you laugh or cry (and how and when), the career you choose, the kind of partner you find attractive, and your goals in life. These ideals represent an unreachable pinnacle of expectations for and about women and men—expectations that no real human being is able to fulfill.[11]

There are, of course, variations on the ideals for men and women because the ideals vary across different cultures and subcultures.[12] For example, in the United States, how you are supposed to look and act in order to be an ideal woman changes somewhat if you are black or Asian, Mormon or Unitarian, in the Army or a civilian. Likewise, what it means to be an ideal man in rural New Cordell, Oklahoma, is socially constructed differently from the ideal man in a city like Oakland, California. However, whatever your ethnicity and religious beliefs and no matter where you live, people in Western culture are taught standards for being a woman that differ from the standards for being a man. That each gender is so clearly recognizable by its prescribed type is testament to the strength and reach of the binary. Whether you subscribe to or resist the ideals that are presented to you by your primary culture and subcultures does not diminish their impact. There is still always a system of ideals in place as models for both masculine and feminine genders.

According to the master narrative of the binary, an ideal man is active, aggressive, athletic, competitive, dominant, independent, logical, self-confident, and unemotional. These ideal attributes of a masculine personality mean that the ideal man is expected to rely on himself (never asking for directions); to do whatever it takes to win and dominate; and above all, to do nothing—such as crying, begging, or backing down—that would earn him the label of *sissy*. The ideal man is a leader—the initiator in dating, sex, and business—and the provider for and head of his household. Certain tasks are perceived to be within his domain—running world governments, designing new technologies, and repairing machines—and he may be rewarded, by peers at least, for having multiple sexual partners. The ideal man may be physically attractive, but attractiveness based on appearance is less important than the attractiveness that comes because of achievements, status, and power. He is, above all, to be manly in everything he does—from the way he parts his hair to how he strides confidently down the street to how he holds a woman when he kisses her.

The binary says that the ideal woman is passive, cooperative, emotional, submissive, and dependent. She is supposed to be sensitive, understanding, tactful, and supportive. A consequence of these prescribed characteristics is that a woman is presumed to be better than a man—or even a natural—at caretaking. The ideal woman takes responsibility for her family's emotional and physical well-being. Whether she has a career or not and whether or not her partner helps her, the household, according to the ideals of the binary, is the woman's domain. She is supposed to manage the housework, laundry, and meals expertly; keep track of the family's social calendar; buy cards and gifts for birthdays and holidays; and coordinate the activities and gatherings that occur at the house, including children's sleepovers, dinner parties, and family celebrations. In terms of appearance, the ideal woman is sexually attractive to men, and she is expected to devote time and money to her appearance—shaving her legs and armpits, putting on makeup, and dressing in a feminine style. During sex, the ideal woman lets the man take the lead.

There is an obvious symmetry to this binary gender narrative: Ideal men and ideal women are socially constructed as complementary opposites. He leads and she follows; he is independent and she is dependent; he is unemotional and she is sensitive; and he is the head of the family—the breadwinner and decision maker—and she is the body, doing the work required to take care of the home and the people in the family. While the ideal man organizes and maintains the world, the ideal woman organizes and maintains the domestic sphere. The binary dictates that ideal femininity is virtually the mirror opposite of ideal masculinity. Together, the ideal man and woman form a whole entity that is fundamentally important to the Western way of life. The classic master narrative provides for the continuance of culture through the courtship of heterosexual couples, marriage, the birth of children, and the stability of the family unit. In other words, the binary gender master narrative not only tells you who to be, but it also provides an ideal lifelong script that culminates in one man and one woman falling in love, uniting for life, and bearing children.

Earlier, we referred to the binary's masculine and feminine ideals as an *unreachable pinnacle* of expectations that no real human can totally fulfill. No real woman is perfectly beautiful and sexy, in control of every dynamic in her family, and totally submissive and happy to follow a man.

No real man is competent in every area of life, a good leader at all times, and always unemotional. If you notice, the Western master narrative leaves a lot of real people out—those who are single; people without children; gay and lesbian people; and those without the economic resources to fulfill the expectations of courtship, home ownership, and children, to name a few. You probably agree that some of the ideal attributes of men and women are fitting goals for you as a person, and you probably find some of the ideal attributes humorous and others offensive. No matter how you judge them, however, you are aware of some version of these ideals because you have grown up in the binary system. You are familiar with this narrative whether you agree or disagree with the standards it presents. Even if you believe things have changed—that equality between the genders has been achieved and people can be and do whatever they want in terms of gender expression—you know the master narrative of the gender binary because you are immersed in it and its ongoing influence.

Why do all people in Western culture, regardless of their genders or the ways they actually live their lives, know this narrative so well? We turn now to how—ever since you were born—you have been exposed to and have internalized the ideals of the binary's master narrative. The media, a major source of information about the binary, will be addressed in a later chapter; for now, we focus on the way relationships, artifacts, systems, and institutions perpetuate feminine and masculine gender ideals through communication.

LIFE IN THE GENDER BINARY

The binary influences your entire life—from before birth, through childhood and adolescence, and into your adulthood and old age. At each stage of life, communication in relationships, artifacts, social systems, and institutions construct and reinforce a social reality of you as a gendered person. As an infant and a child, the binary system affected everything from how you were named and cared for to the language and religion you were taught to how your family life and education were managed. During your adolescence, the binary played a primary role in instructing you how to be a young woman or a young man, how to date and enter romantic relationships, and how to prepare for adulthood through coming-of-age rituals. Now that you are an adult, the binary continues to play a major role in defining who you are as a person as well as prescribing behaviors in your relationships, work, and career. The influence of the gender binary will continue as long as you live.

In the following sections, we discuss each of these stages—infancy and childhood, adolescence and young adulthood, and adulthood and old age—and give examples of how the binary master narrative plays out in individual lives. We are, of course, unable to fully account for how the binary master narrative specifically may have influenced and continues to influence you personally. For each stage, we present a range of details that reflect common Western experiences, and we encourage you to think beyond what you encounter on these pages to how the gender binary has played out in your unique life.

INFANCY AND CHILDHOOD

Your parent or parents might have had a gender preference and might have chosen to learn your gender during an ultrasound exam before you were born. Today, a gender-detection kit is available on the Internet that reveals whether a seven-week-old fetus is male or female.[13] Expectant parents buy these kits because they are curious about or have a preference for their baby's gender. In cultures where males have considerably more opportunities and status than females, there is a preference for sons over daughters. Even in the United States, many men say they want a son to play basketball or baseball with and someone who will carry on the family name. Many women say they want daughters so they can dress them in cute, frilly clothes; because they think raising a girl will be easier than raising a boy; and because they think they will have a special lifetime bond with a daughter that they will not have with a son.[14]

Once they know the gender of their child, parents typically put into place all kinds of binary gender practices, often without being aware that they are doing so. Education professor Kara Smith found that before an ultrasound, people use gender-neutral language to refer to a baby—*baby, the kidlet, little one,* or just *it*. After an ultrasound, however, when the baby's gender is known, mothers tend to talk to boy babies in a low voice and to girls in a higher voice. Mothers even touch their bellies differently after learning the gender of a child—boys get firm pats, and girls receive gentle caresses.[15] These patterns of talk and touch indicate not only that mothers think differently about girl babies and boy babies but that they also believe that the differences are significant enough to require different kinds of interaction.

That differently gendered parents have different roles to play in a child's life is reinforced before babies are born by various cultural rituals such as the baby shower. Although some baby showers are now given for couples, many are still female-only affairs designed to "shower" the expectant mother with things she needs to take care of a baby—baby clothes, diapers, blankets, furniture, and advice about how to be a mother. Karen's recent experience at a baby shower is not atypical. While the female relatives and friends of the expectant mother gathered for the shower, their male spouses and partners went to Hooters. There is no cultural ritual equivalent to a baby shower for men. They are congratulated with cigars for having "caused" the pregnancy, but the master narrative does not include a plot line for showering men with gifts and advice in preparation for fatherhood. Fathers to be are given the message that—while they can anticipate being breadwinners and heads of their households—they also can expect to be the somewhat peripheral parent when their child is born.

At birth, other expectations of the gender binary come into play. When you were born, you were given a name; in all likelihood, that name reflects the binary. Pick up any book or go to any website of baby names, and you will find separate sections for girls' and boys' names. In *The Perfect Baby Name*, Jeanine Cox notes that parents tend to name girls with exotic or unique names, but they want familiar, strong names for boys. Girls' names often end in *a* sounds and are softer sounding than boys' names—*Anna, Juanita, Hannah,* and *Sophia,* for example. Flower names are popular for girls—*Lily, Rose, Heather,* and *Jasmine*—and signal a delicate and feminine nature. Boys' names often end in consonants, giving the impression of being stronger, firmer, and hardier: *Nathan, Adam, Behruz, Ramón,* and *John.* The social construction of names, in other words, involves separating babies into two types—females and males.

Admittedly, increasing numbers of names are used for both girls and boys—*Rory, Quinn, Casey,* and *Rowan,* for example—but in all of these cases, a masculine name has become a feminine name; female-associated names rarely are given to boys. Furthermore, even when parents have different last names, children are most often given the last names of their fathers. The father's last name—not the mother's—is the one that will be passed on, suggesting that names have very different meanings and significance for women and men in the binary.

The different gendering of boys and girls continues in the treatment newborns receive. Mothers talk more with their girl babies and are more attentive to changes in their daughters' facial expressions than in their sons'. Even at birth, boy babies are considered stronger and more capable and are treated more roughly than are baby girls. In one study of thirty newborns, parents were asked to describe their babies within twenty-four hours of birth. They used words like "firmer, more alert, stronger, hardier" for boys and words like "softer, more awkward and inattentive, weaker, and more delicate" for girls. These descriptions were given despite the fact that hospital records showed that the fifteen girls and fifteen boys were virtually indistinguishable in terms of weight, height, reflexes, and activity level.[16] The knowledge that their baby was female or male—and not the appearance and behavior of the infant—was enough to cause parents to perceive substantial differences in girls and boys.

Different perceptions of and expectations for gender continue as a child grows. In one study of gender expectations, a six-month-old baby, dressed in blue pants, was introduced as *Adam* to one group of young mothers and, dressed in a pink dress, as *Beth* to another group. In each case, the mothers were given three toys to offer to the baby—a fish, a doll, and a train. When the women thought the baby was a girl, they gave the baby the doll; when they assumed the baby was a boy, they most often gave the baby the train. When asked how they knew the baby was a girl (the baby was, in fact, a boy), one mother said she knew because the baby was "sweet" and cried like a girl.[17] Fathers also bring expectations to parenting. Fathers touch their baby boys more than their baby girls, play with sons more than with daughters at the age of one, and roughhouse with their sons while treating infant daughters more gently.[18] Parents' gendered expectations, then, are more predictive of how they interact with their children than are the children's own abilities and behaviors.

Not only did your parents or caretakers have different expectations of you and treat you differently because of the gender binary, but the language you learned reinforced gender differences as well. As soon as you began to speak, your language gave you clear and different categories for male and female. You were taught that people who looked like your mother were one thing, and people like your father were an entirely different thing. In English, the standard form of many words is the masculine—*waiter, poet,* and *actor,* for example—and the inherent assumption used to be that these roles were inhabited by only men. When women began to participate in these roles, a suffix was added to denote that someone other than a man was filling the role, so the words for the roles when women performed them became *waitress, poetess,* and *actress.* Although the words designating some roles are becoming more gender neutral—*server, poet,* and *actor* can be used for both genders, for example—this is not a consistent practice. When you were a child, what did you call the person who delivered the mail or the person who drove the big noisy truck and put out fires? The shift from *mailman* and *fireman* to the genderless *mail carrier* and *firefighter* continues to feel unnatural to and be resisted by many people. The point is, as a child, you were taught gendered words for different categories of people, which helped to divide your world into the two different spheres according to the gender binary.

The two categories of words your language gave you, like all binary oppositions, also contain the message that some words are more valuable than others. That the masculine form of words is valued more than the feminine form is apparent in the use of *man* and *mankind* as universal terms that mean *all people*, both men and women. When Apollo 11 astronaut Neil Armstrong stepped on the moon, he said, "That's one small step for [a] man, one giant leap for mankind"—using masculine generic language, where the masculine form is employed to describe both men and women. Presumably, at this important event, Armstrong intended to include women in his poetic reflection. Perhaps you are thinking that this kind of masculine form no longer applies—it is decades old, and many people now say *humankind* or *people* instead of *man*. But consider that space flights are still talked about as *manned*—you *man* the controls and *man* the booth—and city workers remove *manhole* covers to fix the sewer. Consider how many times a day you say *you guys* to mean both women and men. There is not an equivalent term for women—*you gals* is used in some contexts, but it is not nearly as prominent as *you guys* and would never stand for both genders. Further, if you want to refer to one individual when the gender is unmarked—"each student should bring his book to class"—you are probably accustomed to using this masculinized form. If you want to avoid the masculine form, you might say the awkward "his or her" or violate rules of grammar by using the plural pronoun—"each student should bring their book to class." Another option is to convert the sentence to plural: "Students should bring *their* books to class." But you probably would not say, "Each student should bring her book to class" if you meant a class of both men and women. Masculine language, then, is still very much in use; avoiding it often requires conscious effort, and the results are often unwieldy.

The ways in which the binary divides the world into masculine and feminine spheres extend to the environments in which you live and the objects in those environments. The gender master narrative constructs different spaces for girls, boys, women, and men. Do you remember your room when you were little? If you're female, it might have been pink and purple, maybe with dainty flowers on the wallpaper, lots of ruffles on the pillows, and stuffed animals on the bed. The clothes in your dresser and closet also may have been pink and frilly. Your toys were similarly designed for girls—Barbie dolls and baby dolls, Disney movies about and accessories for princesses, toy makeup kits, and sparkly plastic high heels. Everything suggested that you as a girl are dreamy, soft, and beautiful. If you're male, your room might have had a theme of sports, *Star Wars,* or jungle animals with strong colors—blue, green, or yellow. Your drawers probably were full of jeans and T-shirts with animals and sports items on them, and the toys you were given included footballs and baseballs, Hot Wheels and GI Joe action figures, hammers and dump trucks, and video games. Together, the décor, clothes, and toys communicated the expectations of the gender binary for you as a boy. You should be tough, strong, and adventurous.

Your childhood room was not the only space that gave you messages about what it meant to be gendered one way or the other. Perhaps the spaces your parents inhabited in your home were gendered, too. Did your father have a woodworking shop, an area to work on cars in the garage, or a room with a pool table and a big-screen TV? Was your mother's domain the kitchen? In many households, the woman is responsible for everything that occurs in or is related to the kitchen—shopping, putting groceries away, cooking, and cleaning—as well as activities not necessarily connected to cooking such as overseeing children's homework, paying bills, and sewing. Men might have a study or library in a home, whereas many women use the kitchen table for their projects.

The same is true of other rooms in the house. Sharon and Patrick, who are both professors, are expecting their first child. They live in a three-bedroom house, and before the pregnancy, they shared a bedroom and each had an office. With the impending birth of the baby, Sharon has made her study into a dual-use space—both the nursery and her study. The message to the child who shares the room with her will be that mothers are primarily responsible for parenting and that women can work with interruptions. Environments are not neutral spaces; they are places that demonstrate the gender binary, and you learned important lessons about gender from how your childhood home was used differently by the people in your life.

Religion is another part of life that may have taught you the roles expected of men and women in the binary. If you were raised in a formal religion, you have been exposed to the binary in gender stories as told in sacred texts and by priests, rabbis, or imams. Many religious traditions, for example, consider the male and female genders to be equal before God. The two genders are seen as physically and emotionally different, however, so this equality is complementary and is the basis for a division of labor by gender. The ideal woman in these religions accepts that her primary responsibility is to fulfill her roles as wife and mother and to care for her husband, their children, and the home. The ideal man is supposed to assume authority over and guardianship of his wife and children, and his primary role is to work outside the home to support his wife and family. Kathy provides an example of how the roles taught by some religions communicate the gender binary to children. She grew up in a highly religious home, and she literally believed what she heard in church about men being responsible for work outside the home and women responsible for work within the home: "When my mom quit being a stay-at-home mom and went to work, I was really confused about why she was working and my older brother was watching me after school. I thought my mom should stay home with me, and my brother should go to work because he was the 'man.'" If, as a child, you were taught how to be a female or male person according to a particular religion, you may have internalized very clear notions of what those roles entail.

Schools are also places in which the influence of the gender binary is evident. Because schools have a strong normative and socializing function, they are one of the primary institutions through which the binary master narrative is communicated to children. One of the messages schools reinforce is not unlike the one that most children learn at home— that there are two separate and distinct spheres for males and females. Teachers often refer to the students in their classes not as *students* but as *girls and boys*,[19] which reinforces the differences rather than the similarities between them. When being assigned seats in class, playing, working, and standing in line, children often are grouped or segregated by gender.[20] School is one of the first places where children learn that they must strictly divide themselves along gender lines not only to use toilets but also to comb their hair and wash their hands.

Sports in school are often divided—some schools offer football only for boys and stickball for girls, for example—but the notion of two separate spheres is reinforced even when children are allowed to play the same games and sports. They often are divided by gender into teams, assigned to use separate equipment, and segregated into different locker rooms. When interactions are so segregated in one of their primary environments, children cannot help but think of the other gender as very different in every way. Marta's recollection of grade school captures how powerfully this distinction can play out: "As a child, I thought boys had 'cooties,' so I didn't want to have anything to do with them. So many things in my life made me very aware that boys were not like me."

The socializing power of the gender binary is especially apparent—at home, in schools, and elsewhere—when a child deviates from traditional gender expectations. When children try to cross genders in terms of activities, they are often reprimanded by adults. The girl who tries to play football is admonished for getting dirty and encouraged to play on the swings instead; the boy who wants to take up ballroom dancing instead of karate is called a *sissy* by his father. Casey told us of seeing a mother in a library who "kept calling her son a 'girl' because he was crying." If a child is really good at a behavior associated with the other gender, those involved may comment on it. This was the case with Brittany, who said, "I started playing sports at age eight, and the coaches would say, 'You're an athlete, not a girl.' To be athletic meant to be as different as possible from a girl." André recounts being five years old when he learned the clear difference between girl and boy activities: "I saw the *Nutcracker* ballet for the first time and was so enchanted by the male dancers that I asked for lessons. The first day, I showed up in tights and slippers, and I was the only boy in a sea of pink tutus. I didn't last long."

Children also keep each other in line as a way to demonstrate adherence to their appropriate gender roles. Shane recounts how "one of my male cousins would pretend he was a mother dog and would line up his stuffed animals like babies nursing. My other male cousins and I never physically assaulted him, but, verbally, we were very mean." Shane and his cousins stopped short of physical assault in this instance, but it is employed by many children as well as adults to intimidate children into following gender norms. In the binary, children are given strong messages about how to fit into the gender master narrative and are punished in both subtle and overt ways if they don't conform.

From the time you were born, you learned what it means to be feminine or masculine. From your parents, your religion, and your interactions at school, you were instructed to see humans as two distinct types that require different rooms, clothing, and activities. The ways your mother, father, teachers, religious leaders, and other adults looked and behaved communicated strong messages to you about how to be a boy or a girl. Regardless of how your infancy and childhood may have varied from the ones described above, because you were a baby and a child living in the binary, you could not help learning that being female means something vastly different from being male. So effectively was the binary's master narrative communicated to you that, within a few years of being born, you knew how to discriminate between and label people as one or the other gender, and you could identify the various roles that males and females should fulfill. You, like everyone else in the binary, came to see that ways of appearing and acting normal for one gender are constructed differently from ways of appearing and acting normal for the other.

As we discussed in chapter 1, childhood is a foundational time in the development of gender identity. Identity is a social phenomenon that is socially constructed through communication, which means that your sense of self as a gendered child developed as a result of your relationships with other people. You learned to be who you are by how other people treated and talked to you and by observing others and imitating them, and you were rewarded and punished accordingly. The themes of the master gender narrative that were communicated to you in your home, at church, and at school, then, became not only the expectations of the external binary but part of your own internalized sense of being gendered as well.

ADOLESCENCE

Adolescence in Western culture is the stage of life when young people are prepared for the roles they will assume as adults. While the binary distinguishes girls from boys throughout childhood, adolescence is a time when the gender messages and expectations of the binary are especially powerful in directing both males and females toward ideal expectations for courtship, marriage, and parenthood. Adolescents continue to learn the master narrative of the binary at home, in church, at school, and in all other institutions, but the relative importance and influence of these sources usually shifts as peers become more central. Teenagers are more likely to turn to other teens for clues about how to do gender appropriately and are particularly sensitive to being evaluated by each other. Fitting in and being popular are largely matters of adhering to the demands of the gender binary.

Adolescent girls and boys learn that they will be evaluated according to binary standards for appearance and behaviors. Teenage girls learn that ideal women are thin, well dressed, and sexy. Girls learn to walk, eat, and talk in certain ways and learn that belching, scratching, and spitting are inappropriate. Elizabeth remembers learning that unladylike behavior reflects poorly on a girl and her friends: "I had a friend who was the most vulgar girl I'd ever met. At first, I thought she acted vulgar just around other girls, but she continued her trash talk even with guys around. Sometimes, it embarrassed me because she was so unladylike—and I didn't want people to think I was like that, too." Being appropriately female as a teen also means not "going too far"—in how you dress and how you behave sexually, for example. A teenage girl learns that she is supposed to be sexy but not trampy, open and fun but not too loud or physical. She is supposed to be heterosexual and want attention from boys, but she has to be in charge of her sexuality and make sure nothing inappropriate happens. The line between these categories can be subtle and confusing.

Adolescent boys are supposed to live up to another set of binary standards for appearance and behavior. Teenage boys learn that the ideal man is tall, muscular, and athletic. Teenage boys learn behaviors that distinguish them from girls—they learn manly ways to belch, scratch, and spit. Adolescence for boys also involves learning to walk, eat, and talk in certain ways that make clear that they are becoming men. Aggression is often considered a necessary dimension of manhood in interactions with other men. Acting tough, being willing to fight, and engaging in extreme acts of violence are ways to prove one's manliness in some cultures and groups. Neil's experience illustrates the kinds of constraints the binary puts on men's behaviors. When he started dating, Neil's father told him to follow three rules: "(1) Never just pull up at a girl's house and honk the horn; get out of the car, go to the door, and introduce yourself to her parents; (2) Always open the door for her; and (3) If you go to kiss her and she says to stop, stop." Neil's father was expressing an important theme from the binary's narrative—that boys pick girls up, open doors, and initiate kisses. In the binary, boys learn to initiate, and girls are responsible for exercising control.

Definitions of popularity for teens are usually tied to how well they align with masculinity and femininity as defined by a family, group, or culture. Becoming a cheerleader or winning beauty pageants is the epitome of femininity in some families, while becoming the quarterback of the high school football team or going along with the guys is the mark of manhood. Expectations to adhere to the ways in which the binary defines masculinity and femininity can be extremely powerful and difficult to resist. Teens who meet gender expectations as well as those who choose to defy them face challenges in the need to continually work to maintain and uphold the gender stances they have created for themselves. Quan's experience—that of someone who did not meet conventional gender expectations—shows how influential institutions can be in asserting the expectations of the binary.

> The school reinforced one way of being a girl, and that was to be physically attractive, wear the right style of clothing, and know how to be socially adept. If you enacted these qualities, you were asked to dances, crowned queen of the prom, selected to be a cheerleader, and elected to student council. On Valentine's Day, it was really clear

which girls were doing gender appropriately and which were not. Boys could buy a rose for a girl and have it delivered to home room. In each home room, several girls (including me) sat there with no flowers. Not only did this make it very obvious that we didn't conform, but it made us feel even more inadequate than we had before.

The school's ritualized practice effectively conveys a number of binary messages to girls: Heterosexual relationships are desirable and expected; if you want to have such a relationship, you need to look and act in normative ways; and boys are expected to spend money on girls. The tradition effectively tells boys: You should be with a girl; you should be with a girl who is pretty and knows how to act; and to show a girl you like her, you do things like give her flowers (that cost money). Notice that boys are not sending flowers to other boys, and girls are not sending flowers to anyone. Adolescence is a primary time in life when the binary—as communicated through peers, schools, and rituals—stresses that heterosexuality is the standard, acceptable behavior for expressing sexuality.

Coming-of-age rituals often reinforce the messages peers and schools give about meeting the expectations of the gender binary, providing another way of molding teens to assume adult binary roles. Although many of these rituals are being rewritten to address shifting gender roles, most still contain many dimensions that respond to the binary. Perhaps you participated in a Bar Mitzvah when you turned thirteen or celebrated your fifteenth birthday with a *quinceañera*. The Bar Mitzvah is a symbol that a young Jewish man is now responsible for his actions and can participate fully in Jewish community life. The *quinceañera,* common in Hispanic and Latino communities, acknowledges that the girl has become a woman and, at the same time, reminds her of the responsibilities attached to that role.[21] The *quinceañera* illustrates the kind of learning that is expected to take place during such events. The young woman is expected to follow the teachings of the church in regard to sexual activity, should not become pregnant before marriage, and must present herself as a lady when in public. Although a *quinceañera* is specifically for young women, their escorts are being taught about gender expectations as well. Eduardo, thinking back to the *quinceañeras* in which he served as an escort, notes, "It taught me that men should be the ones taking care of women. Even when I was learning to waltz, which is a really important deal, I was told it was my job to lead and make sure the girl looked good."

Debutante balls and proms also teach binary gender roles. Debutante balls mark a young woman's debut or entrance into society and traditionally signaled that she is of marriageable age. Now, these events do not usually indicate a readiness to be married and are often simply occasions for parties, donations to charity, and a way of keeping prominent society families in the news. Maybe you were not presented at a debutante ball, but you might well have gone to your high school prom. If you participated in any of these coming-of-age rituals, you are familiar with the strong messages such ceremonies communicate about female and male roles. For young women, these rituals emphasize the importance of appearance (she is to be beautiful and perfectly coifed), being accompanied by a male (while she can go to a prom without a male date, to do so is a social failure), and proper comportment (she knows what she should and should not do now that she is a woman). Young men similarly learn their roles in these rituals—he asks the young woman to accompany him (he is the leader and initiator); he brings her a corsage and buys her dinner (he is economically responsible for her); and he escorts her and is expected to bring her home safely at the evening's end (he is stronger, more capable, and in charge). All of these expectations for coming-of-age rituals are in line with the gender ideals for men and women, and they prepare teens to assume adult roles in the binary.

Even if your experiences as a teen did not match the ones discussed above, you could not avoid messages about how to be a young man or a young woman. For example, if you are gay, have never dated, or didn't participate in any of the rituals we just described, you nonetheless learned from the binary how females and males are supposed to look and behave, to whom you are supposed to be attracted, and how you were supposed to express that attraction. You also experienced the consequences of not measuring up to these ideals—you may have, like Quan, received negative judgments from peers or been made to feel unattractive and unpopular. Or, like Tyler, you may have felt you had to hide how you deviated from gender norms: "My passion is fashion design, but when I was in high school, I kept my sketchbooks full of dresses and high heels a secret from even my best friends." Quan and Tyler, like many teens, knew they were not measuring up to normative gender ideals.

Adolescence and young adulthood are particularly critical times for identity development, fraught with persistent questions of. "Who am I?" and "How do I fit in the adult world?"[22] Adolescence—a time when so many influences in your life reflected and reinforced the binary master narrative—is also when you began to make decisions about what kind of a gendered person you would become. As you became more schooled in the ideals for being an ideal male or ideal female, you started to figure out who you were in relation to those gender ideals.

ADULTHOOD AND OLD AGE

The master narrative of the binary continues to operate in adulthood, strongly influencing you to be a certain person who adopts certain appearances, behaviors, and roles. Women continue to feel pressured to look and act in appropriate ways, which means continuing to interpret the subtle lines between being assertive and bitchy, smart but not too smart, and sexually attractive but not slutty. Maureen puts it this way: "With every task, from getting dressed to presenting myself, I have to be careful. I have to be sure I'm feminine and sexy but not too revealing or inviting men to approach me—at work, at my husband's company party, even when I'm out shopping." Although adult men in the gender binary don't have as many pressures to maintain a certain look, they have many other pressures to conform. The ideal man is supposed to be competitive and aggressive, a go-getter, and someone who is socially and economically successful. Ideal men are able to support themselves and their families financially and to save money to secure the future. They should have nice cars, nice houses, attractive wives, and well-behaved children. Men who have been raised in the binary know they are most attractive not when they have a good haircut or an expensive suit but when they have social status and power.

Although most professions are now open to both women and men, the existence of the gender binary means that some occupations are still considered to be more masculine and others more feminine. Someone who participates in a job traditionally associated with the other gender may be subject to scrutiny. Until recently, elementary school teaching was seen as primarily a female occupation, and men who chose to teach at this level were considered somehow suspect. Jane notes that women in the military are often evaluated differently from men because they are doing what is considered a male job: "Being in the army, if you do something wrong or with not enough strength, a lot of the males automatically attribute that to your being a female and not having the ability to keep up with them." Lex, a labor and delivery nurse, feels judged as a man because his occupation is seen as feminine: "When my wife and I were dating, her friends tried hard to convince her that she shouldn't be with me; I wasn't a 'real man' because my field isn't masculine. Not only am I a nurse, but I help deliver babies!"

As an adult, the lessons you learned as a child and teen about being a female or a male continue to influence you, and the script for adult ideal expectations—that you will fall in love, get married, and have children—

become especially salient. The pinnacle of the binary gender is to become the ideal man or the ideal women who forms a perfect union with your opposite, to establish a stable domestic unit, and to perpetuate culture through having offspring. When we asked students whether this ideal script continues to exert pressure—if they think they have to get married and be parents—their responses confirmed that, even as adults, binary expectations have a strong influence. "I don't know if it's a pressure," Cliff said. "I want to be married someday, but not until I am settled into a career and can afford a wife and kids." Dagny told us she is a feminist who does not ever plan to be a traditional wife. "Despite my strong feelings, though, in my heart I feel like I'll somehow be a failure if I don't end up in a stable, long-term relationship." Caroline, who lives with her partner Ali, phrased her awareness of binary ideals like this: "Many of our gay and lesbian friends are having commitment ceremonies or are getting married, whether or not they want kids. To say Ali and I aren't pressured by gender norms would be a lie—everyone is supposed to be a couple!" Anushka—who has been married and is a divorced, single parent—told us: "Yes, the constant message I get from everyone is that I won't be doing life right until I'm a wife again and my son has a new dad."

In the binary, marrying completes the coming-of-age process that began with Bar Mitzvahs, *quinceañeras,* and proms. For many young women, their wedding day seems like the most important day of their lives because it is the completion of a certain set of gender expectations. Karen knows a family with three daughters, all of whom chose elaborate, expensive weddings with which to celebrate their marriages. When she asked them what they would have done if their parents had offered them the down payment on a house instead of a lavish wedding, they all said they still would have chosen the wedding. Not only does a wedding signal that a woman has arrived at what a culture expects her to be and do as a woman, but it also tells a man what his proper role is. The bride is "given away" to the groom by her father, suggesting she must be in the company of or even under the guardianship of a man throughout her life. In Jewish weddings, the groom places the veil over the face of his bride, literally signaling his commitment to clothe and protect her. In traditional Christian ceremonies, the woman promises to *obey* the man, and they are pronounced *man and wife.* He enters the ritual as a man and leaves as a man; she enters as a woman and leaves as a wife. The bride often takes her husband's surname, and the couple is introduced as "Mr. and Mrs. John Doe" at the end of the ceremony, subsuming her identity in his and signaling that she has joined him in his life.

Joelle shared her experience with the binary expectations around marriage: "I just got married, and everyone keeps calling me 'Mrs.' I am not going by 'Mrs.,' nor am I taking my husband's name. I've been pressured to take his last name, and it's frustrating." Although many couples, like Joelle and her husband, deliberately disrupt traditional symbols, they must address and justify their choices to clergy, family members, and the community. Other women like taking their husbands' names. Bianca says: "I want us to be one, not two people, and I especially want the children I give him to have my husband's name. I think it is very confusing when parents don't have the same name—what kind of message is that for a child?"

Parenting responsibilities also are affected by the gender binary. A large part of meeting the ideal standard for being a successful father revolves around providing economically for a wife and children. This ideal translates into pressure on adult men to become and stay successful. Men often feel stuck in jobs that do not stimulate or fulfill them because job satisfaction falls below being a good provider in the hierarchy of prescribed values. A man can be very involved in taking care of his children and sharing housework, but those activities are not prescribed in the binary master narrative. While that means there is no pressure to perform those behaviors, it also means there are no rewards for doing so. If trying to meet the dictates of the master narrative to be successful at work prohibits involvement with his children, a man could feel emotionally distant from his family.

Because the ideal women should consider taking care of people as her most important responsibility, women often feel pressured to be good mothers in ways that differ from what is expected of a good father. Susana's comment is typical: "I often feel judged by other mothers about what is adequate in terms of behavior, duties, and obligations." Mothers are often the parent who quits work for several years to stay home with children, in part because the binary expectation is that women are naturally more caring and nurturing and thus better suited to parenting. In fact, throughout her adult life in the gender binary, a woman is expected to take care of other people. If her husband gets a new job in another location, she is expected to follow him, and women are more likely than men to become caretakers of elderly parents. These disruptions of job or career have consequences for women's career advancement, pensions, and Social Security benefits. If a marriage ends in divorce and a woman did not work outside the home or took time off to care for children, she is likely to experience lifelong economic difficulties. A woman, in other words, often must choose between having a successful career or meeting the ideal standards of caring for her children, husband, and elderly parents.

Becoming elderly in the binary can be difficult for both men and women. When a woman is widowed (and 41 percent of women 65 years and older are compared to 13 percent of men), she may see a dramatic loss of income, especially if she has not been in the workforce or has not worked for many years.[23] A woman who is accustomed to having a man take care of the finances may not know how to manage her money. Men who are widowed lack other skills—some elderly men do not know how to cook eggs, launder sheets, or clean house for themselves. Because a married man may have relied on his wife to meet all of his physical, emotional, and social needs, he may be left not knowing how to do even the most basic domestic tasks or how to manage friendships on his own.

Throughout life in the binary, you receive instructions from many sources about what is appropriate for women and men. Relationships, social systems, and institutions coalesce to create an ideal picture for you—a picture of who you are supposed to be as a woman or as a man in terms of appearance, personality, and behaviors. The master narrative about gender results in both females and males learning to perform proper genders in childhood that are rehearsed in adolescence and cemented in adulthood. These ideal standards affect every area and era of life.

Because of a lifetime spent in the binary, you learn the ideal characteristics of each gender whether or not you attempt to live up to them and whether or not your life actually follows the ideal scripts. Again, we want to point out that binary gender ideals construct and prescribe a certain type of life that is different for men and women, which you may or may not choose to accept. In fact, nobody—even if you ascribe to the binary gender system and try hard to meet it—completely lives the life of an ideal woman or an ideal man because that life is impossible. Some people don't want to conform to the ideals and don't try, refusing to adopt the prescribed standards for appearance or behavior. But the pervasiveness of the gender binary is a force that must be negotiated by every person in Western culture because everyone learns and internalizes some form of the same ideal standards. The gender binary is, in fact, so pervasive that it forms a matrix for your life.

BINARY AS MATRIX

Just as you are not always aware of the physical laws you take for granted—the pull of gravity, for example—you probably are not always cognizant of the functioning of the gender binary. Gender theorist Judith

Butler used the term *matrix* to capture the sense of the gender binary as foundational and not always consciously apparent.[24] A matrix is an environment, substance, or site in which something originates, develops, or is formed. Because it is a matrix, the gender binary is the background field in which your gender plays out, beginning with your birth, when you were assigned one gender label or the other.

In the futuristic film *The Matrix,* a computer hacker named Neo realizes that the environment in which he lives and that he has considered real is actually a digital simulation designed and controlled by machines with brains.[25] Similarly, in *The Truman Show,* Truman Burbank discovers that he is the star of a reality television show that began with his birth and is being broadcast twenty-four hours a day around the globe. What he thought was his unique life, motivated by his impulses and desires, is scripted for him by the writers and directors of the show.[26] The gender system is similar to the hidden realities that Neo and Truman discover—a system that you may not have realized is guiding and influencing your entire life. Judith Lorber, a professor of sociology and women's studies, summarizes the gender binary system when she says that it "creates structure and stability, seeps into the practices of many social roles, has a long history, and is virtually unquestioned."[27]

The matrix that is the gender binary might seem like it no longer applies because your experience is not like our description above. On the surface, the Western world does not always clearly reflect the division of all people into two distinct genders. Maybe you were raised by a feminist mother who worked hard to ensure you were treated the same as every other individual and repeatedly told you that you could grow up to be anything you wanted to be. Perhaps your father raised you alone or with his same-gender partner, or you may have attended a Montessori school where gender differences were minimized. In today's world, a girl can be a football player, and a woman can open doors for men or be the CEO of a large corporation. A boy can be a ballet dancer, and a man can be a stay-at-home father or a nurse. If your life experiences are similar to these, you might think there are no gender scripts to follow or pressures to conform to cultural norms of femininity and masculinity.

You also might think that the binary gender system no longer applies because there is now a fairly widespread consciousness that every person has both masculine and feminine qualities. You know that you have the ability to make choices about behaviors that are considered masculine or feminine—you can be gentle or firm, emotionally open or reserved, nurturing or tough. You also are aware that there are gay men, lesbian women, bisexual persons, and transgendered people whose appearances and behaviors are different from or a mixture of the qualities that the binary assigns to male and female.

When we started writing this book, we imagined that—due to their experiences in the contemporary world—students might think that the binary isn't very strong anymore and has little impact on how they view gender. However, when we asked students in colleges and universities across the United States about their gendered experiences, students like you confirmed that the gender binary is alive and well. We share statements throughout this book from the surveys students completed for us, and here we give you a sampling to illustrate how your peers told us the binary matrix affects their lives.

Many women talked about the pressures they are under to live up to the binary's ideals of femininity. One woman described feeling pressured when getting dressed in the morning, a process that for her involves "consciously trying to look attractive and feminine." Another woman said she feels the need to "clean house every single day," even though her boyfriend doesn't have this expectation of her. A student reported that she feels the need in her family to "act like the ideal wife and mother by being nurturing and creative," and many women said they must not to do anything in public that makes them appear unladylike. Our respondents talked about believing that they are treated differently simply because they are female—one woman said her father doesn't listen to her or take her "seriously"—and another described how her coach takes her out of co-ed soccer games when the play "gets too rowdy."

We learned that the pressures of the gender binary are equally intense for men. Many of our surveys noted the pressure for a man to always be a "real man"—at the gym, at work, and when out with the guys. The men told us that they feel like they have to "perform at the top of moral, mental, and physical capabilities" at all times and must avoid doing anything that would make them appear to be "pussies." The boy who wanted to get his ears pierced and collected Precious Moments dolls rather than action figures as a child grew up to be the "fag" of his high school, laughed at and condemned for not performing masculinity correctly. The student who likes to garden and bake said he hides these activities from his father and brothers. Many male students reported that they continue to feel, as men, that they alone are responsible for initiating relationships and sex.

The survey responses indicated that the gender matrix is alive and well, but this is not to say that you are totally governed or controlled by it.

You have a unique way of making sense of gender that is the result of all kinds of factors and influences, including how you were raised and how you interpret and respond to the gender messages you received. The gender binary intersects with innumerable other systems to create a system of characteristics that is unique to you. You live in particular subcultures defined by your nationality, ethnicity, religion, age, education, sexual orientation, and socioeconomic class, and each of these factors intersects with and affects your gender identity. You have been affected by relationships with family, friends, and intimate partners in various ways, and you have been influenced by different places you have lived and worked and by your exposure to different cultures. As a unique person, you also have made individualized choices about your gender.

Your approach to gender, however distinctive it is given your personal life experiences, cannot make the gender binary disappear. The gender binary is an all-encompassing, ever-present system that operates all around you whether you are conscious of it or not. Despite changes in the Western world and an increased awareness of having a choice in how much the binary influences behavior, survey responses from your peers show that the gender binary continues to function as the backdrop to people's lives and as the standards of appearance and behavior people are pressured to meet. Its expectations have "choreographed our lives. . . . We have practiced their confining . . . steps, day by day and year by year, all our lives. When we danced them awkwardly we were laughed at and felt miserable; when we danced them well we were popular and happy. Now, as adults, we know their curious steps and complex cadence by heart."[28]

■ NOTES

[1] Phillip L. Hammock, "Narrative and the Cultural Psychology of Identity," *Personality and Social Psychology Review* 12 (2008): 224.

[2] M. Theodora Pintzuk, "Identity and Cultural Narrative in a Lesbian Relationship," *Journal of Couple & Relationship Therapy* 3 (2004): 28.

[3] Pintzuk, "Identity and Cultural Narrative in a Lesbian Relationship," 28.

[4] Bruce Ryder, "Straight Talk: Male Heterosexual Privilege," *Queen's Law Journal* 16 (1991): 288.

[5] Anne Fausto-Sterling, *Sexing the Body: Gender Politics and the Construction of Sexuality* (New York: Basic, 2000), 51. Cheryl Chase, born intersexed and described as an individual who "almost single-handedly changed both the dialogue on the subject and the surgical practice itself," believes the number of intersexed individuals to be as high as 1 out of 5 births. See Amy Bloom, *Normal: Transsexual CEOs, Cross-Dressing Cops, and Hermaphrodites with Attitude* (New York: Random House, 2002), 127.

[6] Robin Tolmach Lakoff, *Talking Power: The Politics of Language* (New York: Basic, 1990), 203.

[7] Peter Osborne and Lynne Segal, "Gender as Performance: An Interview with Judith Butler," in *Readings on Rhetoric and Performance*, ed. Stephen Olbrys Gencarella and Phaedra C. Pezzullo (State College, PA: Strata, 2010), 208.

[8] Jane M. Simoni and Karina L. Walters, "Heterosexual Identity and Heterosexism: Recognizing Privilege to Reduce Prejudice," *Journal of Homosexuality* 41 (2001): 159.

[9] Simoni and Walters, "Heterosexual Identity and Heterosexism," 159.

[10] Anita Superson, "Privilege, Immorality, and Responsibility for Attending to the 'Facts about Humanity,'" *Journal of Social Philosophy* 35 (2004): 37.

[11] Deborah S. David and Robert Brannon, *The Forty-Nine Percent Majority: The Male Sex Role* (Reading, MA: 1976), 36.

[12] For a discussion of cross-cultural similarities and differences in gender stereotypes, see Mary Crawford, *Transformations: Women, Gender, and Psychology* (New York: McGraw-Hill, 2006), 80–82.

[13] These kits use a simple blood test to indicate gender; they were originally designed to detect fetal abnormalities. Because the test results are 95 percent accurate, there is some concern that the test will be used to select one sex over the other, with parents aborting the child if it is not the sex they want. See "In-Vitro Gender Testing Raises Ethical Concerns," *The Denver Post,* August 10, 2011, 4A.

[14] Cordelia Fine, *Delusions of Gender: How Our Minds, Society, and Neurosexism Create Difference* (New York: W. W. Norton, 2010), 192.

[15] Claire Damken Brown and Audrey Nelson, *Code Switching: How to Talk So Men Will Listen* (New York: Penguin, 2009), 3.

[16] Letty Cottin Pogrebin, *Growing Up Free: Raising Your Child in the 80s* (New York: Bantam/McGraw-Hill, 1980), 123.

[17] Pogrebin, *Growing Up Free*, 124–25.

[18] Pogrebin, *Growing Up Free,* 127.

[19] Rebecca Bigler, "Good Morning Boys and Girls," *Teaching Tolerance* 28 (2005), http://www.tolerance.org/magazine/number-28-fall-2005/good-morning-boys-and-girls

[20] Barrie Thorne and Zella Luria, "Sexuality and Gender in Children's Daily Worlds," *Social Problems* 33 (February 1986): 176–90.

[21] Ruth Horowitz, "The Power of Ritual in a Chicano Community: A Young Woman's Status and Expanding Family Ties," in *Quinceañera*, ed. Ilan Stavans (Santa Barbara, CA: Greenwood, 2010), 36.

[22] Jess K. Alberts, Thomas K. Nakayama, and Judith N. Martin, *Human Communication in Society,* 2nd ed. (Boston: Allyn & Bacon, 2010), 67–76.

[23] White House Council on Women and Girls, Women in America: Indicators of Social and Economic Well-Being (March 2011), pp. 6, 9, http://www.whitehouse.gov/administration/eop/cwg/data-on-women

[24] Judith Butler, *Gender Trouble: Feminism and the Subversion of Identity* (New York: Routledge, 1990), 35–38. Butler now uses the term *hegemony* rather than *matrix* to suggest a fluid, malleable gender system, capable of rearticulation. See Osborne and Segal, "Gender as Performance," 208.

[25] *The Matrix*, directed by Andy Wachowski and Lana (formerly Larry) Wachowski (Burbank, CA: Warner Brothers Pictures, 1999).

[26] *The Truman Show,* directed by Peter Weir (Los Angeles, CA: Paramount, 1998).

[27] Judith Lorber, *Breaking the Bowls: Degendering and Feminist Change* (New York: W. W. Norton, 2005), 13–14.

[28] David and Brannon, *The Forty-Nine Percent Majority,* 41.

four

SCIENCE FICTION
GENDER STORIES IN SCIENTIFIC RESEARCH

*Scientists, like all people, have strong expectations
about the way the world works, and perhaps especially
about the things that we choose to study.*

Rebecca Jordan-Young, *Brain Storm*

It is a dark and stormy night, and in his laboratory, Dr. Frankenstein huddles over the pinnacle project of his life as a scientist—a human form he has created with bones and body parts from dissecting rooms and slaughter houses. With his knowledge of alchemy, mineralogy, and chemistry, Dr. Frankenstein is about to accomplish what has never before been done—to bring inanimate material to life. If you've read or seen Mary Shelley's science-fiction classic, you know that his experiment does not turn out as planned. Instead of a beautiful creature that confirms his superiority as a scientist, Dr. Frankenstein creates a hideous monster that terrifies and kills people. The tale works—we continue to be fascinated by it—because Shelley draws on science to create a captivating imaginary world.

Research on gender differences—findings that prove how inherently different women are from men—functions much as science fiction does by also creating fantasies based in science. Myths about gender differences are able to achieve some degree of believability because they are backed up by scientific studies. You've undoubtedly heard about studies on gender differences through the media and popular culture, and you've probably accepted them as true because you have repeatedly been told that they are based on objective data. These studies report substantial—and usually biological—differences between men and women. Just as Dr. Frankenstein used science to create something that resembled a human being, research on gender differences uses science to create versions of women and men that resemble real people.

Dr. Frankenstein collected bits and pieces of dead bodies to create his version of a human being in a process not unlike the one that gender researchers use to create their own equally skewed versions. Gender researchers also work with bits and pieces. They study isolated behaviors, look for one cause, and limit their explanations to one result to explain complex human processes. Just as the eight-foot monster ended up being larger than life, gender research exaggerates some aspects of people. With body parts and human processes being isolated, fragmented, and often out of proportion, the studies produce monsters of their own—disproportionate claims that cannot fully explain human life. Constructed—like Dr. Frankenstein's monster—in the image of a scientific fantasy, the human beings described in gender research are simplified caricatures of real people.

The creation of the monster had more far-reaching results than Dr. Frankenstein ever intended, which is also true of research on gender differences. After Dr. Frankenstein saw what he had created, he abandoned the monster, but it went on to do many things that he never anticipated and certainly did not intend, including murdering his brother. So, too, the scientific research about gender differences often has a much greater and more detrimental impact than the researchers intend. The stories they construct about gender have significant consequences in the world, especially when those stories are picked up by the media and widely disseminated. Those consequences are not always desirable.

In this chapter, we explore three science-fiction stories about gender differences with the intent of showing how, like *Frankenstein*, much of this research results in a fantasy created from science—something compelling and believable but often not entirely true. We present three such stories about research on gender differences: "Of Math and Men," "The Girl Who Talked Too Much," and "The Curse of the Hormones." The first of these tales concerns male math superiority, the second tells of the belief that women talk more than men, and the third is the story of how sex hormones dictate human behavior. At the heart of each story is the social construction of research to align with expectations of the binary. In the first story, scientific data about boys' and girls' mathematical abilities are oversimplified as the story moves out into the world, and the findings reported are not adequately qualified or nuanced. In the story about women talking more than men, data are ignored in order to preserve the expectations of the gender binary. The research story about hormones and their effect on behavior contains data that are exaggerated in ways that minimize other possible explanations. These are only three of the many science-fiction stories circulating about gender. We use them to represent a large body of scientific literature that creates fantasies around gender differences that affect how gender is understood and experienced.

OF MATH AND MEN

"Of Math and Men" is a story about how males are superior to females in mathematical ability. It is also a story about oversimplification of research findings. Although many studies have found that boys perform better than girls in mathematics, researchers have not been able to identify conclusively the environmental, biological, or combination of factors that account for this finding. They have identified and eliminated some factors as possible causes, but the conclusions are far from definitive. In addition, some studies have found no differences in math ability between girls and boys. When the story of mathematical ability is reported by the media and moves through popular culture, however, these nuances are lost, and people end up thinking that boys are better at math because of innate biological factors.

The narrative about math and gender is complicated and began with a large research project—the Study of Mathematically Precocious Youth (SMPY)—in 1971. Educational psychologist Julian Stanley at Johns Hopkins University started the project, which is ongoing. In the initial phase, seventh- and eighth-grade students who scored in the top 2 to 5 percent of standardized math achievement tests were invited to take the math portion of the Scholastic Aptitude Test (SAT-M) so that researchers could see whether gender differences existed in math ability.

In 1980, Camilla Benbow and Julian Stanley published the first results from the project.[1] The basic claim in "Sex Differences in Mathematical Reasoning: Fact or Artifact?" was that "large sex differences in mathematical aptitude are observed in boys and girls with essentially identical formal educational experiences."[2] In every year in which the seventh- and eighth-grade students were studied, a large gender difference "in favor of boys"[3] was observed. The smallest average difference between girls' and boys' scores was 32 points in 1979, and the largest difference was 55 points in 1973; the average difference was 40 points. In addition, 27.1 percent of eighth-grade boys scored over 600 on the SAT-M, and not a single girl did. Not one top score was earned by a girl in any of the years that Benbow and Stanley studied the children's math scores.[4] When they surveyed these same students in the eleventh grade, they still found strong gender differences in math scores; in fact, those differences had become even larger over time. Whereas a 40-point difference in mean scores on the SAT-M separated the boys and girls in the eighth grade, a 50-point difference separated them at the time of their graduation from high school.

In their first series of studies, Benbow and Stanley were primarily interested in whether students' completion of different or greater numbers of math courses was a major factor in the lower scores girls earn for mathematical reasoning on the SAT-M. They found, however, that the girls and boys in their studies typically took the same number and types of mathematics courses, eliminating the number of math courses as an explanation for the different scores.[5] Benbow and Stanley then pursued several other possible explanations for their finding of gender differences in mathematical ability, finally concluding that they did not know what caused the differences in scores. They left open how best to account for these gender differences, suggesting that male math superiority is probably due to a combination of both internal and external variables such as biology and socialization. They also made clear that alternative hypotheses could very well explain their results.[6]

Benbow and her colleagues in SMPY continued their research on gender differences in math. In 1988 and again in 2007, summaries of the longitudinal research from SMPY were published that continued to report gender differences in mathematical ability. In the 1988 report, authored by Benbow, she stated: "Sex differences in SAT-M scores among adolescents are not temporary trends. They have been stable even in times of great change in attitudes toward women."[7] Benbow reviewed possible environmental explanations for this finding, including attitudes toward math, views about the importance of math to future careers, self-confidence about math abilities, the stereotyping of math as masculine, expectations and encouragement from parents and teachers, and the completion of different types and numbers of math courses. Of all of these possible explanations, only self-confidence was found to distinguish SMPY males from SMPY females. On all of the other variables, there were no strong indicators or significant results that could point to any of them as reliable explanations for gender differences in mathematical reasoning ability.

Because of their inability to find strong environmental correlations for mathematical ability, Benbow and her colleagues also investigated potential biological factors. The fact that left-handedness, allergies, and myopia had previously been correlated with high mathematical reasoning ability led them to wonder if there could be biological factors that explained their results. In Benbow's report in 1988, she concluded that both environmental and biological factors need to be considered as explanations for the differences between girls and boys:

> To date a primarily environmental explanation for the difference has not received support from the numerous studies conducted over many years by the staff of SMPY and by others. This and the identification of several physiological correlates of extremely high mathematical reasoning ability lend credence to the view that these sex differences may partly be biologically induced. Because there are well-documented differences in the socialization as well as in the biology of boys and girls, it is proposed that a combination of both of these factors causes the sex difference in mathematical reasoning ability.[8]

The researchers, in other words, were unable to specify what factors might cause the consistent findings of male math superiority.

A decade later, in the 2007 summary of the SMPY research prepared by Diane Halpern and her colleagues, the researchers' intent was to present a "consensus statement"[9] about "what is known about sex differences in mathematics and science achievement and abilities based on a review and evaluation of the best available scientific evidence."[10] In this summary, they noted that "the question of sex differences in mathematical and science achievements is really a set of embedded questions, because the answer depends on (a) which mathematical and science achievements are studied, (b) how those achievements are assessed, (c) when in the life span they are assessed, (d) which portion of the achievement/ability distribution is investigated, and (e) the context in which the achievement is assessed."[11]

The researchers explored possible explanations for the findings about gender differences in three areas—verbal, visuospatial, and quantitative abilities—all of which contribute to success in learning and doing science and mathematics. They reviewed biological research that explores the role that sex hormones, brain structure, and brain function might play in mathematical ability. They discussed possible sociocultural factors, including the influence of family and peers, single-sex education, and the degree to which a culture values math and science. Factors that might negatively affect women were given special attention, including discrimination against women who enter careers in math and science and stereotype threat—when a negative stereotype leads to self-doubt and poor performance. They also investigated the penalty threat "in the marriage market" that women who choose nontraditional careers might experience.[12] Although they enlarged their research scope to include more factors, the researchers again concluded that they could not yet explain the reason for gender differences in mathematical ability:

> There cannot be any single or simple answer to the many complex questions about sex differences in math and science. Readers expecting a single conclusion—such as that we can explain sex differences in science and math by knowing about hormones, or by knowing how stereotypes affect performance, or by knowing how our ancestors met the challenges in their lives—are surely disappointed. Just as there are many related questions about sex differences in test scores and career choices, there are many variables that work together to present a level of complexity that is inherent in understanding complicated questions about the way people think and behave.[13]

In sum, the research originally reported by Benbow and Stanley in *Science* and continued by Benbow and her colleagues found gender differences in mathematical reasoning among females and males in middle school and as seniors in high school that typically lead to substantial gender differences in career choices. Nowhere do these researchers claim such differences are genetic or innate. Rather, they clearly assert that multiple factors probably contribute to these gender differences, some of which may have a basis in biology and some of which appear to be environmental in origin.

. . . THE REST OF THE STORY

Benbow and Stanley and their subsequent colleagues were careful to discuss the complexity of the issue of gender differences in mathematical ability. The media, however, oversimplified the information they disseminated—turning scientific research into science fiction. Within days of the release of the findings of the 1980 study, major news magazines such as *Time* and *Newsweek* reported on the research with headlines such as "Do Males Have a Math Gene?"[14] and "The Gender Factor in Math: A New Study Says Males May Be Naturally Abler than Females."[15] The content of many of these articles stated or implied an innate genetic or biological basis for gender differences in math ability. An article in *Family Weekly*, for example, reported that "boys are born with greater math ability,"[16] and the *Time* article summarized the findings as "males inherently have more mathematical ability than females."[17] Rather than describing all of the factors identified by researchers that might contribute to gender differences in mathematical ability, the media resorted to oversimplification in reporting that genetic or biological factors can explain why boys are better at math than girls.

In response to the media's oversimplification of the findings of their study, Benbow wrote a letter to the editor of *Science*, in which she corrected several inaccuracies in the media's reports on the research.[18] She noted the "hazards of inaccurate or sensational publicity," especially in regard to the phrase *math gene*, and stated that SMPY researchers had always "carefully avoided" the use of the phrase. She reiterated: "Our view is still as follows. It 'seems likely that putting one's faith in boy-versus-girl socialization processes as the *only* permissible explanation of the sex difference in mathematic[al reasoning ability] is *premature*.'"[19] A great number of biological, environmental, and social factors were still possible, she asserted, as explanations for male math superiority.

Other research done after the SMPY studies found no differences between girls and boys in terms of math scores. In an article published in *Science* in 2008, psychologist Janet Hyde and her colleagues reported the results of a review of math scores from the annual math tests mandated by No Child Left Behind.[20] They examined math scores of students from the second to the eleventh grades in ten states for the years 2005, 2006, and 2007 for a sample size of seven million students. Whether they examined the scores of average students, the scores of the most gifted students, or students' abilities to solve complex math problems, there was no measurable difference between girls and boys. Social psychologists Tony Scafidi and Khanh Bui replicated Hyde's study using national data from the National Education Longitudinal Study rather than data from just ten states.[21] Math scores for over 9,000 students in the eighth, tenth, and twelfth grades served as the data set. The researchers found gender similarities in performance on these math tests across all three grades. Moreover, they determined that these findings were not affected by correlations with race, socioeconomic status, or math level.

Psychologist Nicole Else-Quest and her colleagues employed meta-analysis (the study of research findings across multiple studies) to reexamine gender differences and math scores across countries.[22] In a 2010 study of 493,495 students between the ages of fourteen and sixteen from sixty-nine countries, they found only miniscule differences between the boys and the girls in terms of math ability, but they did find that boys displayed more confidence about their abilities than did girls. They also determined that cultural variations are significant in predicting and explaining girls' scores in math studies, including girls' access to education, whether women held research jobs in the culture in which the girls grew up, and the extent of women's representation in their countries' governments.

Despite efforts by Benbow and her colleagues to counter media over-simplification of their research findings and despite studies that show no differences in math ability between girls and boys, the belief in innate male math superiority has persisted, sometimes with far-reaching impact. Psychologists Janis Jacobs and Jacquelynne Eccles found that media coverage affected parents' beliefs about the mathematical abilities of their children as well as their stereotypes about gender differences in math. Jacobs and Eccles had surveyed parents in 1979 and 1980 to determine their beliefs about their children's mathematical abilities. Three months after the *Science* article was published, they surveyed parents again. One fourth of the parents said they had heard of the research, suggesting the widespread coverage the Benbow and Stanley article received. Both the mothers of daughters and the fathers of sons who knew of the research became more stereotypical in their beliefs—they believed boys were inherently better at math. Mothers became more conscious of gender differences, making statements such as, "Boys have a tendency to *understand* the principles (of math) but girls are trying to just *memorize* the principles."[23] Surprisingly, fathers who knew of the report expected their daughters to perform better in future math classes than did the fathers who had not heard of the report.

In 2008, psychologist Sara Lindberg and her colleagues demonstrated the impact on both mothers and children of the belief that boys are better at math. These researchers studied mothers as they helped their fifth-grade children with math homework.[24] Although the researchers found no significant differences in the amount of time boys and girls spent on math homework each day, the amount of help they received, or their standardized test scores, the mothers said that mathematics was more difficult for their daughters than for their sons. This opinion was consistent across mothers, no matter how much math training or ability the mothers themselves had had. In fact, the mothers with higher levels of math education showed the most gender differentiation in interacting with their daughters and sons. They spent more time with their daughters, giving them both more math instruction and more emotional support in terms of math homework. The children in the study held similar gender stereotypes about mathematics. The boys reported greater math ability and higher expectations for future success in math than the girls did, and the boys also said that math was easier for them than it was for the girls. Both the mothers and their children acted in ways that confirmed the social construction of male math superiority, despite the fact that test scores revealed no difference between the genders in the study.

When a cultural belief—such as that of innate male math superiority—gains a foothold, it is extremely difficult to dislodge. A university president might even believe it. When Lawrence Summers was the president of Harvard University, he sought to explain the low percentages of women in academic positions in math and science. Summers suggested that women are unwilling to give up time with their families to pursue high-level academic careers in science, women and men are socialized differently, and women may be discriminated against during the hiring process. His primary claim, however, was that innate differences between men and women might be the reason why women lag behind men in careers in math and science.[25] His remarks prompted considerable discussion of gender differences in math at academic forums nationwide. Jo Boaler, a mathematics education professor at Stanford University, noted at one such event: "There is a huge belief that boys are better at math which is vastly out of proportion to any data that we have. . . . And yet people believe it. You go into schools and the children will tell you that."[26]

"Of Math and Men" is a story not only about gender differences in mathematical reasoning but also about how such research is reported and disseminated. The belief that men are better at math than women persists in large part because of the widespread circulation and oversimplification of Benbow and Stanley's work. The media typically oversimplify explanations for male math superiority, claiming it is entirely biological. They also fail to report on studies that suggest that environmental or social factors may be responsible for gender differences or on studies that show no gender differences at all in mathematical ability. "Of Math and Men" is a much more complicated story than what has been reported in the media. Nevertheless, oversimplified media reports continue to impact the attitudes and behaviors of children, parents, and educators.

THE GIRL WHO TALKED TOO MUCH

Many cultures have proverbs about how much women talk. The English, for example, say, "Women's tongues are like lambs' tails—they are never still." In Jutland, a region of Denmark, there is a saying that "the North Sea will sooner be found wanting in water than a woman at a loss for words." In the Maori culture of New Zealand, a proverb states, "The woman with active hands and feet, marry her, but the woman with over-active mouth, leave well alone." The idea that women talk more than men is the story of "The Girl Who Talked Too Much." It is also a story about ignoring the actual evidence about who talks more because that evidence does not fit cultural biases about gender and talk. Whereas scientific findings consistently report that men talk more than women in many contexts, these data are not what circulate throughout the culture.

The belief that women talk more than men stems from a long-standing expectation that women not only talk a lot but talk excessively. In both Europe and in the American colonies, actual physical punishments were devised for women who were called *nags*, *scolds*, *gossips*, and *shrews*. The ducking stool, for example, was a chair at the end of a pole that could be plunged into water to punish women who were perceived to talk a lot. Another such punishment was a scold's bridle, which consisted of an iron cage placed on a talkative woman's head. Attached to the cage was a sharp bit that was inserted into her mouth to literally force her to hold her tongue.[27] The assumption that women talk too much has resulted in various kinds of censure and punishment over the years to curb their talk.

Women today are not publicly punished for how much they talk, but the assumption is still widespread that girls and women like to spend time gabbing, visiting, gossiping, and chatting with one another. Many boys and girls talk a lot, but the talk of girls is often labeled *girl talk* and is viewed as something different from boys' talk in content and amount. Images of girls and women talking with their friends are commonplace in popular culture—in advertising and on sitcoms, for example. Such images of women's talk are also reproduced for girls and teenagers in various forms. Telephone Tag, a board game directed at girls, requires a player to receive three phone messages from her boyfriend in order to win the game. There are several versions of another game, Girl Talk; in all of them, players are asked to answer a question or perform a stunt. They are penalized for not talking; if they refuse to talk about what the spinning dial tells them to talk about, they must wear a "zit sticker" for the rest of the game.

The widespread assumptions about women and amount of talk were captured in John Gray's book, *Men are From Mars, Women are From Venus,* published in 1992.[28] According to Gray (a relationship counselor, lecturer, and author), women and men are so different they might as well be from different planets. Men and women differ in how they conceptualize and deal with love and romance, problem solving, stress, and communication. In chapter 3 of his book, "Men Go to Their Caves and Women Talk," Gray suggests that men become noncommunicative when faced with difficult problems, retreating until they have figured out what to do. Women, on the other hand, want to talk things out. They like to be allowed to talk through a problem, even if there is no immediate solution or resolution, and they enjoy talking for its own sake. The impression that emerges from the book is that men are doers, and women are talkers.

Another example of this same assumption, also widely circulating in pop culture, is Chaz Bono's description of the changes in his level of talkativeness following his gender transition. You will meet Bono again in chapter 5, but what is important here is that Bono says he has become much less talkative and more action oriented following surgery to transition from a woman to a man:

> Communication is also a bit different for me as well. I can't or don't like to talk as much as I used to. I find that women seem to have the ability to talk endlessly about things, recounting every little detail. I no longer have that ability. In fact when I'm around such chatter, it starts to drive me crazy. When I'm with a group of women . . . I often hit a wall, where I just can't talk or listen to others talk anymore. I start to feel like I want to jump out of my skin and I have to get up and do something physical, such as clear everyone's dishes from the table.[29]

Bono's anecdotal evidence lends credence to the idea that women talk more than men and that this greater talkativeness is somehow biological. There was no challenge to Bono's assertion that he became less talkative simply because he now has a more male body because it is a claim in keeping with cultural expectations.

The belief that women talk more than men is a cultural truism, so obvious and self-evident that it seems to need no investigation or explanation. Thus, when neuropsychologist Louann Brizendine suggested in her book, *The Female Brain,* that girls and women speak 20,000 words a day to men's 7,000,[30] there was little motivation to question this figure because it resonated with general societal beliefs about gender differences in talk. The specificity of Brizendine's statistics suggested that there must be considerable scientific data available to support her claim. But Mark Liberman, a phonetics professor who works with recorded speech in his own linguistics research, became suspicious of Brizendine's assertion that women talk more than three times as much as men and went to the footnotes of *The Female Brain* so he could read her sources himself. What he found were references to self-help books and academic studies that had nothing to do with measurement of the amount of talk by women and men. As far as Liberman could tell, "All these numbers were plucked from thin air: In no case did anyone cite any actual research to back them up."[31] Later editions of the book do not provide this specific statistic and simply state that women talk two to three times as much as men, which is still an unsupported claim. In both the first and later editions of her book, Brizendine believed so strongly in the existence of a gender difference in amount of talk that she did not feel the need to provide any real evidence for that claim.[32]

. . . THE REST OF THE STORY

The consistently told science-fiction tale of "The Girl Who Talked Too Much" seems to be based on scientific data, but those data are a fiction. The conclusion that women talk more than men do is not drawn from actual research but from cultural beliefs; it reflects cultural biases rather than actual gender differences in amount of talk. In fact, the data from actual scientific studies suggest that men talk more than women in some contexts and that both women and men talk about the same amount in many other contexts.

Dale Spender, an Australian linguist, is one researcher who has challenged the story that women talk more than men. As a result of her own experiences with men's and women's conversational patterns, she speculated that men talk considerably more than women, and she decided to test her hypothesis for herself. For two years, Spender carried around a tape recorder and recorded all the conversations she had with men. At the end of each conversation, when possible, she asked her male conversational partner whom he thought had talked more. With few exceptions, the men claimed that Spender had done most of the talking. When she totaled the talking time on the recordings and calculated the percentages, however, the men talked much more than she did in the conversations. Spender then began to try to contribute 50 percent to each conversation she had with a man, but she never could—she reached only 40 percent in some conversations. Furthermore, she reported feeling like a real "bitch" in her efforts to hold the conversational floor—interrupting, talking over the man, raising her voice, and doing everything she could think of that might allow her to participate equally with her male conversational partner.[33]

Meta-analyses of gender differences in talk support Spender's claims. Linguistics professor Deborah James and social psychologist Janice Drakich reviewed 56 research studies conducted between 1951 and 1991 that dealt with gender differences in amount of talk. In 24 of the studies, men talked more than women, and in 10 studies, men talked more than women in some circumstances. An additional 16 studies reported that women and men talked the same amount, and 2 studies reported that women talked more than men.[34] In direct contradiction of cultural beliefs, many different kinds of studies found that there were not substantial differences in the amount of talk by men and women.

Psychologists Campbell Leaper and Melanie Ayers collected data from 70 scientific studies that spanned several decades and totaled 4,385 participants for their meta-analysis of talkativeness published in 2007. When they tested the hypothesis that women talk more than men, they found exactly the opposite—that men are significantly more talkative than women. Leaper and Ayres found that men talk more than women during mixed-gender interactions, and there was no significant difference in talkativeness between women and men in same-gender interactions.[35]

Research on gender differences in amount of talk suggests that context is critical in assessing whether men or women talk more. In the studies reviewed by James and Drakich, context was significant in several studies. In one study, psychologist Matthias Mehl and his colleagues asked almost 400 participants to wear voice recorders for several days in order to calculate their daily word use. The researchers found that both men and women talk, on average, about 16,000 words per day. Mehl and his colleagues found no significant differences between how much women talk and how much men talk. Their findings suggest that contextual factors such as circumstances, familiarity with the subject, and whether someone is in a position of leadership—not gender—determine who talks more.[36]

Although the belief that women talk more than men is pervasive, it is a fiction that is not supported by science—a contradiction between cultural "knowledge" and research findings. The cultural bias that women talk more than men is so strong that some researchers simply construct evidence to support the claim. When research shows that men talk as much as or more than women, those findings are not widely reported, and people continue to assert and believe just the opposite. The media do not report the findings because they do not fit with cultural biases and expectations, which allows the science-fiction tale of "The Girl Who Talked Too Much" to persist unchallenged and unquestioned.

THE CURSE OF THE HORMONES

Jokes about PMS or premenstrual syndrome abound: "They call it PMS because 'mad cow disease' was already taken"; "I have PMS and a gun"; and "I have PMS and GPS, which means I am a bitch and will find you." Then there is the list of things *PMS* stands for: "Perpetual Munching Sprees," "Puffy Mid-Section," "People Make me Sick," "Provide Me with Sweets," "Pissy Mood Syndrome," and "Pardon My Sobbing." Men are shown to be equally at the mercy of male hormones, showcased in "testosterone-fueled" action flicks starring Bruce Willis, Matt Damon, or Ryan Gosling. According to "The Curse of the Hormones," women are crazy with PMS five days a month because of the effects of estrogen, and men cannot control their aggressive urges because of their high levels of testosterone. This science-fiction story is the story of how women and men are affected—or cursed—by their hormones. It is also the story of the exaggeration of the effects of these hormones on human behavior. A fictional world is created based on scientific research without an acknowledgment of all sorts of complicating factors—environmental factors that affect levels of hormones in the body, elements that may mitigate the impact of hormones, and variables other than hormones that may be responsible for the behaviors of men and women.

"The Curse of the Hormones" is based on the belief that each gender is differentially impacted by its particular sex hormone. For women, this means being subject to premenstrual syndrome or PMS. British physician Katharina Dalton used the term *Pre-Menstrual Syndrome* in 1964 to refer to a combination of emotional and physical symptoms that, in some women, surface a few days prior to and end with menstruation.[37] The most common emotional symptoms of PMS are irritability, emotional sensitivity, and unhappiness, while frequent physical symptoms consist of fatigue, headaches, and insomnia. After Dalton named PMS a medical disorder, the diagnosis became popular with physicians and researchers alike to the point that many came to believe that all women suffer from PMS. Physician Eduard Eichner, studying what he called *premenstrual tension syndrome (PTS)*, summarized this belief: "There is ample evidence that women in general . . . experience symptoms of premenstrual tension. Many are not aware that they suffer, but their coworkers know and often feel the full effects of the irritability and irascibility manifested by the patient. Interpersonal relationships are frequently inharmonious, and many domestic tragedies result in part from PTS."[38] Women are told that they suffer from PMS even if they do not.

So strong is the science-fiction tale about the premenstrual impact of hormones on women that court cases have made profitable use of it with clients. Dalton testified at the trial of a woman who had run over her boyfriend with a car. Dalton argued that the defendant was suffering from PMS at the time and should not be held legally responsible for her acts. In large part because of Dalton's testimony, the defendant was discharged from jail. In another case, a judge dismissed charges against a man accused of raping and sodomizing his girlfriend after he argued that she had filed the charges during a period of PMS.[39] The widespread belief in PMS reinforces a belief in the inescapable and largely uncontrollable influence of estrogen on women's emotions and actions. According to this science-fiction tale, women are cursed by the "curse."

Beliefs and research about aggression in men follow a similar trajectory to those regarding the effects of estrogen on women, although the absence of a clear indicator like menstruation to signal phases of the hormone cycle makes this version of the hormone curse less obvious. In this iteration of the tale, men are subject to the rages of testosterone, which causes them to be aggressive and violent. The work of psychologists Eleanor Maccoby and Carol Jacklin provides a starting point for understanding studies on aggression and male behavior. In their review of 94 studies dealing with aggression, they found 52 studies that showed males to be more aggressive than females, 5 that showed the reverse, and 37 that showed no gender differences in aggression whatsoever.[40] Although many of the studies they reviewed showed that men are not more aggressive than women, the story being told in "The Curse of the Hormones" ignores those findings. When scientific studies are ignored, the belief that men are more aggressive than women and that their aggression is caused by hormones continues to be the dominant story available within the binary.

Despite the mixed results of their investigation, Maccoby and Jacklin claimed that there is a biological basis for aggression in men and supported their assertion with three reasons: Males are more aggressive than females in all human and primate societies; aggression can be changed by administration of sex hormones; and aggression shows up early, before socializing factors begin to function.[41] In subsequent research, Maccoby and Jacklin continued to assert a strong link between hormones and aggression, claiming that "males are the more aggressive sex and that this sex difference is evident as early as the preschool years and continues through subsequent phases of development. . . . We also believe it is highly likely that there is a biological component underlying the sex difference."[42] Despite evidence to the contrary, Maccoby and Jacklin asserted that men are more aggressive than women because of testosterone.

In numerous other studies that found correlations between testosterone levels and violent behavior, a biological basis for aggression was the standard conclusion. In their study of prison inmates, psychologist Joel Ehrenkranz and his colleagues found that 12 prisoners with histories of chronic violent behavior and another 12 socially dominant prisoners had higher blood levels of testosterone than a group of 12 nonviolent prisoners.[43] In another study, Richard Rada and his colleagues (psychiatrists who study rapists and child molesters) identified a small group of five such offenders judged to be the most violent according to clinical classification, police records, and interviews. This group showed significantly higher levels of testosterone than three other groups—less violent rapists, adult male volunteers, and convicted child molesters.[44] In both of these studies, the powerful influence of testosterone on male bodies was linked to particular kinds of behavior in men, and men's violence was seen to be caused by the hormone simply because it was present in higher levels in those who were the most violent. The moral of "The Curse of the Hormones," as these studies indicate, is that both women and men are "out of control" because of the influence of their hormones.

. . . THE REST OF THE STORY

That both women and men are affected by sex hormones appears to be a well-established plotline in "The Curse of the Hormones." The presence of estrogen in women and testosterone in men causes them to exhibit certain behaviors, the story goes. But because the belief in the biological force that estrogen and testosterone exert on human behavior is so strong, evidence about hormones and behavior is being ignored in this story—for example, that both men and women have both testosterone and estrogen, that not all women experience PMS and not all men are aggressive, and that there may be factors other than biology that mitigate the impact of hormones on behavior.

The alternative story to "The Curse of the Hormones" begins with correction of a misconception about estrogen and testosterone. Many people believe that only females have estrogen, and only males have testosterone. In actuality, both hormones exist in men and women, but because they were labeled *sex hormones* when they were discovered, each hormone is assumed to be unique to each gender and to affect unique biological processes in women's and men's bodies. Not only are estrogen and testosterone found in both genders, but some women have higher levels of testosterone than some men, and some men have higher levels of estrogen than some women. In addition, the amount of each hormone in the body changes in both men and women throughout the course of a day and across the lifespan. An episode of the radio show *This American Life* provides anecdotal evidence of the widely varying amounts of testosterone and estrogen found in women and men. One segment of the show discussed the decision of the show's staff (five men and four women) to have their testosterone levels tested. The testing revealed considerable variation across individuals, with a gay man having more than twice as much testosterone as anyone else and a pregnant woman having a higher level of testosterone than any of the other women.[45]

The hormones referred to as *sex hormones* affect far more than sex organs and reproductive processes. In fact, testosterone contributes to various reproductive organs and functions in both women and men. It affects sex-organ development, increased body hair, and a deeper voice at puberty in males; in women, it stimulates pubic-hair growth, the enlargement of the clitoris, and proper ovarian functioning.[46] Testosterone is necessary in both women and men for the development of bones and muscles, for the distribution of fat, and for maintaining energy levels. Estrogens, on the other hand, are crucial for the proper functioning of virtually every organ in the bodies of both men and women, including the thymus gland, the kidneys, the liver, and the heart. Estrogens are responsible for increases in high-density lipoprotein or HDL cholesterol (the good kind), blood clotting, and soaking up free radicals in the blood.[47] When both women and men have both estrogen and testosterone in their bodies, the claim that typically links their different behaviors to their different hormones becomes harder to support.

"The Curse of the Hormones" also ignores environmental factors that can moderate the effects of hormones on the body. A number of these factors have been found to affect levels of hormones in both men and women and thus potentially to affect resultant behaviors. Exercise is one factor that alters hormone levels in the body. Levels of both testosterone and estrogen increase in the bloodstream of women and men as a result of sustained exercise and remain elevated for several hours following the exercise period.[48] Caring for children is also a factor that seems to affect hormone levels in men. Anthropologist Christopher Kuzawa and his colleagues studied almost 900 young men in the Philippines and found that the testosterone levels in men who are fathers were lower than the levels

in men who did not have children.[49] In fact, in their study, men's testosterone levels were found to fall by about a third in the days and months after
their partners gave birth, additional evidence that life experiences and
activities affect testosterone levels.

Even something as seemingly insignificant as playing video games
can change the amount of testosterone and estrogen in the body. Psychologists Steven Stanton and Oliver Schultheiss were interested in whether
there was a hormonal basis for power seeking and dominance in women,
similar to the effect that testosterone seems to have on men. They asked
power-motivated women to play video games with one another and discovered that when they won a round, their levels of estrogen increased
dramatically. Conversely, their estrogen levels plunged when they lost. In
competitive situations, men tend to experience a rise in testosterone levels, and after winning a contest or game, the winner's testosterone level
increases even more while that of the loser decreases.[50] Again, environmental factors appear to affect hormone levels and thus to mitigate whatever effects those levels have on bodies.

But the interaction effect between hormones and behaviors is not the
only explanation that counters the impact of hormones on human behavior. Human consciousness is another. Humans have a unique capacity to
influence and overcome physical and biological limitations by creatively
thinking about and responding to their environments.[51] Humans can modify the impacts of bodily processes and bodily limitations through their
mental abilities. In the case of the effects of hormones on behavior, humans
can use their capacities to develop processes and strategies that mitigate or
moderate any effects that are experienced. Physician Lucille Peszat suggests that the use of stress-management techniques and increased sleep at
the time of women's periods can lessen the effects of PMS.[52] Similarly, men
need not be at the mercy of testosterone; they also can manage whatever
impacts it may have on them. Anger-management training has been found
to be effective in controlling aggression in young men, for example.[53] Meditation also has been found to be effective for moderating the manifesta-
tions of premenstrual symptoms in women and aggression in men.[54]

In "The Curse of the Hormones," the science-fiction story relies on an
exaggeration of the link between hormones and behavior. The fact that
two events occur together does not mean that there is a cause-and-effect
relationship between them. Simply because high levels of testosterone
exist in the bodies of men who are violent doesn't mean that testosterone
causes the violence, but this is what usually gets reported in the tale. The
science fiction about hormones also ignores other factors that could cause

irritability in women and violence in men. A third variable, sometimes called a *confounding* or a *lurking* variable, is an unintentional variable that is unseen and thus not measured that is actually determining the findings of a study.[55] A simple example of a third variable is the claim that playing video games causes heart attacks. In this claim, the kind and amount of food eaten while playing video games might be a confounding or an unintentional third variable that is more likely responsible for the heart attacks than are the games themselves. Any number of variables may be responsible for men's aggression and women's irritability rather than their hormones. Acknowledgment of possible third variables, which are beginning to be identified in studies of environmental factors, does not occur in "The Curse of the Hormones."

Until alternative ways of seeing the relationship between hormones and behavior become acceptable and accessible, "The Curse of the Hormones" will continue to reign as the prevailing interpretation of hormones and behavior. Like "Of Math and Men" and "The Girl Who Talked Too Much," this is a science-fiction story in which a particular worldview or set of beliefs is crafted from the findings of scientific studies. In this instance, the exaggeration of the effects of hormones creates the widespread impression that both men and women are out of control for biological reasons. There is virtually no recognition in the story that the differences between women and men in terms of types of hormones in their bodies are not nearly as pronounced as is typically assumed or that nonbiological variables may mitigate hormone levels and effects of hormones.

FICTIONS FROM SCIENCE

The science-fiction stories we have discussed here are only three examples of the many popular stories circulating that suggest that women and men are very different from one another in almost every human trait and behavior. In each case, science is simplified, ignored, or exaggerated as it intersects with culture. Not unlike *Frankenstein*, a story in which disparate body parts created a malformed specimen, these studies create a body of knowledge that does not add up to an accurate picture of gender. Despite claims of objectivity for science, social expectations that focus on difference are affecting the results of these research studies and are creating a fantasy world around gender differences.

Social expectations play a role both in the scientific studies themselves and the media's coverage of them. "Of Math and Men" offers a clear example in which the media reported a genetic explanation for male math superiority, which was not what the researchers claimed but that fit with social expectations. In the case of women talking more than men, because the belief that women talk all the time is so strong, a researcher generated her own statistics to make this claim, despite actual research to the contrary. There is also no acknowledgment in the story as it plays out in media coverage and in popular culture of the considerable amount of research that shows exactly the opposite of what is believed. In "The Curse of the Hormones," social expectations continue to reinforce the idea that women's behavior is governed by estrogen and men's behavior by testosterone, despite mitigating factors.

A primary reason why the three science-fiction stories tend to be believed is that they align with the binary's emphasis on significant differences between men and women. There is considerable research that suggests how much more similar than different women and men are on virtually every characteristic imaginable, yet societal expectations discourage a focus on these similarities. Researchers look for the gender differences that exist between men and women and see within-group differences or gender similarities as uninteresting. The preference for studying gender differences is compounded by the fact that studies that report significant gender differences are published more frequently than those that do not. The *file-drawer problem* aptly labels this phenomenon. Studies that find no or small gender differences end up in researchers' file drawers rather than in scientific journals.[56] The information available to both scientists and the general public is weighted in favor of gender differences.

The work of psychologist Janet Shibley Hyde offers an example of how different gender research might look if its focus were on similarities rather than differences. Hyde has proposed a gender-similarities hypothesis that asserts that women and men are far more alike than different on most psychological variables.[57] Hyde developed her gender-similarities hypothesis after engaging in a meta-analysis of a large number of studies of psychological gender differences. She reviewed studies of cognitive variables (such as math and verbal abilities), verbal and nonverbal communication, social and personality variables (such as aggression and leadership), measures of psychological well-being (such as self-esteem), motor behaviors (such as throwing distance), and miscellaneous constructs (such as moral reasoning). Across the studies she analyzed, 30 percent showed gender differences near zero, and 48 percent showed differences in the small range. This means that 78 percent of the gender differences she was studying were small or nonexistent. Hyde did find significant differences in motor abilities between the genders—many men can throw a ball farther than many women—but this is hardly a psychological variable, and some women in the study could throw a ball farther than some men. On verbal and communication skills, Hyde found that women smiled more and spelled better, but these were the only traits that showed moderate gender differences.[58] Again, not all women smiled more and spelled better than all men.

That the very small gender differences found in some studies continue to make news in a binary world says more about the nature of the binary than about the differences themselves. With an understanding of how social expectations affect inquiry, researchers might envision new options outside of the binary to get to "the place where difference does not make quite so much difference."[59] Scientists then might ask questions about gender that explore and admit the complexity, creativity, and flexibility of human behavior, no matter the gender. With such questions prompting research, there may come a time when fictions are no longer created out of scientific findings about gender differences. When this happens, thinking about the "opposite sex" or the "opposite gender" will sound strange, and talk about "neighboring" genders [60] may come to be the most natural thing in the world. *Individuals* or *people* will populate the research world rather than *men* and *women*, and science-fiction tales will be used for popular entertainment rather than for spreading fantasies about gender differences.

■ NOTES

[1] Camilla Persson Benbow and Julian C. Stanley, "Sex Differences in Mathematical Ability: Fact or Artifact?" *Science* 210 (December 12, 1980): 1262–64. Researchers associated with the SMPY project deliberately have chosen not to make strong distinctions between sex and gender, in agreement with those who argue that "the distinction between *sex* and *gender* may have outlived its usefulness, because biology cannot be separated from its cultural influences." They use the term *sex*—"perhaps arbitrarily but for the sake of clarity." See Diane F. Halpern, Camilla P. Benbow, David C. Geary, Ruben C. Gur, Janet Shibley Hyde, and Morton Ann Gernsbacher, "The Science of Sex Differences in Science and Mathematics," *Psychological Science in the Public Interest* 8 (2007): 2–3. We have chosen, on the other hand, to consistently use the term *gender* because we believe it more adequately captures the constructed nature of both biology and human social life.

[2] Benbow and Stanley, "Sex Differences in Mathematical Ability," 1262.

[3] Benbow and Stanley, "Sex Differences in Mathematical Ability," 1263.

[4] Benbow and Stanley, "Sex Differences in Mathematical Ability," 1263.

[5] Benbow and Stanley, "Sex Differences in Mathematical Ability," 1263.

[6] Benbow and Stanley, "Sex Differences in Mathematical Ability," 1264.

[7] Camilla Persson Benbow, "Sex Differences in Mathematical Reasoning Ability in Intellectually Talented Preadolescents: Their Nature, Effects, and Possible Causes," *Behavioral and Brain Sciences* 11 (1988): 172.

[8] Benbow, "Sex Differences in Mathematical Reasoning Ability in Intellectually Talented Preadolescents," 182.

[9] Halpern, Benbow, Geary, Gur, Hyde, and Gernsbacher, "The Science of Sex Differences in Science and Mathematics," 1.

[10] Halpern, Benbow, Geary, Gur, Hyde, and Gernsbacher, "The Science of Sex Differences in Science and Mathematics," 2.

[11] Halpern, Benbow, Geary, Gur, Hyde, and Gernsbacher, "The Science of Sex Differences in Science and Mathematics," 5.

[12] Halpern, Benbow, Geary, Gur, Hyde, and Gernsbacher, "The Science of Sex Differences in Science and Mathematics," 39.

[13] Halpern, Benbow, Geary, Gur, Hyde, and Gernsbacher, "The Science of Sex Differences in Science and Mathematics," 41.

[14] Dennis A. Williams with Patricia King, "Do Males Have a Math Gene?" *Newsweek*, December 15, 1980, 73.

[15] "The Gender Factor in Math," *Time*, December 15, 1980, 57.

[16] "Sex + Math = ?" *Family Weekly*, January 25, 1981.

[17] "The Gender Factor in Math," 57.

[18] Camilla Persson Benbow, "Achievement in Mathematics," *Science* 223 (March 23, 1984): 1247–48.

[19] Benbow, "Achievement in Mathematics," 1248.

[20] Janet S. Hyde, Sara M. Lindberg, Marcia C. Linn, Amy B. Ellis, and Caroline C. Williams, "Gender Similarities Characterize Math Performance," *Science* 321 (July 25, 2008), 494–95.

[21] Tony Scafidi and Khanh Bui, "Gender Similarities in Math Performance from Middle School Through High School," *Journal of Instructional Psychology* 37 (2008): 252–55.

[22] Nicole M. Else-Quest, Janet Shibley Hyde, and Marcia C. Linn, "Cross-National Patterns of Gender Differences in Mathematics: A Meta-Analysis," *Psychological Bulletin* 136 (2010): 103–27.

[23] Janis E. Jacobs and Jacquelynne Eccles, "Science and the Media: Benbow and Stanley Revisited" (Washington, DC: National Institute of Education, 1982), 7.

[24] Sara M. Lindberg, Janet Shibley Hyde, and Liza M. Hirsch. "Gender and Mother-Child Interactions during Mathematics Homework: The Importance of Individual Differences," *Merrill-Palmer Quarterly* 54 (2008): 232–55.

[25] Marcella Bombardieri and Maria Sacchetti, "Summers to Step Down, Ending Tumult at Harvard," *Boston Globe*, February 22, 2006, http://www.boston.com/news/education/higher/articles/2006/02/22/summers_to_step_down_ending_tumult_at_harvard/

[26] Teresa Johnston, "In Wake of Harvard President's Comments, Stanford Professors Discuss Gender in Math, Science and Engineering Education," *Stanford New Service*, February 8, 2005, news.stanford.edu/pr/2005/pr-math-020905.html

[27] Una Stannard, *Mrs. Man* (San Francisco: Germainbooks, 1977), 53.

[28] John Gray, *Men are From Mars, Women are From Venus* (New York: HarperCollins, 1992).

[29] Chaz Bono with Billie Fitzpatrick, *Transition: The Story of How I Became a Man* (New York: Dutton/Penguin, 2011), 228.

[30] Louann Brizendine, *The Female Brain* (New York: Broadway, 2006). This account is provided by Deborah Cameron, *The Myth of Mars and Venus* (New York: Oxford University Press, 2008), 19–20.

[31] Mark Liberman, "The Main Job of the Girl Brain," *Language Log*, September 2, 2006, http://itre.cis.upenn.edu/~myl/languagelog/archives/003530.html

[32] When confronted by Liberman, Brizendine admitted that her claim was not supported by evidence and agreed to remove this statistic about a gender difference in amount of talk from subsequent printings and editions of her book. See Cameron, *The Myth of Mars and Venus*, 20.

[33] Dale Spender, "Keynote Address," Conference on Gender and Communication, Eugene, OR, March 1989.

[34] Deborah James and Janice Drakich, ""Understanding Gender Differences in Amount of Talk: A Critical Review of Research," in *Gender and Conversational Interaction*, ed. Deborah Tannen (New York: Oxford University Press, 1993), 284.

[35] Campbell Leaper and Melanie M. Ayres, "A Meta-Analytic Review of Gender Variations in Adults' Language Use: Talkativeness, Affiliative Speech, and Assertive Speech," *Personality and Social Psychology Review* 11 (2007): 328–63.

[36] Matthias R. Mehl, Simine Vazire, Nairán Ramírez-Esparza, Richard B. Slatcher, and James W. Pennebaker, "Are Women Really More Talkative Than Men?" *Science* 317 (July 6, 2007): 82.

[37] Katharina Dalton, *The Premenstrual Syndrome* (London: William Heinemann Medical Books, 1964).

[38] Eduard Eichner, "The Premenstrual Tension Syndrome—Fact or Fancy?" in *Psychosomatic Obstetrics, Gynecology and Endocrinology*, ed. William S. Kroger (Springfield, IL: Charles C. Thomas, 1962), 319.

[39] These examples are discussed by Anne Fausto-Sterling, *Myths of Gender: Biological Theories About Women and Men* (New York: Basic, 1985), 5.

[40] Eleanor Emmons Maccoby and Carol Nagy Jacklin, *The Psychology of Sex Differences* (Palo Alto, CA: Stanford University Press, 1974). Maccoby and Jacklin's work is reviewed by Todd Tieger in "On the Biological Basis for Sex Differences in Aggression," *Child Development* 51 (1980): 943.

[41] Maccoby and Jacklin, *The Psychology of Sex Differences*.

[42] Eleanor E. Maccoby and Carol Nagy Jacklin, "Sex Differences in Aggression: A Rejoinder and Reprieve," *Child Development* 51 (1980): 964.

[43] Joel Ehrenkranz, Eugene Bliss, and Michael H. Sheard, "Plasma Testosterone: Correlation with Aggressive Behavior and Social Dominance in Man," *Psychosomatic Medicine* 36 (1974): 469–75.

[44] Richard Rada, D. R. Laws, and Robert Kellner, "Plasma Testosterone Levels in the Rapist," *Psychosomatic Medicine* 38 (1976): 257–68.

[45] Ira Glass, host, *This American Life* (Chicago, IL: Chicago Public Media, August 30, 2002).

[46] Paula J. Caplan and Jeremy B. Caplan, *Thinking Critically about Research on Sex and Gender*, 3rd ed. (Boston: Pearson, 2009), 66.

[47] Free radicals are unstable molecules that bond with other molecules, damaging cells and contributing to the development of diseases and aging.

[48] Greg Landry, "Eight Hormones and Exercise," 2002, http://liftforlife.com/content/bodybuilding-fitness-diet-health-articles/alternative-health/709-hormones-and-exercise

[49] Christopher W. Kuzawa, Lee T. Gettler, Martin N. Muller, Thomas W. McDade, and Alan B. Feranil, "Fatherhood, Pairbonding and Testosterone in the Philippines," *Hormones and Behavior* 56 (2009): 429–35.

[50] David A. Edwards, "Competition and Testosterone," *Hormones and Behavior* 50 (2006): 681–83; Michael Elias, "Serum Cortisol Testosterone and Testosterone-Bind-

ing Globulin Responses to Competitive Fighting in Human Males," *Aggressive Behavior* 7 (1981): 215–24; and Alicia Salvador, Vicente Simón, Fernando Suay, and Luis Llorens, "Testosterone and Cortisol Responses to Competitive Fighting in Human Males: A Pilot Study," *Aggressive Behavior* 13 (1985): 9–13.

[51] R. C. Lewontin, *Biology as Ideology: The Doctrine of DNA* (New York: HarperCollins, 1990), 121.

[52] Julie Clow, "Managing Moodiness: How to Lighten the Darker Side of PMS," http://www.homemakers.com/health-and-nutrition/disease-prevention/managing-moodiness-how-to-lighten-the-darker-side-of-pms/a/26371

[53] Leona L. Eggert, *Anger Management for Youth: Stemming Aggression and Violence* (Bloomington, IN: National Educational Service, 1994); and Eva L. Feindler, Suzanne A. Marriot, and Margaret Iwata, "Group Anger Control for Junior High School Delinquents," *Cognitive Therapy & Research* 8 (1984): 299–311.

[54] Paul Grossman, Ludger Niemann, Stefan Schmidt, and Harald Walach, "Mindfulness-Based Stress Reduction and Health Benefits: A Meta-Analysis," *Journal of Psychosomatic Research* 57 (2004): 35–43; and Elizabeth Monk-Turner, "The Benefits of Meditation: Experimental Findings," *The Social Science Journal* 40 (2003): 465–70.

[55] Caplan and Caplan, *Thinking Critically about Research on Sex and Gender*, 30.

[56] Caplan and Caplan, *Thinking Critically about Research on Sex and Gender*, 34.

[57] Janet Shibley Hyde, "The Gender Similarities Hypothesis," *American Psychologist* 60 (2005): 581–92.

[58] Cameron, *The Myth of Mars and Venus*, 43.

[59] Jacquelyn B. James, "What Are the Social Issues Involved in Focusing on *Difference* in the Study of Gender?" *Journal of Social Issues* 53 (1997): 228.

[60] Dorothy L. Sayers, *Are Women Human?* (Grand Rapids, MI: William B. Eerdmans, 1971), 37.

five

BEST SELLERS
GENDER STORIES
IN POPULAR CULTURE

When will I learn? The answer to life's problems
aren't at the bottom of a bottle, they're on TV!

Homer Simpson, *The Simpsons*

You get dressed watching Brad and Angelina interviewed on *Good Morning America*. You drive to school listening to the top 40, singing along when your favorite Beyoncé song comes on. You drive through a landscape of billboards advertising everything from Pabst Blue Ribbon to T-Mobile. You stop at Starbucks to get coffee and check out a couple of your friends' Facebook pages before class begins. Television, music, advertisements, coffee shops, and the Internet are just a few of the sources of messages competing to sell you various visions of who you should be. All of these forms of entertainment—the "best sellers" of popular culture—are the stories you are supposed to "buy" about how to be attractive, sexy, fulfilled, and successful.

Many of the stories the best sellers of pop culture tell are about gender. As you watch, buy, listen to, and participate in them, these stories employ a variety of strategies to invite you to accept the perspectives on gender they offer. Some of these stories retell the binary, reinforcing in various ways the expectations of the binary for gender roles. Other stories revise the binary, suggesting that the categories of this matrix can be modified. A third type of story rewrites the binary, challenging and overturning it. We turn now to an explanation of each of these strategies and how they function in the best sellers of pop culture to retell, revise, or rewrite the binary. We obviously can't include all of the media stories that are out there, but we encourage you to look for the stories that are most influential for you and to reflect on the types of stories they are.

Our goal in presenting these samples is to provide you with a framework for analyzing and evaluating the texts that are delivered to you through mass media, digital media, and all forms of popular culture. We hope that the gender literacy you develop as a result encourages you to ask questions about what you watch, hear, and read and prompts you to be more aware of the role of mass media and pop culture in constructing your views of reality around gender. If you are able to analyze critically the messages being offered you in the form of gender stories throughout the culture, you will be able to make more informed choices about the kinds of stories in which you want to participate and the ones you want to use as resources for constructing your own gender stories.

GENDER STORIES THAT RETELL THE BINARY

Many of the gender stories that are offered to you in pop culture retell the binary—in other words, their messages about gender align with the prescriptions of the master narrative of the binary. These stories encourage you to conform to traditional, normative gender expectations by telling stories of men and women who meet those expectations and who are rewarded for doing so. Stories that retell the binary use three primary mechanisms to encourage you to adhere to the binary's expectations for gender: (1) preparation; (2) prescription; and (3) reinscription.

PREPARATION

One mechanism for retelling the story of the binary is preparation, a strategy directed primarily at children and teens. Pop-culture stories of preparation socialize children in anticipation of adulthood in the binary, telling children that they will be expected to look and act in certain ways. This preparation assumes many forms, including explaining how children should be as adults, actually modeling the expected behavior, showing the rewards to be gained from following the binary, and projecting negative consequences for those who do not conform. Dr. Seuss's books and Taylor Swift's music are examples of the strategy of preparation employed in gender stories that retell the binary's expectations for women and men.

DR. SEUSS Disney movies — pre-pixar

The Dr. Seuss books not only introduce children to the fun of language and a set of wacky characters, but they communicate a clear message about gender differences. They anticipate substantial variation between the kinds of lives men and women are expected to live. They illustrate the binary's hierarchical value of the masculine over the feminine in stories that show that males are more important than females, and boys will have more adventures and more say about what goes on in the world than girls.

Dr. Seuss's books preview the greater importance of males in the adult world through the predominance of male characters in his books. All of the active roles in his books are performed by males, as novelist Alison Lurie notes: "There is the almost total lack of female protagonists; indeed, many of his stories have no female characters at all. . . . The typical Seuss hero is a small boy or a male animal."[1] In fact, not one of the 42 children's books written by Dr. Seuss has a female title character.[2] In the few Dr. Seuss books where female characters assume relatively major roles, those characters are unlikable. In *Horton Hatches the Egg*, Mayzie is a lazy bird who traps Horton into sitting on her egg while she flies off to Palm Beach, and Gertrude McFuzz in *Yertle the Turtle and Other Stories* is "vain, envious, greedy, stupid, and fashion-mad. She gorges on magic berries to increase the size of her tail, and ends up unable to walk."[3]

The female characters in his books are not only largely absent and unpleasant, but when they are present, they appear as "mostly silent sidekicks."[4] The lack of words spoken by female characters in Dr. Seuss's books is striking. Of the 170 speaking parts in his children's books, 148 of them are male. Of all the words spoken in the books, 86.9 percent are spoken by males, 10.4 percent by characters of uncertain gender, and 2.7 percent by females.[5]

Some specific examples clearly point to the message of Dr. Seuss's books that men matter more and that boys will play a more active role in the world when they grow up. In *The Cat in the Hat*, the two main characters are a boy and his sister Sally. The boy narrates the story and is the one who captures Thing One and Thing Two, while Sally hides behind her brother and doesn't say anything throughout the entire story. Similarly, Peter, the main character in *Scrambled Eggs Super*, spends the book explaining what a wonderful cook he is to Liz, who remains silent. In *The*

Glunk That Got Thunk, a girl with a powerful imagination conjures up a monstrous, green glunk. When she is unable to unthink the monster, she is rescued by her brother, who turns on his Un-thinker so they can unthink the glunk together. He then advises her not to take any more risks: "Then I gave her/Quite a talking to/About her Thinker-Upper."[6] The pattern continues in *You're Only Old Once!*, which contains a female receptionist (although only her arm is visible) and a female nurse; all of the other characters are male—a patient, an orderly, doctors, technicians, and a fish.

Using the strategy of preparation, Dr. Seuss's books explain to children the kind of world in which they will live as adults and how important they will be in that world. Boys will become men who will matter the most and will have adventures that make them central to the world, while girls will have minimal participation in the world. These messages align with the binary's evaluation of men as more important than women and its prescription that men are the ones who do the major and most visible work of the world.

TAYLOR SWIFT   Counter - Pink, Dua Lipa

Pop culture offers every generation of girls and boys models for them to use for growing into adulthood. The music of country and pop singer Taylor Swift resonates particularly with today's pre-teen girls, and it is likely to constitute a formative musical experience for many of them. Swift's musical stories introduce girls to some key components of the binary's expectations for them as women. In particular, she previews a key role she says girls should play when they grow up—the princess— a role Swift models in her songs and videos. In "Love Story," she calls herself *Juliet* and her boyfriend *Romeo* and sings: "I'm standing there, on a balcony in summer air. I see the lights; see the party, the ball gowns." She develops the princess theme even more explicitly in these lyrics: "You'll be the prince and I'll be the princess. It's a love story, baby, just say yes." Swift's modeling of the princess role is evident as well in "Today Was a Fairytale": "Today was a fairytale, you were the prince. I used to be a damsel in distress. You took me by the hand, and you picked me up at six." Swift also dresses like a princess in her photograph on the bottle of her perfume, the name of which, *Wonderstruck,* alludes to life as a princess.

Swift's songs play out the binary script by suggesting that love and romance are the most important concerns for girls and women. These are far more important, for example, than studying and excelling at school. In her videos, Swift often is shown exchanging her books and her studies for a romantic relationship. Several videos begin with Swift walking to class or studying in a library while wearing a school uniform and glasses. In the video for the song "Love Story," Swift is walking across campus with schoolbooks when she sees the man of her dreams. Both are instantly transported to a castle setting, where everyone is dressed in sixteenth-century clothing, including Swift, whose almost-strapless ball gown makes her look every bit the princess. Love, romance, and attracting a man are all that matter as Swift flits among lantern-lit gardens and lingers on the balcony of the castle with her prince.

Swift's lyrics often present marriage as the ultimate goal for women. The lyrics for "Love Story," for example, describe a marriage proposal: "He knelt to the ground and pulled out a ring and said/Marry me Juliet, you'll never have to be alone./I love you, and that's all I really know./I talked to your dad—go pick out a white dress." In the video for "You Belong With Me," which deals with Swift's unrequited love for the boy next door, she wins him when she appears at a dance dressed in a white, strapless gown very much like a wedding dress. He likewise wears a wedding-like tux complete with boutonniere. Swift's music offers a clear preparatory message to young girls—a message that aligns with the prescriptions of the master narrative of the binary: Dress like a princess and be beautiful so that you can be the center of attention and attract and marry a prince. The result will be a happily-ever-after world, according to Swift's music. For young boys, the message of Swift's music is complementary: You are expected to do the choosing in romantic relationships, and your choices are to be based on the beauty and appearance of the woman.

PRESCRIPTION Fifty Shades of Grey

Other best sellers are marketed toward adults and explicitly prescribe how men and women should be. These narratives depict adult masculinity and femininity in ways that conform to the gender binary and often reveal the rewards to be reaped from meeting the binary's expectations. The music of rapper Pitbull, the articles and ads in *Cosmo* magazine, and the sport of snowboarding illustrate stories that give advice on appropriate behavior for women and men and, in the process, retell the binary using prescription.

PITBULL

Rapper Pitbull's songs and videos prescribe that masculinity is constituted largely by sexual prowess and the achievement of material success, two key ingredients that are requirements for normative masculinity in the binary. Sexual prowess is accompanied by aggressiveness and confidence, and Pitbull's lyrics and videos clearly suggest that he can have sex whenever and with whomever he chooses—single women, groups of women, and even women who have other boyfriends. The lyrics to "Hey Baby" are typical of his demonstration of confident sexuality: "Hey baby girl, what you doin' tonight?/I wanna see what you got in store/Hey baby, givin' it your all when you're dancin' on me/I wanna see if you can give me some more." In "Give Me Everything," he sings, "Tonight I want all of you tonight/Give me everything tonight," and the implication is that she will not refuse. The video for "Hotel Room Service" also makes explicit the idea that he is sexually active as he is joined in a hotel room by a number of women dancing, taking bubble baths, and inviting him to participate in group sex.

The binary's requirement that men be materially successful is also evident in Pitbull's lyrics and videos. He is shown in many of his videos dressed in an impeccably tailored suit, suggesting a high income. In the video for "Hotel Room Service," he is seen driving a sleek black car, another typical symbol of success. When he enters an opulent high-rise hotel, he shows the hotel clerk his ID, which has the name *Armando Bond* on it. *Armando* is Pitbull's first name; *Bond*, of course, references the charming, successful, and idealized James Bond. Pitbull reinforces his status as a successful man in the lyrics to "Go Girl": "Baby, I'm a superstar/ Always posted at the bar." Because of his status, he has leisure time and sufficient money to spend his days drinking and entertaining himself with women.

The proper role for women in Pitbull's music and videos is complementary to men's roles. If men are supposed to be sexually confident and aggressive, women are supposed to be sexually available so they can satisfy men's appetites. "I know you want me, want me/You know I want cha, want cha," he sings in "I Know You Want Me," suggesting that women are willing to engage in sex with him. In his videos, Pitbull is typically shown at the center of a group of women, all of whom are focused on him as they dance suggestively. Women dressed in strapless minidresses dance behind him in "Go Girl" and, at the end of the video, they encircle him, much as football players in a huddle. Pitbull emerges with lipstick kisses all over his face. In the video for "Hey Baby," women at one of his performances are seen doing the same things as the women in most of his videos—dancing suggestively with their attention focused exclusively on him, signaling their availability. Because women's primary function is to satisfy men sexually, women are interchangeable, as seen in "Hotel Room Service," in which Pitbull sings "Mujeres!" and follows it with the names of many different women: *Roslin, Zulema, Christina, Carolina, Sofia,* and *Stefany*. The prescription offered by Pitbull's music, then, focuses largely on the nature of masculinity as rooted in sexual prowess and wealth. Women's place, according to this gender story, is to be sexually available to men.

COSMO

Using the strategy of prescription, *Cosmopolitan* magazine tells its female readers that life is about making themselves sexually attractive to men as girlfriends or wives. The primary duty for women, according to the magazine, is to create a body that is sexually appealing to men, a task that is accomplished by buying and applying a wide array of beauty products. Ads appear every second or third page in the magazine, promoting the products that women need to develop or enhance their physical beauty. Women's faces are a particular focus of attention, so there are ads for all kinds of makeup—foundation, eye shadow, lipstick, moisturizer, facial hair remover, eyeliner pencil, and mascara. Hair plays a big role in sexual attractiveness, evident in the ads for shampoo, hair spray, hair fortifier, hair color, conditioner, moisturizer, hair-repair treatment, and anti-frizz cream. Ads for jeans, shoes, watches, and bras and panties help women construct their wardrobes in ways that enhance their appearance according to the magazine's particular standards. Diet aids offer help to remain thin (one of the prescribed attributes). Ads for nail-polish strips and grow-faster base coats depict the accepted appearance for nails. Women are encouraged to buy perfumes with names such as *Seductive, Lovestruck,* and *Forbidden Euphoria,* reminding women of the goal of being sexually attractive. Most important, the *Cosmo* women are sporting engagement rings and wearing diamond bracelets, earrings, and necklaces—rewards for their superb performances as *Cosmo* women.

That shopping is the key route to sexual attractiveness can be seen not only in the ads but in feature articles that promote beauty products— often the very ones being advertised in the magazine. "Beauty: His Picks" discusses "lipstick shades he likes" and tells where to buy them. "The Cosmo Beauty Awards" describe sexy lip shades that will make the *Cosmo* woman "more kissable," false eye lashes in a tube, and lip gloss that stays put all night long. The article "Ssseriously Sssexy" suggests that wearing snakeskin "can morph you from girl next door to total temptress." It includes photographs of skirts, blouses, dresses, shoes, pants, and belts that look like snakeskin and provides information on where they can be purchased. Not only the ads but the articles themselves provide information about what to buy so that women can make themselves sexually attractive.

Cosmo women are supposed to be sexually attractive for one reason: to be available to perform sexually in ways that are pleasing to men. Most of the feature articles in the magazine help women achieve this goal by offering advice about sex. "Naughty Sex Tips" contains ideas about how to make sex as exciting as possible, such as doing it in a "teeny, tiny space" or on a skateboard. Another article offers "Four Words that Seduce Any Man . . . Anytime," while in "The Lap Dance He's Dying to Get," a dance instructor teaches readers how to do men's favorite parts of a lap dance. The importance of performing sexually is underscored by the question-and-answer columns in *Cosmo*, where many of the questions and concerns deal with sex: "I'm dating a new guy, and we're having a ton of sex . . . like, up to four times a day. Is it possible to do it too much?," asks one reader. "I want to handcuff my husband to the bed, but I feel weird initiating it. What's the best way?," asks another. *Cosmo* women have sex on their minds because, according to the magazine, that's what concerns and attracts men.

Cosmo advises women on how to be sexually attractive: Purchase the right makeup, hair products, clothing, and perfume, and the result is an engagement or wedding ring. This is the reward for women's focus on their man's sexual needs and desires. Using the strategy of prescription, *Cosmo* asserts and reinforces women's primary activities in the binary—applying beauty products and performing sexually in the service of a goal the binary says is all important for women—being in a relationship with a man.[7]

SNOWBOARDING   *Serena Williams*

Sports are a common way in which the prescriptions of the binary for boys and men are transmitted. Men's sports such as football and hockey clearly present and reinforce a view of masculinity as aggressive, violent, and competitive, with women as attractive cheerleaders and spectators. In contrast to many sports, snowboarding is a gender-integrated activity with male and female boarders participating next to one another. But the snowboarding culture nonetheless employs a variety of strategies both to prescribe a particular type of masculinity for male participants and to reinforce a masculine culture for the sport.

The masculinization of the sport began in its early years when the core snowboarders—largely men at the time—were "at the forefront of developing athletic expressions, style, and jargon."[8] They appropriated elements of two existing cultural versions of masculinity—the "skater kid" and the "gangsta"—to help develop the stereotypical masculine snowboarder. By stressing that a skateboarding background was an essential requirement for success in snowboarding, male participants connected snowboarding to an almost exclusively male sport and discouraged women from believing that they could be as successful. As a woman boarder explained, "I think most of the girls that I know don't have any kind of a skating background, and I didn't either, and it helps you so much. The guys who started skating just like stepped on a board and rode it."[9] Snowboarders also co-opted elements of the urban "gangsta"—fearless, aggressive, and heterosexual. The clothing, styles, and tastes of gangstas—such as "'dressing all street style, wearing T-shirts on their heads and headbands,' baggy clothing, low riding pants with exposed boxer shorts, gold chains and listening to rap and hip hop music"[10]—helped communicate that snowboarding is a masculine sport.

As the sport grew, masculinity—and a particular type of masculinity—was enforced in other ways. One was snowboarding's privileging of physical strength and toughness, characteristics the binary assigns to men. Toughness is emphasized in the glorification of injuries that characterizes the sport. Because "tolerance of physical risk carries enormous symbolic capital" among men, male athletes are encouraged "to ignore or deny injuries and pain," and "admitting to injury or suffering is seen as an admission of weakness."[11] Interviews in snowboarding magazines usually include questions about worst injuries, with replies reported in gory detail. Also included are pictures of riders displaying their gashes, black eyes, bruises, stitches, and broken bones. Likewise, most snowboard films include a slam section that features crashes and injuries.

In contrast, the media direct very little attention to female riders' injuries. Professional rider Tara Dakides recalls the injuries she has suffered over her career: "I've fractured my back, dislocated elbows, and torn ligaments in both knees. I've gotten whiplash six or seven times this year and who knows how many concussions."[12] Instead of proclaiming such women to be tough, strong, and daring, the snowboarding media rarely discuss their injuries. As a result, the media strengthen the image of the male rider who is tough and courageous and who is a more legitimate participant in the sport.

The metaphors used in snowboarding idealize and valorize men and masculinity.[13] Terms such as *killing, slashing, destroying, ripping, slaughtering, fresh kill,* and *tearing it up* are used to describe good performances,[14] suggesting that men are supposed to be aggressive and even violent. The names of and graphics on the snowboards for men reinforce the appropriateness of aggressiveness for men. Men's boards are named *K2, Attack Banana, Horrorscope, Destroyer, Youngblood, Ultrafear, Garage Rocker, Happy Hour, Flying V, Buckwild, Crush, Bully, Goliath,* and *Evil Twin* and feature images of skeletons, guns, monsters, comic-book graphics of action figures, graffiti, and frightened faces. Women's boards, in contrast, carry names such as *Diva, Lily, Diamond, Biddy, OMG, Lip-Stick, Feather, B-Nice,* and *Snowbunny* and are adorned with birds, flowers, cats, snowflakes, and sewing machines. Despite the presence of large numbers of women in the sport of snowboarding, female riders must fit into space constructed as masculine, which is defined as physically tough, fearless, and aggressive. The story of snowboarding, then, retells and reinforces notions of masculinity despite the participation of women in the sport.

REINSCRIPTION Hillary Clinton for President?

Reinscription is a strategy that retells the binary but in a more complex way than the strategies of preparation and prescription. The best sellers that employ this strategy use two steps to achieve reinscription. The first step is to tell a story that challenges binary guidelines, introducing gendered ways of being that violate the expectations of the binary. They encourage audiences to challenge the binary's expectations or to engage in a subversive or oppositional reading to these expectations. As a result, audiences position themselves as smart and enlightened because they recognize the binary's limitations. A story that makes use of reinscription, for example, might depict women and men in ways that the audience views as "retrograde or exaggerated or unrepresentative," [15] thereby suggesting that the binary should be mocked and dismissed because it is outdated.

The second step of reinscription involves reinforcement for the binary at the same time it challenges it. Reinscription revives the binary and encourages the audience to embrace it by offering an equally (or more) compelling message with which to identify. This message takes precedence over the audience's earlier dismissal of the binary. As a result, audiences are encouraged to align with the very binary they rejected earlier. Reinscription, for example, might depict women as housewives concerned only with cleaning products, encouraging the audience to see such a portrayal as limiting and silly, at the same time that it brings the audience around to supporting that very portrayal of women. An episode of *The Simpsons,* an issue of *Us Weekly* magazine, the Japanese graphic novel *Ouran High School Host Club,* and Chaz Bono's narrative of his gender-transition surgery illustrate how the strategy of reinscription appears to challenge but ultimately reinscribes the gender binary, bringing the audience back to adherence with its norms and expectations.

THE SIMPSONS

Homer and Marge and their children Lisa, Bart, and Maggie star in the longest-running comedy on American television, *The Simpsons*. An episode from the eighth season, "Homer's Phobia,"[16] revolves around Homer's efforts to keep Bart from becoming homosexual after a gay man, John, enters the Simpsons's lives. The episode illustrates the strategy of reinscription first by encouraging viewers to see homophobia and heterosexism as silly and ridiculous but, ultimately, asking them to see homosexuality as abnormal and undesirable. It both challenges and reinforces the binary's heteronormativity (the idea that heterosexuality is the norm), but reinforcement of the binary wins out at the end of the episode.

One way in which "Homer's Phobia" challenges the binary's stance toward homosexuality is to show how ridiculous prejudice toward gay men is by making fun of homophobic people like Homer. When Bart appears to identify with John, Homer reacts negatively, behaving in a stereotypically homophobic way. He criticizes Bart's Hawaiian shirt as gay, for example, and he is horrified when Bart chooses a pink snowball instead of a chocolate cupcake for dessert. He sees both Bart's dessert and clothing preferences as signs of homosexuality and therefore of deviance from the gender norm. Homer's intolerant, narrow-minded behavior toward what he sees as Bart's budding homosexuality is depicted as stupid and foolish.

A second way in which "Homer's Phobia" encourages the audience to challenge the binary is by presenting positive ways to think about gay men. After John saves Homer from attack by a pack of reindeer, his friends Barney and Moe lament, "We were saved by a sissy. We'll never live it down." Homer's reply calls them on their negative attitude toward gay men: "Hey! We owe this guy, and I don't want you calling him a *sissy.* This guy's a fruit, and a . . . no, wait, wait, wait, queer, queer, queer! That's what you like to be called, right?" He uses a term that many gay men and lesbians prefer to be called, suggesting that the audience knows about and is accepting of gay men. The show's references to filmmaker John Waters, a gay icon, also acknowledge gay culture. Because the episode shows both how ugly homophobia is and, in contrast, what an open, insider perspective on gay men looks like, it allows audiences to position themselves as progressive, sophisticated viewers who know more than Homer does about gay men and, unlike Homer, treat them with respect.

At the same time that it encourages a disruption of the binary's negative attitude toward homosexuality, "Homer's Phobia" is designed to reinscribe or reinstate homophobia. As the episode ends, audiences that earlier were critiquing homophobia and congratulating themselves on their openness toward gay men are encouraged to support the binary's norms of heteronormativity. In the concluding dialogue between Homer and Bart, Homer's attitudes toward John seem to have changed when he tells his son, "You know, Bart, maybe it's the concussion talking, but any way you choose to live your life is okay with me." This ostensibly open stance toward homosexuality is undermined by the word *concussion*. Homer suffered a concussion when he was rescued from the reindeer, and his reference to it suggests that his moment of transformation is the side effect of an injury and thus is likely to be fleeting. To hold an enlightened, accepting stance toward homosexuality, he suggests, is a result of something awry in the brain.

Heteronormativity is highlighted and seen as the superior attitude as well when Bart wonders what Homer means by his statement encouraging him to live as he chooses. When Lisa clarifies by whispering, "He thinks you're gay," Bart appears shocked and confusedly proclaims, "He thinks I'm gay?!" Bart's shock indicates that being presumed to be gay is an insult and cause for consternation; it clearly is inferior to being heterosexual. As TV critics Steve Williams and Ian Jones observe, the episode "leaves such a nasty taste in the mouth"[17] precisely because, at the same time that it encourages audiences to break with the binary and to see homosexuality as a legitimate alternative to heterosexuality, it reinscribes the norms of the binary. Audience members are brought back to a place where they are asked to see homosexuality as deviant and abnormal.[18]

US WEEKLY

As you wait in the checkout line at the grocery store, you are likely to encounter stories of gender told in celebrity magazines or celeb-azines such as *Us Weekly*. Although these magazines include stories about both men and women, women are much more frequently the subjects of the articles and features. Readers might learn about Sean Kingston's jet-ski accident or the expensive necklace Justin Bieber purchased, but men are not the focus of attention and are not subjected to the same kind of scrutiny as women. This scrutiny is at the heart of the reinscription strategy employed by *Us Weekly* that ultimately retells the story of the binary.

The women who are the focus of *Us Weekly* earned their celebrity status because of prominence in their fields. They excel in their careers as actors, models, business executives, and working mothers and are accomplished, confident, powerful, and economically independent. They also have worked hard to achieve their success and fame. Although audiences may read these magazines thinking that the content is silly and frivolous, they implicitly recognize that the women in them are featured because they are successful professionals in their fields. One story that *Us Weekly* tells is that the binary's ideal of women as dependent, nonprofessional housekeepers can be challenged by women who are independent, accomplished professionals.

But the binary is reinscribed in the gender stories that *Us Weekly* tells because of their focus on whether or not the women meet the standards for ideal feminine beauty. Their careers and their professional success are undermined in that the women featured are judged and defined exclusively by their bodies and their appearance. As the binary dictates, they must be gorgeous, sexually alluring, thin, and perfectly attired. The magazine prompts audiences to scrutinize the women through an intimate and direct mode of address that encourages them to call the celebrities by their first names or nicknames. Headlines such as "Zoë's Sexy Breakthrough" and "Jen's New Love," for example, assume that readers know these women personally. Because they do, they can monitor and discipline them, just as a close friend might do, to make sure they conform to the ideal of feminine beauty.

Readers are encouraged to scrutinize the women microscopically, looking "for signs of insufficient adherence to this forceful, pointed code of femininity."[19] They are prompted to judge the celebrities on their figures, weight gain, faces, hair styles, clothing, and the time and effort they put into maintaining their appearance. "Passion Adds Pounds," for example, is the headline of one story that features four women who have gained weight since they started dating or got married. Readers are encouraged to applaud celebrities when they don't gain weight, illustrated by "The Little Black Bikini," which shows ten celebrity women who look thin and toned in their bathing suits.

In "Who Wore It Best?," readers are asked to study juxtaposed photographs of celebrities wearing identical outfits and to decide whether Katie Holmes or Jessica Simpson looks the best "in an Isabel Marant jacket." Staff at the magazine ostensibly asked 100 people in New York City's Rockefeller Center to render their judgments on the question, and the percentages are reported under the pictures of the women; Jessica Simpson won 57 percent of the votes to Katie Holmes's 43 percent. The judgment is even more explicit in "Fashion Police," in which women are chastised for what they are wearing with taglines like "Perfect for dusting the red carpet" or "The love child of Barney and Big Bird."

The magazine explicitly undermines women's professional success through its focus on weight and clothing. Although they have the freedom and independence that come with success, thus disrupting the binary's expectations for women, the binary's norms for physical appearance for women are revived when readers are asked to focus their attention not on the women's talent and hard work but solely on their physical appearance. As a result, despite its focus on successful, professional women, *Us Weekly* ultimately reinscribes or retells the binary's expectations for women.[20]

OURAN HIGH SCHOOL HOST CLUB

Japanese graphic novels known as *gender benders*, a subgenre of *shōjo manga*, also exemplify the strategy of reinscription. Exported to the United States and translated into English, the novels are first serialized in magazines and later published as paperback novels. When published in the United States, they retain the Japanese layout, so English readers begin at what they would consider the back of the book, reading sequentially right to left and ending at the front. Written by women for a female audience, these graphic novels feature relatively empowered and often cross-dressing female protagonists.

The graphic novel *Ouran High School Host Club* by Bisco Hatori is an example of these gender benders. In *Ouran*, the protagonist is Haruhi, the poorest girl in an elite high school, who breaks an expensive vase. To pay off her debt, she is forced to join the all-male Host Club, which provides dating services for female students. Haruhi is initially mistaken as male by the other characters in the novel (and probably by most readers), thus expanding gender boundaries simply because she successfully passes as another gender. Haruhi considers herself androgynous and explains that she doesn't "fully appreciate the perceived differences between the sexes"[21] as a rationale for why she typically dresses in men's clothing. The novel thus challenges the assumption "that gender is natural and predetermined by biology, suggesting instead that females can be masculine and males can be feminine" because these are "socially constructed categories, not physiological states."[22]

Even as *Ouran* challenges and extends gender norms, however, it reinscribes the binary. Although the novel suggests that gender roles can be reversed, it does not challenge biological sex as the basis for gender. Haruhi eventually becomes romantically involved with another member of the Host Club, and when her boyfriend walks in on her while she is changing clothes, her biological sex is revealed. This act not only establishes biological sex as the basis for establishing someone's "true" gender but "removes any gendered ambiguity between the primary characters."[23] The notion that there is a real gender that is based on biological sex is also reinforced when straight men in the novel respond to Haruhi (often falling in love with her) as if they are somehow aware of her biological sex. In constructing a biological basis for gender for Haruhi, *Ouran* reaffirms the gender binary and a required alignment between the physical body and gender.

Ouran also reinforces heterosexuality and thus the binary's heteronormativity in that romantic relationships in the novel are seen to be appropriate only between women and men—same-sex couples are not taken seriously and serve as a source of comedy. For example, two members of the Host Club—twins Hikaru and Kaoru—perform a fake homosexual relationship with one another to entertain their female clients, and the novel depicts them as deviant and amusing. Likewise, Haruhi's father is a bisexual man who is a professional drag queen; he, too, is presented in a humorous light. Although the presentation of ambiguous gender, homosexual relationships, and transgendered persons expands the ways in which the genders may act, it also suggests that these are not real or significant gender portrayals, thus expanding the binary but reinscribing the norms of the binary as well.

CHAZ BONO

Chaz Bono, who was born *Chastity Bono* in 1969, is a celebrity whose gender transition has attracted media attention because he is the child of the pop singing duo Sonny and Cher. A female-to-male transgender person, he is an advocate for LGBTQ rights, a speaker, and an author. Bono's story of his gender transition is another example of the strategy of reinscription in that his narrative modifies the binary by enlarging the categories of men and women. But, at the same time, it checks that expansion and encourages the audience to align once again with the norms and expectations of the binary.

Bono's narrative of his gender transition begins with an expansion of the kinds of feelings and activities that the binary links to female bodies. Although he was born with female genitals and was assigned female at birth, he did not follow normalized gender roles and chose to dress and act like a boy: "As soon as I was able to dress myself, my self-image was clear: I chose boys' clothes, boys' shoes and sneakers, and was interested in boys' toys, games, and other preferences."[24] As Bono grew older, these feelings did not change: "Over time, it began to dawn on me that though embodied as a female, I was not a woman at all. That despite my breasts, my curves, and my female genitalia, inside, I identified as a man. This meant, of course, that I was transgender, literally a man living in a woman's body."[25] In such statements, Bono expands the gender binary, assuming a gender that does not have to match the biological sex characteristics with which he was born. Whereas the binary dictates that biological sex is the basis for the determination of gender, Bono disagreed, believing that his feelings, activities, and appearance could be masculine even though his body was feminine.

Bono began transitioning to male at the age of thirty-nine, undergoing counseling, hormone therapy, and top surgery to remove his breasts and to sculpt a male chest. His transition was completed on May 7, 2010, when a California court granted his request to change his gender and his name. He found adapting to the life of a man very easy: "I didn't really have to learn how to act like a man because in my head I'd always been one. I already knew how a man stands, dresses, combs his hair, and hails a cab. I was born with this knowledge, and as soon as I stopped trying to pass as a woman, I knew how to live as a man."[26]

In the story he tells following his surgery, Bono reinscribes the tenets of the binary that he previously rejected, encouraging his audience members to do the same. Bono asserts that a certain gender identity and certain kinds of activities and roles can only be performed by someone with a certain body. To do conventionally male things or act in a masculine way, a person must have a male body. Individuals need not engage in activities that match their bodies, he suggested earlier, but when he tells how his new more-male body creates activities that align with the binary, he reverts back to conventional views about the link between behavior and bodies.

Bono offers many examples of how his gender transition has transformed his personality, reflecting his perspective that a biologically male body determines personality traits. He asserts that he is "more gadget oriented now,"[27] and he reports an increased sex drive.[28] He reports that his girlfriend says his "smile is not as big as it used to be"[29] and perceives him as "less sweet."[30] Bono's challenge to the link between body and gender prior to his sex change is reversed when he reconnects biology and gender following the procedure.

Three mechanisms are used by the best sellers of pop culture to retell the binary's narrative—preparation, prescription, and reinscription. As pop culture acts on you with these strategies that retell the binary, you are exposed to the binary's expectations for women and men and are reinforced for accepting them. Preparation prepares boys and girls for how they are expected to be as adults, prescription advises them on how they should look and behave as adults, and reinscription revives the binary even as it allows audiences to feel temporarily progressive and enlightened for rejecting it.

GENDER STORIES THAT REVISE THE BINARY

Best sellers also offer you gender stories that revise the binary—stories that stretch or modify it in some way. The binary stays in place, but it is challenged and expanded in these revisionist narratives. Two primary mechanisms used in pop culture to revise the binary are: (1) critique; and (2) expansion.

CRITIQUE   ORANGE IS THE NEW BLACK

Sometimes, forms of pop culture critique the binary, questioning its utility, appropriateness, and consequences. As they do, these stories encourage audiences to interrogate the matrix that is the binary, questioning what they might earlier have taken for granted. Gender stories of critique encourage audiences to ask questions such as "Is the binary useful?" "Is it appropriate?" "What does a binary system do to individual identity and to relationships?" and "Are the consequences of the binary positive or negative?" Such questions revise the binary by raising questions for audiences about the system in which they have been participating. The paintings of Jean-Michel Basquiat and a J. Crew advertisement that sparked controversy over appropriate gender activities illustrate the strategy of critique.

JEAN-MICHEL BASQUIAT

The paintings of Jean-Michel Basquiat tell a gender story that critiques and thus revises the binary. Because his paintings tell about the cost to black men of attempts to live the ideal binary script, they provide a critique of the normative masculine ideal through the lens of the black man's experience. Many of his paintings depict the nature of the gender binary as it intersects with race to construct unique requirements for black men. They depict the stereotyped ways in which black men are often viewed—fighting, boxing, playing basketball, driving cars, shooting guns, and playing the saxophone. Basquiat points in his paintings to some of the qualities black men are asked to adopt as well. Many of the men he depicts have gold crowns hovering over their heads, as though status and dominance over others have not yet been achieved but are primary goals. The crowns also suggest that men should seek glory and status and should strive to be rich, successful, and powerful, competing with other men to be seen as legitimate and successful.

Basquiat not only identifies and explicates the binary that requires black men to act in narrowly confined, stereotyped ways but challenges the system as well. His paintings tell a story about the costs—incompleteness and fragmentation—to black men of the roles they are asked to adopt. Black men's bodies are often shown fragmented in his paintings, with feet, legs, arms, and heads isolated and disconnected. "Appearing always in these paintings as half-formed or somehow mutilated, the black male body becomes," as feminist theorist bell hooks observes, "incomplete, not fulfilled, never a full image."[31] Basquiat exposes the binary system as shallow and superficial when he depicts black men as stick figures, painted flat and without perspective in a childlike manner. Black men cannot be whole, adult, full human beings when they are caught in the requirements of the binary. That many of the black men have skulls for faces in Basquiat's works also suggests that black men can never become live, fully human men under current conditions. They lack the flesh that marks embodied, living persons and are simply caricatures of human beings.

In *Napoleonic Stereotype Circa '44*, which Basquiat painted in 1983, he illustrates both his portrayal and his critique of the binary. The painting shows two men fighting each other, and words such as *bip, bop,* and *splat* fly between them. They fight against a background grid of tiny squares, and a list of very large numbers runs down the left side of the scene. Black men are shown as confined to stereotyped boxes or in roles that involve fighting and aggression in which they must compete with each other to dominate and to win monetary rewards. At the bottom of the painting is the head of boxer Joe Louis depicted as a skull with the word *crown* written under it. The word *boxed* runs down the left side of this panel, repeated six times, with each letter in a small square. Even the successful boxer is confined, and the costs of his success in the binary clearly have been high. His body is neither complete nor alive, suggesting that those who fight for and achieve success, as defined by the binary's dictates for black men, ultimately lose their wholeness and their humanity. Because Basquiat's paintings critique the system in which black men are required to live, they revise the binary, suggesting the negative consequences for following its prescriptions. As a result, they challenge the hold of the binary on viewers' conceptions of gender.

J. CREW AD

An advertisement for J. Crew that was e-mailed to customers in April 2011 is an example of the strategy of critique because it invites—and almost demands—contemplation of and reflection on the binary. The ad features Jenna Lyons, president and creative director of J. Crew, and her five-year-old son Beckett, who is pictured with bright pink polish on his toenails. The tagline reads, "Saturday with Jenna . . . See how she and son Beckett go off duty in style." Below the picture is a quote from Lyons: "Lucky for me, I ended up with a boy whose favorite color is pink. Toenail painting is way more fun in neon."

For many viewers, the ad is not one they can easily ignore because something about the ad is likely to strike them as wrong, puzzling, or intriguing. They see a mother painting the toenails of her child—not an unusual act—but then they see that the child is a boy, and boys don't usually have their toenails painted. A mother is playing with her child—not an unusual act—but mothers don't usually play with their sons in ways that encourage them to dress and act in feminine ways. Also surprising is that the color of the polish she is painting on his toenails is pink, usually associated with girls and not boys, and the mother seems to be flaunting her son's preference for that color. Readers are also likely to wonder why J. Crew chose to advertise its clothing using this particular strategy. Beckett's mother seems to be advertising her delight that her son does not conform to gender prescriptions. Is the company thus aligning with a particular position on gender? Is it saying that breaking gender norms should be encouraged?

The controversy that erupted over the ad suggests that the strategy of critique was, indeed, effective because it encouraged viewers to reflect on gender roles. Some viewers responded negatively to the ad, claiming that it celebrates transgendered identity and that Lyons's act is likely to result in negative psychological consequences for Beckett as he grows older. Commentator Erin R. Brown of the Media Research Center, for example, saw the ad as supporting the expansion of gender roles when she suggested that J. Crew has "a new demographic—mothers of gender-confused young boys."[32] Psychologist Keith Ablow also reacted negatively to the ad: "Yeah, well, it may be fun and games now, Jenna, but at least put some money aside for psychotherapy for the kid—and maybe a little for others who'll be affected by your 'innocent' pleasure." He predicted highly negative outcomes for Beckett and other children whose mothers allow expanded gender options for them: "This is a dramatic example of the way that our culture is being encouraged to abandon all trappings of gender identity—homogenizing males and females when the outcome of such 'psychological sterilization' . . . is not known."[33]

Other viewers answered the questions the ad raised about gender in more neutral or positive ways. Psychiatrist Jack Drescher explained that most research on gender identity and sexual orientation concludes that neither is a choice and that a parent's behavior does not cause these conditions: "I can say with 100 percent certainty that a mother painting her children's toenails pink does not cause transgenderism or homosexuality."[34] Many online readers responded in similar ways to the ad: "A small child, with no secondary sexual characteristics, cannot be considered 'transgendered' or even a transvestite," wrote one.[35] Another commented: "I don't think it's all that uncommon for little boys to want their toenails painted 'like mommy's.' Kids are kids—my daughter sees me with colorful toenails and wants to copy me. If I am using a power tool, she wants to copy me. I guess that makes us both transgender in some people's eyes."[36] Because viewers of the J. Crew ad cannot easily dismiss it, they are asked to question and reflect on appropriate ways for being gendered. They are asked to contemplate the binary and the degree to which they see themselves aligning with or challenging it.

EXPANSION — Glee

Stories of pop culture that expand the binary remake the two gender categories of male and female. They suggest that there are multiple ways of being a man and a woman—ways that expand the prescriptions of the binary. Such stories allow the categories of female and male to become larger and to encompass more characteristics and qualities appropriate to the genders than the binary usually allows. In this way, stories of revision open up the categories of the gender binary. The movie *Fast Five* and *Men's Health* magazine offer different approaches to revising the binary through the strategy of expansion.

FAST FIVE

Fast Five, the 2011 installment in *The Fast and the Furious* franchise, expands the binary and thus models new ways of doing gender for moviegoers. Written by Chris Morgan and directed by Justin Lin, the movie revolves around the efforts of Dominic Toretto, his friend Brian O'Connor, and his sister Mia Toretto to steal $100 million from a corrupt businessman in Rio de Janeiro. The trio recruits seven additional people to help with the heist, one of whom is a woman, Gisele. As the plans for the heist unfold, the team members must contend not only with the cunning businessman and his partners but also with a US Diplomatic Security Service agent who is pursuing them.

Fast Five is an example of the action-film genre, which usually provides standard binary messages about masculinity with car chases, explosions, gun fights, brawls, and close escapes. The movie has all of these, suggesting a view of masculinity that means brawn, aggressiveness, courage, and the capacity to drive anything with an engine at high speed. At the same time, however, the movie expands the message of the binary concerning both femininity and masculinity.

Fast Five deviates from the master narrative of the binary in terms of femininity because the two women characters—Mia and Gisele—do exactly the same things in the film as the men. Admittedly, they meet expectations of femininity in terms of appearance, but they drive souped-up cars and motorcycles expertly and fast (Gisele, in fact, arrives on a motorcycle after being recruited for the team). The women are pursued by the bad guys, plot the next moves, and escape, just like the men do. They are just as competent as the men at all of the activities of the team, and this remains true even after Mia announces her pregnancy. She continues to drive fast cars and to participate in brazen and risky escapes, defying the conventional notion that pregnant women are fragile and in need of protection. Whereas the binary suggests that masculinity involves speed, aggression, and daring—and femininity precisely the opposite—*Fast Five* disagrees. It says that femininity may involve the very same qualities as masculinity, challenging the binary's division of traits and activities into one gender or the other.

Not only is the appropriate role for women stretched to include typically masculine activities, but men's roles are expanded in the film as well. Brian, a former FBI agent turned criminal, is of slight build, wears a beard that would be more likely to characterize a professor than an outlaw, and is more feminine in appearance than the men who usually star in these movies. He does everything, however, that the large, heavily muscled men do. He is just as able to drive cars fast, to fight and outmaneuver the villains, and to survive. A man who might be seen by the binary as marginally masculine because of his slight stature is shown in *Fast Five* to be quite capable of performing aggressively. Masculinity thus expands to include body types and appearances that deviate in some key ways from the binary's ideal presentation of the masculine.

Fast Five, an action film that, at first glance, seems to be a conventionally masculine film, offers audiences a disruption of the binary. The film says that women and all kinds of men can be aggressive, physically powerful, cunning fighters, and action heroes. The kinds of bodies typically thought to be required for these kinds of roles are seen in the film, but so are bodies that definitely are not associated with this kind of masculinity—male bodies that are small and slight and women's bodies. Employing the strategy of expansion, *Fast Five* broadens the meanings of both masculinity and femininity in terms of body and personality.

MEN'S HEALTH

Men's Health is a magazine that also expands the binary, seesawing between reinforcement of conventional masculine roles and qualities and expansion of them to include new (and conventionally feminine) activities and qualities. For men, reinforcement of the binary can be seen in the feature articles and ads in the magazine that assume that men are rich and sexy. Ads for watches, razors, colognes, and body washes suggest that men are to be well groomed and sophisticated in how they dress. Ads for athletic shoes, sunscreen, breakfast cereal, power drinks, pre-workout energy bars, and dietary supplements indicate that men are physically active. According to the ads, their primary interests, aside from work and sports, are cars and music (or at least portable digital music systems).

Another message the magazine gives readers is that men are expected to perform sexually. The article "Limp to the Bedroom" discusses how over-the-counter pain relievers, taken for athletic injuries, can cause erectile dysfunction. That the ideal man is heterosexual is clear in that one of men's major goals is to attract a "perfect beach babe." In one article, pro surfer Maya Gabeira gives tips on how to meet and keep such a babe happy by zeroing in, breaking the ice, cozying up, and mixing sexy beach cocktails. "Thirty-Nine Things She Wishes You Knew" begins, "You've admired, explored, stroked, cupped, and caressed women's bodies since you were first able to get away with it. But you can still learn. We enlisted the help of 2,439 women to point out what you may have missed." Men's performances in the bedroom, then, are expected to satisfy.

According to *Men's Health*, men are to be rich, sexy, physically active, and able to perform sexually, all of which reinforce the binary's conception of masculinity. But some of the articles in the magazine expand the binary by suggesting that men can and should do things that once were considered to be the exclusive domain of women. In other words, the magazine breaks with stereotypes of masculinity to expand the roles available to men. Articles about which exotic vegetables at the grocery store have the best antioxidant properties (Tatsoi, Peruvian purple potato, tomatillo, and kohlrabi) suggest that men are not just grilling but are cooking elaborate meals—typically considered the purview of women. Ads tout various skin-care products for men, including face cream, eye-lift cream, overnight renewal serum, and hair removal cream—products that are largely associated with women's efforts to stay young and sexually attractive. Men are also choosing clothes that make them look good and are even advised to wear pink, the color traditionally associated with femininity, because "it gives a warm glow to your face."

Some of the articles in *Men's Health* expand the binary in that they implicitly acknowledge that there are things that men do not know, in contrast to the expectations of the binary that men have all the answers. Men are shown as not always knowledgeable about even some basic things. "Rocket Fuel for Your Workday" tells men how they can "move mountains" or accomplish their goals by maintaining a steady to-do list, becoming friends with fear, and assessing their potential speed. "How to Do Everything Better" explains to readers how to tune up a bike, shine shoes, keep beach sand out of a car, mix sangria, move furniture, impress upper management, spot a bench press, and take a woman to a baseball game. Men are also told how to find their way around airports, large cities, and theme parks in "Never Ask for Directions Again," suggesting that, contrary to the stereotype, they may not always know how to get where they are going. The gender binary is being expanded, then, in *Men's Health* to include activities and interests once considered the exclusive domain of women, even as its gender stories simultaneously reference some key aspects of the binary for men.[37]

You encounter many gender stories that revise the binary in some way. Some modify it by providing a critique of it. They point to the power of the binary and scrutinize and assess it, suggesting some damaging and harmful impacts it has on people. Still others stretch the binary's options for men and women, suggesting that you can be a woman or a man even though you are not conforming precisely to the binary's rules for your gender. The binary has not disappeared in the revisionist gender stories told by pop culture, but it has been questioned, modified, and expanded. Such stories make that category larger and allow some traits or behaviors that normally would not be seen as appropriate to be exhibited by all human beings.

GENDER STORIES THAT REWRITE THE BINARY

A third group of stories told in pop culture rewrites the binary. These stories disrupt any connection between bodies and gender expectations, suggesting that any behavior, any quality, and any kind of appearance is appropriate for any body. By constructing alternative versions of gender and opening up possibilities for new kinds of gender performances, these narratives ignore, defy, or undo the binary system of gender that delineates two gender categories and prescribes how they should be. In these stories, gender truly is fluid, ambiguous, and multiple within the same person. Two mechanisms are used for conveying messages that rewrite the gender binary: (1) synthesis; and (2) innovation.

SYNTHESIS

Some best sellers from pop culture rewrite the binary by presenting a new gender that includes elements of both the conventionally feminine and the conventionally masculine. Although traces are still evident of the binary in that components of the two genders are synthesized into one, the strategy allows one body to carry markers and meanings of both genders simultaneously without privileging either. These stories, then, create a genuinely ambiguous gender that does not fit into either the female or male category of the binary. The movie *Palindromes* and fashion model Andrej Pejić illustrate the strategy of synthesis that rewrites the binary.

PALINDROMES

The movie *Palindromes* employs synthesis to rewrite the binary. A 2004 film written and directed by Todd Solondz, it traces the adventures of Aviva, a girl whose primary goal in life is to have babies. After having sex as a teenager with a family friend, she becomes pregnant and is forced by her parents to have an abortion that results, unbeknownst to her, in a hysterectomy. She runs away from home, begins a sexual relationship with a truck driver, is taken in by a Christian fundamentalist foster home, watches the truck driver shoot the doctor who performed her abortion, and has sex once again with the young man who impregnated her earlier. The film ends with Aviva's announcement that she has a feeling she's going to be a mom.

The strategy of synthesis that rewrites the binary is employed in the movie in the portrayal of Aviva's character. Aviva is played in the film by eight different actors of different ages, races, and genders. She appears on screen in various scenes as a five-year old black girl, a thirteen-year-old

red-haired white girl, a ten-year-old brown-haired white girl, an obese
adolescent black girl, a white adolescent boy, and a middle-aged white
woman. The movie unfolds in standard narrative fashion, but the form of
the main character keeps shifting among the eight personas. In the final
scene of the movie, the depictions of Aviva switch every few seconds
among six of the versions of her persona. The same character, then, is
shown to contain and to synthesize dramatically different physical and
personality characteristics. The other characters in the movie respond to
her as the same person, despite the substantial variations in her gender
performance, and they never acknowledge her dramatically different gender performances.

As an audience member, watching the character of Aviva switch
among so many different versions of gender is disconcerting simply
because of expectations that a gender performance remains somewhat
consistent across various contexts and life stages. At the beginning of the
film, most audience members might be shocked at the gender multiplicity
displayed by the main character and focus on figuring out what is going
on with this character. They have an initial resistance to the gender instability of the protagonist simply because it disrupts conventional expectations for gender. As the film progresses, however, audience members are
likely to begin to reflect on what the various versions of gender mean
both for the character herself and for standard conceptions of gender.

The most important aspect of the film is that the audience is pre-
vented from stereotyping Aviva. When audience members focus on a pre-
dominant characteristic such as age or race, they tend to attribute certain
qualities to the person as a result of that single characteristic. Audience
members cannot do that with *Palindromes*. Aviva stays complicated and
nuanced as a character and cannot be pigeonholed or caricatured on the
basis of any one identity marker. Audiences are reminded that all people
are complex, and to define them by focusing on one aspect of their identity is to deny them the richness and complexity that characterize all
human beings. The film also emphasizes how identity markers such as
age, race, and size frequently affect judgments on how closely people successfully embody a gender ideal. *Palindromes* rewrites the binary by showing multifaceted gender embodied in the protagonist, and it also
encourages audience members to reflect on any uneasiness they may feel
about this kind of interruption of a conventional gender portrayal.

Some features of *Palindromes* clearly do reference and enact the binary,
but they serve as contrast for the rewriting of the binary that occurs in the
film. The titles for the various sections of the movie are the names of the

main characters, and the boxes around their names are either blue or pink, depending on the gender traditionally associated with the name. But these boxes contrast dramatically with the multiple and fluid form of the gender of the main character and seem old fashioned and outdated as a result. Even the title of the film, *Palindromes*, suggests a rewriting of conventional gender requirements. A palindrome is a word that is the same forwards and backwards, and the names of the main characters in the film—*Aviva*, *Bob*, and *Otto*—are all palindromes. Standard conceptions of gender are rewritten and reordered in the film, questioning the standard ways in which the binary imposes order. That one character can be embodied by individuals of various genders, races, and ages suggests that gender appears and functions differently when it integrates or synthesizes various aspects of the feminine and masculine as well as other aspects of identity. *Palindromes* depicts on screen an example of gender that truly is dynamic, fluid, and multiple.

Andrej Pejić

Andrej Pejić is an androgynous model assigned male at birth whose fashion photographs rewrite the gender binary because his body is a site of synthesis for conventionally feminine and masculine as well as ambiguous genders. He models in both men's and women's shows for fashion houses such as Jean-Paul Gaultier and Marc Jacobs, incorporating into his body female, male, and sometimes androgynous clothing, accessories, postures, and hair styles.

In some photographs, Pejić models women's fashions and looks exactly like the thin, white, young woman who is the ideal of the binary. In these photos, he is typically shown with long, blond, curly hair that covers his chest. He wears eye makeup, pale pink or bright red lipstick, bright red nail polish on long fingernails, and dramatic women's jewelry. He might be modeling, in these photos, a red fur jacket or a form-fitting black leather jacket with a plunging neckline and pink flowered pants. His body postures mimic those traditionally linked to women in the binary—his head is cocked, for example, or his thumb is in his mouth, little-girl style.

In other images, Pejić models men's clothing and performs a conventional male gender wearing traditional male clothing. In these photographs, his hair is pulled back so that it appears to be short, has a side part, and is often brown in color. He wears classic styles of men's clothing such as a long cashmere coat, a gray cable-knit sweater with white pants, a striped sweater and white shirt over gray trousers, a tuxedo, or a letter-man-style jacket. In some photos, all of his clothing and accessories conform to stereotypical male markers of success, but there is one ambiguous aspect. In one such photo, he wears a dark suit, striped shirt, tie, and oversized glasses and is carrying a briefcase and a bouquet of flowers—all elements that contribute to a conventional presentation of professional and successful masculinity. Only his long blonde hair adds a touch of ambiguity to the look.

In some images, Pejić presents as a synthesis of femininity and masculinity, creating an androgynous look. Viewers would have difficulty deciding whether he is male or female, for example, in a photograph for *PF Magazine* in which he wears a white jumpsuit, or in another photo in which he wears jeans, a black print jacket over a sweater, and a scarf casually wrapping his neck. Pejić performs a different kind of androgyny when he does not conceal but exposes his penis and flat chest while wearing women's clothing. In one such photograph, he and model Hannah Holman pose together. Both have long blonde hair parted in the middle, wear red lipstick, and are naked from the waist up; Pejić is wearing white men's briefs, while Holmon wears bikini panties. A white lace mantilla is draped over their heads and shoulders, and they are holding hands. Another image shows Pejić with his long hair in curlers, wearing women's makeup, and his eyes are downcast. He is taking off his top, exposing his flat chest, and his pants are riding below his belly button. In these photos, both male and female gender markers are juxtaposed, and no effort is made to conceal or privilege one or the other.

In his fashion photos, Pejić's gender performances embody both the feminine and masculine within one body, and he performs both equally convincingly. The story the photos tell rewrites the binary that typically allows only one set of characteristics to inhabit a gendered body, allowing masculine, feminine, and androgynous gender forms to be synthesized within a single body. Pejić "admits that his look doesn't just blur the line between male and female, it seems to erase it." When asked if he sees himself as a man or a woman, he responded, "I see myself."[38]

INNOVATION

The stories that employ the strategy of innovation show that individuals can rewrite the gender binary by escaping it altogether. Individuals in these stories no longer follow the binary's prescriptions for being a man or a woman and create or invent their own genders. Gender cannot be linked to any particular kind of body, and the body does not reference any of the conventional types of genders rooted in the binary. Openness and flexibility are the only rules for constructing and performing this kind of gender. The Asexual Visibility and Education Network, genderless children, and CN Lester's genderqueer identity illustrate the strategy of innovation.

ASEXUAL VISIBILITY AND EDUCATION NETWORK

The Asexual Visibility and Education Network (AVEN) not only challenges the binary's expectation that individuals are heterosexual, but it challenges the binary's expectation that individuals are sexual. It simply opts out of the binary's dictates concerning sexuality. Founded by David Jay in 2001, AVEN provides information about and support for people who do not experience sexual attraction and who claim asexuality as their sexual orientation. Asexuality is not celibacy; neither is it something experienced by people because they are defective or late bloomers, are sexually dysfunctional, were abused as children, or are fearful of intimate relationships. For asexual individuals, their orientation is a choice.

Asexual individuals acknowledge the strength and power of the gender binary that expects people to have sex: "See, what all of these sexual people have been told, and what all of us asexual people have been told, is that sex is necessary. In classrooms, in advertisements, in locker rooms and sleepovers we've all been told that everyone needs sex, that it's unavoidable."[39] In the context of a highly sexualized culture, asexuality seems abnormal and strange, but for asexual individuals, having sex seems strange. Kate Goldfield, an asexual college student, offers an analogy to describe how she and other asexual individuals feel about sex: "It's almost as foreign to me as someone saying 'You know, when you're 18 we're going to take you on a space shuttle and we're going to go to Mars.'" Her view of sex as alien is echoed by forty-year-old Angela: "I have never had interest in sex all my life, at all. It's like algebra. I understand the concept, but have no interest."[40] Another asexual person explains: "Perhaps asexuality bothers some because people can be frightened and hostile to anything that is different from the norm. Well, we're here to show that different from the norm isn't bad—it's just different."[41]

Asexual people have romantic relationships; those relationships simply do not include sexual activity. Because they have no models for creating asexual romantic relationships, asexual people believe they have more freedom than sexual people do to create satisfying intimate relationships: "Asexual relationships are a 'blank slate.' There are no rules dictating how nonsexual love is expressed. . . . It's up to us to make up words to describe our bonds with other people."[42] One asexual individual appreciates the freedom that asexuality brings in relationships: "Figuring out how to flirt, to be intimate, or to be monogamous" in a nonsexual relationship "can be challenging, but free of sexual expectations we can form relationships in ways that are grounded in our individual needs and desires."[43]

Using the strategy of innovation, AVEN and asexual individuals invent new ways of doing gender that are not based on and do not even reference sexuality. Engaging in sex is a very important part of the binary's prescriptions—how to look and act in order to get it, who to do it with, and how to do it. AVEN dismisses all of these prescriptions as irrelevant and unnecessary and creates a new gender identity in which sex is absent. Asexuality as an orientation is summarized by one asexual person in this way: "News flash: sex is a choice, and if it's not fun don't have it. . . . If it ever gets boring, if that whole sexual thing ever gets tired and frustrating and you're looking for a good time then, baby, you know where to find us."[44] AVEN thus innovates in the binary, inventing new ways of doing gender entirely apart from its norms and expectations.

GENDERLESS CHILDREN

In 1972, Lois Gould published a story called "X" that began: "Once upon a time, a Baby named X was born. It was named X so that nobody could tell whether it was a boy or a girl. Its parents could tell, of course, but they couldn't tell anybody else. They couldn't even tell Baby X—at least not until much, much later. You see, it was all part of a very important Secret Scientific Xperiment, known officially as Project Baby X."[45] Gould's story follows X through interaction with family members, X's parents' efforts to buy toys and clothes for their child, X's experiences at school, and the negative response of other parents to X. When it was published, "X" seemed like a futuristic fantasy tale that was humorous and bizarre. But some parents are now using the story as a model for raising genderless children. They refuse to assign the label of *female* or *male* to their babies, thus innovating in and rewriting the gender binary that requires the assignment of a child into one of these two categories at birth.

Several years ago, a couple in Sweden decided not to announce the sex of their baby at the time of the child's birth.[46] The pseudonym given to this child in interviews with the parents was *Pop*, and only a handful of close relatives know the nature of the child's genitals. If anyone asks about Pop's gender, Pop's parents simply say that they don't disclose that information, and they plan to identify the child's gender when Pop decides to do so. The parents explained that their decision was rooted in a commitment to disrupt the expectations of the binary: "We want Pop to grow up more freely and avoid being forced into a specific gender mold from the outset. It's cruel to bring a child into the world with a blue or pink stamp on their forehead." Pop's wardrobe includes both trousers and dresses, and Pop decides each morning how to dress. Pop's hairstyle changes regularly, ranging from feminine to masculine to androgynous. Pop's parents never use personal pronouns when referring to the child; they just say *Pop*. Swedish gender-equality consultant Kristina Henkel supports Pop's parents' decision, suggesting that if a child is given no gender, the child "will be seen more as a human" rather than "a stereotype as a boy or girl."[47]

When Kathy Witterick and David Stocker of Toronto, Canada, had a baby in 2011, they named the child *Storm* and also decided not to announce the gender of the child. Storm's brothers, a close family friend, and the two midwives who helped deliver the baby are the only ones who know the nature of Storm's genitals, and they have promised not to tell. Witterick and Stocker sent out this e-mail message after the child's birth: "We decided not to share Storm's sex for now—a tribute to freedom and choice in place of limitation, a standup to what the world could become in Storm's lifetime." Storm's parents explained that children "receive messages from society that encourage them to fit into existing boxes," particularly boxes concerning gender. "We thought if we delayed sharing that information, in this case hopefully, we might knock off a couple million of those messages by the time that Storm decides Storm would like to share." The reaction to the parents' decision illustrates the strength of the binary, as Witterick explains: "Everyone keeps asking us, 'When will this end?' And we always turn the question back. Yeah, when will this end? When will we live in a world where people can make choices to be whoever they are?"[48] As they present a new option for gender, the parents of Pop and Storm are defying and innovating in the binary, substantially rewriting it.

CN LESTER

CN Lester, an alternative singer-songwriter and a mezzo-soprano in the classical music ensemble En Travesti, identifies as neither male nor female. Instead, Lester claims the identity of "both transsexual and transgender" or genderqueer,[49] queering identity and choosing to express gender in nonnormative ways. As such, Lester innovates in the binary, refusing to be categorized as female or male and choosing both a new gender and a new label for that gender. With the introduction of a third gender into the options offered by the binary through these acts, the matrix of the binary is disrupted and rewritten.

Lester enacts genderqueer identity in various ways. One is in a preference for the pronoun *they* instead of *he* or *she* to refer to themself. Another is in their ambiguous performance of gender. Lester has had top surgery to remove their breasts and wears their hair short in the back and sides in a typical male style but with a big shock of hair in the front, closer to a conventional women's style. Lester's gender presentation can be seen in their video *Just Like a Woman*, in which they plays piano and sings Bob Dylan's song by the same name. In the video, Lester wears eye makeup, black pants with suspenders, a black shirt, and a stud in their right ear.

Lester explicitly rejects the two categories of gender articulated by the binary: "I didn't see the world as divided between 'men' and 'women.' Nothing I've ever read or seen has convinced me of those immutable, eternal, external categories. I think that so many of the world's troubles come from trying to force humanity into narrow categories that cannot possibly allow or contain the diversity of the creatures within them, and that a social movement to challenge that process of categorization could do a lot of good."[50] They summarizes: "Urgh, false dichotomies—aren't they disgusting?"[51]

Lester's goal is for each person to do gender in a unique manner, unconfined by the binary—to perform "a big mess of unique."[52] They urges others to "constantly question the 'conventional wisdom' of the static binary sex/gender system" and "to allow each human being (yourself included) the bodily and mental autonomy to follow their own heart, and craft their own future, caring not a jot for the category they were forced into at birth."[53] "I'm not fighting for the right for everyone else to be exactly like me. Not even vaguely like me," Lester explains. "But I would give everything for each person to be wonderfully, and strangely, and totally themselves."[54]

Although more rare than those that retell or revise the binary, gender stories that rewrite the binary are also offered to you in pop culture. Some of them synthesize the conventionally masculine and feminine into one body, allowing it to stand as evidence that an individual cannot be placed into one gender and excluded from the other. In fact, these narratives suggest a synthesis of both genders can produce a third ambiguous gender in which both genders are present simultaneously. A second mechanism for rewriting the binary is innovation. Using this strategy, gender narratives create and embody alternative ways of doing gender to that of the binary, dispensing with key aspects of the binary's prescriptions altogether and operating entirely outside of the system by claiming no gender or a new gender. In these instances, the gender binary has become irrelevant and is no longer undergirding the performance of gender.

You cannot escape the best sellers of pop culture that offer you all sorts of messages about gender and invite you to do gender in various ways. Some of them retell the binary, imploring you to follow its prescriptions for being a man or a woman. Some revise the binary, expanding and modifying it so that expectations for masculinity or femininity are enlarged. A third type of story rewrites the binary, dispensing with it altogether and creating entirely new possibilities for gender. These stories offer models of different ways to relate to the binary, serving as resources for formulating your own gender stories and making your own decisions about how to do gender. This process is the subject of the next chapter, which deals with crafting your gender stories.

■ NOTES

[1] Alison Lurie, "The Cabinet of Dr. Seuss," in *Of Sneetches and Whos and the Good Dr. Seuss: Essays on the Writings and Life of Theodor Geisel*, ed. Thomas Fensch (Jefferson, NC: McFarland, 1997), 159.

[2] Jan Benzel, "Dr. Seuss Finally Transcended the Gender Barrier," in *Of Sneetches and Whos and the Good Dr. Seuss: Essays on the Writings and Life of Theodor Geisel*, ed. Thomas Fensch (Jefferson, NC: McFarland, 1997), 182.

[3] Lurie, "The Cabinet of Dr. Seuss," 159.

[4] Benzel, "Dr. Seuss Finally Transcended the Gender Barrier," 182.

[5] The Kidd, "Reading Dr. Seuss Can Be Dangerous," The Slacktiverse, May 18, 2011, http://slacktivist.typepad.com/slacktivist/2011/05/reading-dr-seuss-can-be-dangerous.html

[6] Dr. Seuss, *I Can Lick 30 Tigers Today! and Other Stories* (New York: Random, 1969), n. p.

[7] All of the examples and quotations from *Cosmopolitan* magazine in this section are from the October 2011 issue.

[8] Mari Kristin Sisjord, "Fast-Girls, Babes and the Invisible Girls: Gender Relations in Snowboarding," *Sport in Society* 12 (2009): 1312.

[9] Kristin L. Anderson, "Snowboarding: The Construction of Gender in an Emerging Sport," *Journal of Sport and Social Issues* 23 (1999): 61.

[10] Holly Thorpe, "Embodied Boarders: Snowboarding, Status and Style," *Waikato Journal of Education* 10 (2004): 186.

[11] Holly Thorpe, "Jibbing the Gender Order: Females in the Snowboarding Culture," *Sport in Society* 8 (2005): 89

[12] Thorpe, "Jibbing the Gender Order," 90.

[13] Thorpe, "Jibbing the Gender Order," 88.

[14] Thorpe, "Jibbing the Gender Order," 88; and Thorpe, "Embodied Boarders," 189.

[15] Susan J. Douglas, *The Rise of Enlightened Sexism: How Pop Culture Took Us from Girl Power to Girls Gone Wild* (New York: St. Martin's Griffin, 2010), 191.

[16] The episode, written by Ron Hauge, originally aired on February 16, 1997.

[17] Steve Williams and Ian Jones, "Five of the Best . . . and Five of the Worst of *The Simpsons*," May 2002, http://www.offthetelly.co.uk/?page_id=382

[18] David Proper's analysis of "Homer's Phobia" informed much of this discussion. See David Proper, "'I Like My Beer Cold, My TV Loud and My Homosexuals Flaming':

Intertextuality and Heterosexism in 'Homer's Phobia,'" Communication Department, University of Colorado Denver, July 2010.

[19] Douglas, *The Rise of Enlightened Sexism*, 218.

[20] All of the examples and quotations from *Us Weekly* in this section are from the June 13, 2011, issue. Susan J. Douglas's analysis of celebrity magazines informed much of this analysis. See Douglas, *The Rise of Enlightened Sexism*, 242–66.

[21] Sarah Kornfield, "Cross-Cultural Cross-Dressing: Japanese Graphic Novels Perform Gender in U.S.," *Critical Studies in Media Communication* 28 (2011): 221.

[22] Kornfield, "Cross-Cultural Cross-Dressing," 220.

[23] Kornfield, "Cross-Cultural Cross-Dressing," 222.

[24] Chaz Bono with Billie Fitzpatrick, *Transition: The Story of How I Became a Man* (New York: Dutton/Penguin, 2011), 13.

[25] Bono with Fitzpatrick, *Transition*, 4.

[26] Bono with Fitzpatrick, *Transition*, 218.

[27] Chaz Bono, Interview, *Jimmy Kimmel Live!*, May 19, 2011.

[28] Bono with Fitzpatrick, *Transition*, 196.

[29] Chaz Bono, Interview, *The Wendy Williams Show*, May 19, 2011.

[30] Bono with Fitzpatrick, *Transition*, 229.

[31] bell hooks, *Art on My Mind: Visual Politics* (New York: New, 1995), 38.

[32] Erin R. Brown, "J. Crew Pushes Transgendered Child Propaganda," April 8, 2011, http://newsbusters.org/blogs/erin-r-brown/2011/04/08/jcrew-pushes-transgendered-child-propaganda

[33] Keith Ablow, "J. Crew Plants the Seeds for Gender Identity," April 11, 2011, http://www.foxnews.com/health/2011/04/11/j-crew-plants-seeds-gender-identity/

[34] Susan Donaldson James, "J. Crew Ad with Boy's Pink Toenails Creates Stir," April 13, 2011, http://abcnews.go.com/Health/crew-ad-boy-painting-toenails-pink-stirs-transgender/story?id=13358903

[35] Quoted in James, "J. Crew Ad with Boy's Pink Toenails Creates Stir."

[36] Comfy1Mom, online comment to James, "J. Crew Ad with Boy's Pink Toenails Creates Stir," posted May 31, 2011.

[37] All of the examples and quotations from *Men's Health* in this section are from the June 2011 issue.

[38] Juju Chang, "Genderless: World's Most Popular Male Model Walks Runways in Heels, Dresses," September 14, 2011, http://abcnews.go.com/Business/genderless-worlds-popular-model-walks-runways-heels/story?id=14522370

[39] The Asexual Visibility and Education Network, "The Movement," http://www.asexuality.org/home/node/25

[40] Sylvia Pagan Westphal, "Glad to Be Asexual," *NewScientist*, October 14, 2004, http://www.newscientist.com/article/dn6533-feature-glad-to-be-asexual.html?full=true

[41] The Asexual Visibility and Education Network, "How Things Change," http://www.asexuality.org/home/node/23

[42] The Asexual Visibility and Education Network, "Relationship FAQ," http://www.asexuality.org/home/relationship.html

[43] The Asexual Visibility and Education Network, "Overview," http://www.sexuality.org/home/overview.html

[44] The Asexual Visibility and Education Network, "The Movement."

[45] Lois Gould, "X," *Ms.*, May 1980, 61.

[46] Lisa Belkin, "Keeping the Gender of a 2-Year-Old Secret," July 1, 2009, http://parenting.blogs.nytimes.com/2009/07/01/keeping-the-sex-of-a-toddler-secret

[47] Kristina Henkel, quoted in Lydia Parafianowicz, "Swedish Parents Keep 2-Year-Old's Gender Secret," June 23, 2009, http://www.thelocal.se/20232/20090623/

[48] Zachary Roth, "Parents Keep Child's Gender Under Wraps," May 24, 2011, http://news.yahoo.com/s/yblog_thelookout20110424/ts_yblog_thelookout/parents-keep-childs-gender-under-wraps

[49] Paris Lees, "Interview: Genderqueer Performer CN Lester," March 11, 2011, http://www.pinknews.co.uk/2011/03/11/interview-genderqueer-performer-cn-lester

[50] CN Lester, "On Being Both Transgender and Transsexual," *A Gentleman and a Scholar* (blog), August 29, 2011, http://cnlester.wordpress.com

[51] Lester, "On Being Both Transgender and Transsexual."

[52] Lester, "On Being Both Transgender and Transsexual."

[53] CN Lester, "How to Be a Transgender Gentleman," *A Gentleman and a Scholar* (blog), May 11, 2011, http://cnlester.wordpress.com/2011/05/11/how-to-be-a-transgender-gentleman

[54] Lester, "On Being Both Transgender and Transsexual."

CRAFTING
DEVELOPING GENDER STORIES

*Our life . . . appears to us as the field of a constructive
activity, borrowed from narrative understanding,
by which we attempt to discover and not simply to impose
from outside the narrative identity which constitutes us.*

Paul Ricoeur, "Life in Quest of Narrative"

Your favorite coffee shop is quiet this Sunday morning. People are drifting in and settling into the cozy armchairs next to the fire. You open your journal or computer, reflecting on what you're going to write. Sam asked you to marry him last night, and you're having a difficult time figuring out how to respond. You begin a new entry: "I love him, and this is very exciting. No one has asked me to marry him before. We've been together two years, but I still don't feel ready. I like the relationship we have. Why change it? Maybe I just don't want to get married. I want to be independent and self-sufficient. Will I have to give up too much of myself if I get married?" As you compose your thoughts, you are working out a story about who you are and who you want to be.

This kind of journaling is similar to the process that is the subject of this chapter—constructing a gender identity by crafting stories about yourself. In chapter 1, we introduced you to the idea of identity as your sense of self or how you define yourself. The focus of this chapter is on how you construct your identity and, in particular, your gender identity. Just as keeping a journal allows you to figure out how you want to look, be, and act, the personal internal narratives you craft also script your sense of yourself. You might think of this process as "inner speech"—you narrate your life story to yourself, constructing an interiorized psychological sense of yourself.[1] This sense of yourself is your identity. The process of constructing an identity might seem like a solitary act because your identity feels like something that is yours alone—something you own. But it's really not. Certainly, your identity is the result of your personal motivations, desires, and creative impulses, but it is also the result of your interactions with other people. Much of this chapter deals with the engagements with others that enable you to create a gendered identity.

The interactions that help you form your identity began when you were very young. From the moment you were born, those around you told you that you were a *boy* or a *girl*, so you learned very early that you belonged in one category rather than the other. Somewhere around the age of eighteen months, you developed a feeling that you were either female or male, although, at that stage, the label you were given was largely empty of meaning. You hadn't had many experiences yet to fill that label with any kinds of associations and identifications for the words *girl* and *boy, female* and *male*.

Psychoanalyst Jessica Benjamin calls the gender identity that children experience in the first couple years of their lives "*nominal* gender identity"[2] because it is a gender identity in name only. Children at this age haven't been exposed yet to many of the ways in which the binary assigns certain characteristics and qualities to the two genders, so at this stage, they are likely to tell the genders apart in some odd and often amusing ways. They use information such as hair length, color, and style; the shape of eyes; and the ability to dance to distinguish men from women.[3] As you grew older and had the opportunity to interact with more people and things in your world, you began to fill in the labels of *male* and *female* with more conventional meanings. You learned society's cultural definitions of femaleness and maleness—an entire network of gender-linked associations that includes "anatomy, reproductive function, division of labor, and personality attributes."[4]

The interactions with others that develop your notions of femininity and masculinity come to you in the form of stories. As you saw in earlier chapters, you encounter stories about the proper ways to be a woman or a man from many sources in your environment. Each of the gender stories you encounter comes with a particular ideology or system of beliefs that asks you to draw particular conclusions about gender. Each narrative, in other words, "becomes the opportunity to imagine, in this or that way, different responses to acting and being-in-the-world,"[5] each offering a "potential horizon or world" [6] for you to enter with a particular perspective and outlook on gender.

The stories that are offered to you by others become the resources or building blocks for you to use in crafting your gender identity. Because your identity is created through the "process of assimilating, interpreting, and integrating contents of the cultural environment,"[7] the gender stories to which you are exposed become the resources you use to give meaning to the labels *male* or *female*. As narrative theorist Paul John Eakin explains, "We do not invent our identities out of whole cloth. Instead, we draw on the resources of the cultures we inhabit to shape them, resources that specify what it means to be a man, a woman, a worker, a person in the settings where we live our lives."[8]

The process by which you make use of the stories circulating in your environment to construct your personal gender stories is the subject of this chapter. Four steps are involved in the process of crafting your gender identity: (1) attending to gender stories; (2) appropriating from gender stories; (3) drafting your own gender stories; and (4) creating a coherent identity. Although we describe it in four sequential steps, the process is not linear or sequential. Because the steps are integrally connected, they can happen in any order, and they are typically happening simultaneously. Keep in mind, then, that although the parts of the process are presented as steps, they are not steps at all but elements of a complex and dynamic process.

ATTENDING TO GENDER STORIES

The first step in the process of constructing your own gender stories is to deal with the sheer quantity of narratives you encounter. There are simply too many demanding your attention, so you manage information coming at you by attending only to some of them. You filter or screen out some gender narratives in your environment, withdrawing your attention from some "in order to deal effectively with others."[9] For example, when you are surfing the Internet to look for material for a paper you have to write, you might pay attention to gender stories that come to you from various websites and the song you are hearing through your ear buds, but you might ignore the story your roommate is telling you or the nonverbal communication of the décor of your dorm room where you are working on your laptop.

As a child, you do make some conscious choices, but your attention to some things rather than others is largely automatic and unconscious. You pay attention to things you have learned and recognize. The subculture in which you grow up directs you to pay attention to some kinds of things in your environment and not to notice others, and these patterns of attending became habitual. Your race, economic status, or religion, for example, probably encouraged you to notice some things and not others. These stories were reinforced by people important to you who wanted you to be a certain kind of person. You were probably attending to whatever these people said was important and acceptable rather than attending consciously and independently to things in your environment.

Even when you grow into adulthood, the process of selective attention can be unconscious. In this case, it may simply be the result of a bodily or an emotional feeling that you have. You don't make careful and deliberate decisions about each story you encounter. You might screen out a story if a behavior triggers a reaction of "I can't imagine ever acting like that" or "Why would anyone dress like that?" Alternatively, you could have a gut feeling that something feels right, and you would then pay attention to that story. You find yourself drawn to, intrigued by, and repulsed by some stories more than others, but you often aren't conscious of the reasons for doing so.

"Millions of items . . . are present to my senses which never properly enter into my experience. Why? Because they have no *interest* for me. *My experience is what I agree to attend to.* Only those items which I *notice* shape my mind."[10] Psychologist William James's statement is a reminder that there are any number of reasons why you might attend—both unconsciously and consciously—to some gender stories in your environment rather than others. Some of the reasons have to do with characteristics or properties of the stories themselves. Something about some stories simply commands your attention. At other times, you pay attention to stories because of something about you as a person. You are motivated, in other words, to pay attention to some narratives because of your own sense of self, goals, and desires. You pay attention to some gender stories and not others because of (1) properties of stories; and (2) properties of the self.

MOTIVATED BY STORIES

A number of properties or characteristics inherent in gender stories themselves can encourage you to pay attention to some over others. One such property has to do with the coercive power of the binary. Because the binary is filling your immediate environment with all sorts of stories about the proper ways to be a woman or a man, you may pay attention to them because they are the only stories you encounter—the only ones you are allowed to experience. You attend to them because they are sanctioned and reinforced in many ways, and you gain approval for attending to them. A desire for affiliation and maybe even a fear of rejection pressure you into noticing them. You focus in certain directions, then, because of the substantial influence of the binary on your attending processes and practices. When you encounter story after story that tells you that women are primarily responsible for parenting and child care, you may not notice a narrative that reveals different aspects of parenting. You encounter stories of the binary everywhere and are heavily reinforced for attending to them, and so you do. These stories seem natural and normal—they are pervasive and prominent in your environment, and so you pay attention to them.

You pay attention to other stories, however, because of the element of surprise. A story that violates your expectations may catch your attention because it is different from most of the stories you encounter. Maybe you go into a restaurant and discover that the waiters are all men in drag, wearing lots of makeup, high heels, and tight-fitting women's clothes over fake breasts. You don't know how to react or what you think of these men, so you pay particular attention to the gender stories they are offering. Other stories might surprise you in similar ways. Only men have been elected to be president of the United States, but one year, you witnessed Hillary Rodham Clinton run for president and almost become the Democratic nominee. Or maybe you are used to seeing only men as commercial pilots, but then you boarded a plane and saw, for the first time, a woman in the cockpit. These gender stories stand out because they deviate from the stories you are accustomed to encountering, so you are likely to pay more attention to them. Because they surprise you, the stories encourage you to think about how you feel about them and to learn more about the people who are performing them.

You may encounter stories among family and friends that stand out because they violate your expectations and are surprising to you. Isaac was in high school when he got to know his Uncle Jared, whom he rarely saw when he was growing up. He discovered that his uncle did gender very differently from the rest of his family. Isaac's immediate family members followed very traditional gender roles, and he was expected to play football and spend his free time watching sports on TV. But Uncle Jared was interested in art and spent time going to art museums and playing the tuba in a quartet; he neither played sports nor was interested in watching them. The gender story he presented seemed fresh and interesting, and Isaac was intrigued by it and was drawn to learn more about his uncle's world. In these cases, the fact that a story is unusual, surprising, or stands out in some way from the typical stories you encounter may prompt you to pay attention to it.

Stories that are characterized by high emotional intensity are also likely to be stories to which you pay attention. You are likely to pay more attention to gender stories that prompt you to feel happy, sad, or angry, for example, than to ones that aren't emotionally involving. When you watch a movie about a princess in love with a prince, and he finally reciprocates her love at the end of the film, you might feel emotions of relief and happiness. You pay more attention to such a gender story than to one that is not as emotionally compelling. If you have a highly negative emotional reaction to the movie—perhaps because it fails to represent genders and sexual orientations with which you identify—you are also likely to pay attention to the story, although in a different way. When you play *Grand Theft Auto* and get to run over people with a police car, earning the points you need to advance to the next level, you feel powerful. This feeling not only encourages you to continue playing but to pay more attention to the gender stories being offered in the video game than to stories that lack such emotional payoff.

Stories that are repeated are also those to which you tend to pay more attention. You selectively attend to the gender stories to which you are exposed over and over rather than to the stories that you rarely or infrequently encounter. If you are told by your parents, your priest, the Pope, and your teachers about how a Catholic woman should think, dress, and act, you are likely to pay attention to that story because you hear it so often. Derek explains how the ubiquitous baseball stories in his house virtually required him to pay attention to them. As a result, they became a primary source of gender information for him: "My family are all Red Sox fans. They watch all the games, make trips to see the team play in person, go absolutely crazy when they win the pennant, and also play fantasy baseball." The individual players presented particular gender stories to him, as did his father and brothers when they sat in front of the TV cheering while his sister and mother prepared snacks for everyone. All of these stories repeated consistent messages about how men and women are supposed to be and the kinds of things in which they are supposed to be interested. Because of the repetitive and accumulative nature of the baseball stories in his environment, he paid attention to them rather than to other stories he encountered less frequently.

Sometimes, gender stories attract your attention because they are flashy, dramatic, potent, or vivid—they have presence.[11] An example of stories that tend to be characterized by such presence are media stories— those presented to you via television, films, video games, and websites. Because these stories often involve motion, color, drama, and sometimes humor and special effects, they are likely to attract your attention because of their striking and exciting characteristics. If you have a choice between listening to your professor lecture or watching a movie, for example, you are likely to want to watch the movie simply because it is more dramatic and entertaining than the lecture. You pay attention to some narratives about gender, then, because of characteristics of the stories themselves— something about them catches and compels your attention.

MOTIVATED BY SELF

You also might choose to pay attention to some stories over others because of properties of the self. Something in you motivates you to pay attention to them. Some gender stories might seem relevant to you simply because of the way you've constructed your gender. You might watch *Mission: Impossible*, *Buffy the Vampire Slayer*, or *Beavis and Butthead*, for example, because you have an affinity for some stories over others. They seem natural to you and seem to fit with who you are or who you want to be.

Another motive for paying attention to some stories over others is that you attend more to stories that come from people who are important to you and less to stories from people who don't matter as much. You are likely to be particularly influenced by people to whom you are emotionally connected and with whom you have close bonds. You tend to internalize aspects of these people, including the gender stories they present. When you were very young, the people with whom you identified were likely your parents or other close family members. You tended to pay attention to their stories because you loved them, needed them, and wanted their approval. As you grew older, you began to pay attention to the gender stories being presented by people you idolized or wanted to be like. Your strong identification with them made you pay particular attention to their stories. Lucy, for example, explains how a professor became a role model for her in terms of gender: "I had a professor in college who was fun and interesting to talk to, commanded respect when she walked into a room, dressed in a really cool style, was married, had kids, and published lots of books and articles. I decided I wanted to be a college professor just like her." As a result, Lucy paid particular attention to how her professor expressed her gender. Similarly, when Max was a teenager, he idolized Alejandro, his next-door neighbor, who was a body builder. Max watched Alejandro closely—how he worked out, prepared for competitions, carried himself, and dressed. That particular gender story, then, resonated for Max because he admired Alejandro and wanted to be like him. Your filtering process can prompt you to pay attention to the gender stories told to you by the people who are most important and influential in your life.

You also might pay attention to the stories told by groups to which you belong that are important to you. Although you are a member of many groups, you especially want to be seen as appropriately gendered in the groups that you value the most, so your peers in these groups are likely to be particularly salient sources of information about gender. Maybe all of the men on your floor of your dorm play video games, so you start playing video games, too. Maybe you're a member of the soccer team, and all the women on the team swear a lot and act tough, so you take on these behaviors as well. Because you want to have a place in the social world of the groups to which you belong, you attend to and try to follow the gender prescriptions being communicated by your peers in these groups.

The gender stories offered by the media also might be ones to which you attend because they fit with your experience or provide models for the kind of person you want to be. The reinforcement you get from participating in these stories often prompts you to pay particular attention to them. When Selena Gomez or Adele sings about falling in love, their songs might be a perfect description of your own experience in love, so you'll pay attention to what the lyrics say about how to be a woman and how to be in a relationship. Or maybe you want to be a man who is confident and powerful, and you might unconsciously use George Clooney's movies as a model for how to look and act. In some cases, you might not have had much experience with some of the stories you see depicted through media, so the gender messages they offer function as guidelines on how to be and act when you do have that particular experience. The media provide you, in other words, with equipment for living—the equivalent of charts, formulas, or manuals—you can use to figure out how you are supposed to act.[12] Because you get information you consider valuable from media stories, you tend to pay attention to them over some other stories.

You are likely to pay more attention to gender stories if you are rewarded for doing so. You are likely to be more motivated to pay attention to some stories rather than others if people like your parents, rabbis, coaches, teachers, and peers reinforce and affirm you for attending to them. Little girls whose parents enter them in beauty pageants like those featured on *Toddlers and Tiaras*, for example, are being introduced to certain kinds of gender stories about women. When their parents and the judges applaud them for wearing makeup and grown-up dresses and dancing suggestively, the girls are likely to continue to pay attention to such narratives because they are reinforced for performing them.

Likewise, if you are punished for your attention to some gender stories, you might choose not to focus on them. When Noah started hanging out with the skateboarders in his middle school, his parents reacted negatively, threatening to cut off his allowance. Because he got such flak from his parents, he developed a different group of friends who presented gender in ways his parents considered more acceptable. If you participate in a workshop on sexual harassment at your frat house and the brothers crack down on making sexual jokes about women, you might pay less attention to stories in which women are presented as sexual objects and more to gender stories in which women are presented as full human beings. You choose not to attend and enact gender stories if, in doing so, you face punishment, conflict, or other negative consequences.

Of course, you might choose to attend to some gender stories precisely because they are prohibited. If you are denied access to some stories, they might become more desirable, intriguing, and compelling for you, and you might work even harder to find and attend to them. If your parents didn't let you watch PG-13 movies when you were young, you probably became very interested in them and devised all sorts of ways to get to see them. You attended to these narratives because they were forbidden, which made them particularly attractive stories to you.

The knowledge you bring to a story also can determine the amount of attention you pay to it. If you are familiar with some aspect of a gender story, you can participate in it easily and feel comfortable with it. If you know a lot about a key aspect of some narrative—one that deals with automobiles, for example—you are more apt to pay attention to it. If you are interested in cooking and know a lot about it, you might be inclined to watch chef Giada De Laurentiis's cooking show and pay attention to the gender story she is performing. If you know little about the subject being featured in a narrative—especially if it is a complex and technical subject—you might find it boring, tedious, or simply uninteresting, and you will quickly turn your attention to another story. Of course, when you don't know much about a story, there can be an element of intrigue. More frequently, however, knowledge and interest are reasons why you might choose to attend to one gender story over another.

Beliefs and attitudes also affect which stories attract your attention and which ones you ignore. If you believe that particular kinds of gender stories are wrong or evil or if you find them repulsive, you probably will not engage with these stories if you encounter them. In contrast, if you believe that stories are right or good and you find them compelling, you are more likely to engage with the stories. If you have strong feelings about pornography and believe it is immoral, you are not likely to search the Internet for porn; if your roommates are watching pornographic movies, you aren't likely to join them. Conversely, you are likely to pay attention to the gender stories about something you really like. Tanya, for example, grew up with Disney movies and toys and loves all things Disney. She pays attention to ads for Disney movies, goes into Disney stores in malls, visited Disneyland during several spring breaks while in high school and college, and takes note whenever she sees a Disney cruise advertised. She even chose to get married at Disneyland. Whatever story about gender Disney is offering, Tanya is likely to attend to it. Your attitude toward a particular kind of gender story, then, can encourage you either to ignore it or to pay attention to it.

The degree of commitment you have to your existing identity also may affect the gender stories to which you pay attention. If you are highly committed to presenting gender in a certain way, you look for and attend to stories that align with and reinforce that identity. You don't pay attention to alternative stories because you aren't interested in questioning your commitments, and you aren't inclined to be open to a wide variety of stories.[13] If you have constructed a Goth identity for yourself, stories about gender that are presented by fraternities are likely to hold little interest for you. You may not even see posters advertising opportunities to rush, and you won't find yourself attracted to fellow students who present the genders valued by Greek campus culture.

In contrast, if you are in a process of exploration and don't have a high commitment to a particular kind of identity, you are likely to be open to different kinds of stories. You might find yourself paying attention to ones that aren't familiar to you and that don't reinforce your current identity, actively looking for and exploring narratives that are different from the ones you usually encounter. You might, for example, explore a variety of groups on campus and engage with all sorts of people representing different perspectives on gender because you haven't excluded any ways of being gendered from your identity.

For whatever reason—whether because of the story itself or your own motives—you sort through the gender stories in your environment and filter some of them out. You pay attention to some stories and not others either because something about the story attracts your attention or because of some motivation on your part. The array of stories that are available to you as a result of this process plays a critical function in your construction of your gender identity because these stories are the building blocks or the resources you use for crafting your personal gender stories. The next step of the process is appropriating pieces from the stories to which you are attending to use in drafting gender stories for yourself.

APPROPRIATING FROM GENDER STORIES

Appropriating is the process of making use of the stories to which you have paid attention. When you appropriate something, you make it your own—absorbing and incorporating it or some portions of it. This is a good description of what you do with the gender stories that have captured your attention. As you craft your own gender stories, you consciously or unconsciously incorporate those parts of the stories that you find particularly salient or compelling and make them your own.

You have likely gathered a vast collection of gender stories from your external environment through selective attention, but, of course, you can't adopt and use all of them in your personal gender stories because there are simply too many. You sort and sift through the stories to which you have paid attention, picking out fragments or bits and pieces that you want to make part of your own gender stories. Sometimes, you reflect on the information about gender presented in the stories you've encountered to decide exactly what you want to integrate into your own stories. At other times, you adopt fragments automatically, not really thinking about what you are picking and why. You select those stories and parts of stories that seem right to you for constructing your gendered self—those details that represent the way you want to be as a gendered person.

To craft your own gender stories, you might appropriate one item from one story, perhaps a couple of pieces from another story, a thread from still another story, an excerpt from another, and so on, taking in particular versions of gender. You might watch a video by the rapper Nelly, for example, and notice how he dresses. You like his style and think he looks sexy, and that look becomes something you want in your personal gender stories. If religion is a major source of gender stories for you, you might sort through the stories you have been told during your religious training and pick out certain aspects of them to incorporate into your gender identity. Maida, for example, chose a particular perspective on sexuality that came from the stories of Islam: "My Muslim faith has certain ideas about gender, especially female sexuality. I see female sexuality as something deep and valuable. I feel in control of my sexuality and that it is powerful. Therefore, only one man, a deserving man, should see me as a sexual being." In this process, you actively appropriate parts of the contents of the stories in your environment, internalizing and assimilating them to use as the building blocks for your own gender stories. As you absorb them, you make them part of your own gender identity.

Similar to the process of focusing attention on some stories and not others, the reasons for selecting particular pieces of gender stories to incorporate will vary. Sometimes the reasons for appropriating will be conscious and deliberate. You might choose to focus on certain aspects of gender stories to make your own because of the influence of someone important in your life. Kirsten, for example, chose to select a particular thread from the gender stories offered in the Bible because of the influence of her mother, who is her best friend and a significant role model for her: "Because my mother is very spiritual, she taught me to be like the virtuous woman from Proverbs 31 in the Bible. I want to be seen as nice, caring, nurturing, and loving. As a result, I don't allow myself to curse, rebel, or question." Maybe you choose to adopt some aspects of other gender stories because of your membership in a group, and that fragment fits with the values and beliefs of the group. If you often go snowboarding with a group of friends, you are likely to adopt elements of their gender stories—their fearlessness on the slopes and their gangsta-inspired clothes, for example.

In other instances, your process of selecting narrative threads for your gender stories is not at all conscious, systematic, or orderly. You don't deliberately reflect on the stories coming to you and rationally appropriate the best stories or the best parts of stories to incorporate into your own. You might simply feel some imperative to be a certain way and to appropriate something that matches the feeling. Perhaps you're walking through the mall and see a jacket that you just have to have. You don't consciously think, "I want that jacket because it fits with my style." Instead, you almost have a "felt sense" or a kind of internal awareness[14] that compels you to buy it. This same kind of sense is present when you feel attracted to someone or when the hair stands up on the back of your neck for some reason. Luke illustrates this kind of bodily knowing when he explains his awareness of his homosexuality: "I just always knew I was gay." His sense that he was gay was something he felt rather than a decision he consciously made. As a result, he found himself drawn to gender stories that involved gay men and their constructions of gender and appropriated components of those stories for his own use. Some choices rather than others simply seem right for you as you borrow from the stories of others, even though you may not be able to articulate why.

You also might select particular narrative threads for constructing your own gender stories because the binary encourages your acceptance of certain fragments rather than others. You saw in chapter 3 the power that the binary has in all areas of your life, so it might very well be directing you to see and to select certain fragments rather than others from the stories you encounter. If the binary has inculcated you with the idea that men are supposed to be physically strong, you might pick up on male strength from external stories as something you believe you need to incorporate into your own gender stories. Similarly, you might select the need to be caring as something that the binary encourages you to select if you are a woman. What you appropriate for your own gender stories may come as much from the gender binary as it does from any unique motives on your part.

You are exposed to an abundance and a multiplicity of gender stories in your environment. From those to which you pay attention, you select—whether consciously or not—parts of those stories that you want to incorporate into your personal gender stories. Just as a number of reasons are possible for why you attend to some stories rather than others, a number of reasons are possible for why you select particular fragments from those stories to make your own. Some derive from your own sense of who you are, and some derive from external forces such as the gender binary that push and pull you in certain directions.

DRAFTING GENDER STORIES

The fragments that you have appropriated from the gender stories in your environment combine into many different stories that represent you as a gendered person. You've probably noticed that we have been talking throughout this chapter about gender *stories* and not just one *story* to describe your process of constructing a gender identity. That's because your gender is multiple and continuously shifting, which means that you are creating many different gender stories for yourself. You synthesize fragments from other stories to create multiple gender stories that constitute your identity.

Each story you create by combining various fragments represents a particular interpretation of how you see yourself as a gendered person. Some of the pieces you have appropriated have to do with settings. You might see yourself, in these stories, on the football field, in the library, in a swanky office on the top floor of a high-rise building, or snuggling on a sofa with someone you love. Other pieces have to do with you as a character and depict your physical characteristics, qualities, and motives. They might show you wearing a particular style of clothing, a particular hairstyle, and having a certain kind of body. Other fragments deal with the actions you choose to do—the kinds of things you perceive yourself doing now or in the future. You might see yourself making the winning touchdown for your team, impressing your work team with your expertise on a project, meeting interesting people because of your eccentric style and outgoing personality, or rocking a crowd with your musical talent.

To create your gender stories, you put together setting fragments, character fragments, and action fragments to complete a particular inter-pretation of gender that represents how you see yourself. You synthesize various fragments that go together or are most congruent to form a set of narratives about your gender. Some of these constructions are ones you create for yourself out of your own desires and interests, and others are constructions you feel pressured to create by people close to you or by societal expectations. One story might show you in casual clothing, playing basketball or volleyball; this might be your athletic gender story. In your devoted-father story, you might perceive yourself interacting with your children and being involved with them at home, in school, in music and arts activities, and at church. Maybe one of your gender sto-ries constructs you as gender ambiguous, so your clothes and hair style are gender neutral, you try not to engage in activities stereotypically seen as either masculine or feminine, and you see yourself comfortable in all different kinds of spaces. Maybe you construct yourself as a fun and eccentric friend to others rather than a romantic partner. You see yourself interacting with and enjoying relationships with all sorts of people. Such stories may not always be positive. You might see yourself in one of your gender stories, for example, as socially inept, self-con-scious, and unpopular. Perhaps you feel pressured to meet the expecta-tions of others, so one of the stories you construct and try to maintain is of a successful corporate executive, wearing professional clothing, work-ing overtime, focused on getting ahead in the corporation, and making lots of money.

The result of the many different pieces of gender stories from which you select certain narrative elements is a set of gender stories about you that constitutes your narrative repertoire or your narrative toolbox. All of these stories represent you in different ways, and all of them are available for you to draw on as sources for your motives and actions and in your interactions with others. They all allow you to be a person with multiple and fluid genders, changing your gender as you alternate among your stories to continually invent and reinvent your gender identity. On the soccer field, you are athletic; at school, you are studious and intellectually engaged; on a date with the new employee at work, you are sexy and witty; and at work, you are a serious professional. But, of course, having all of these different stories about you can make forming a cohesive sense of yourself difficult, so there's one more step in the process of crafting your own gender stories: You configure those different stories into a coherent gender identity.

CREATING A COHERENT IDENTITY

Although your gendered self is made up of multiple gender stories, you don't usually think of yourself as multiple, nor do other people see you that way. To achieve a coherent or stable identity, you combine the seemingly disparate gender stories you craft about yourself into an inner sense or a vision of yourself as a coherent, integrated being. You weave together all of the gender stories into a single primary story or "narrative unity" that allows you to see your "own personal being as an integrated whole, with properties of stability and continuity over time."[15] The vision you create of yourself is like a container that holds you together, giving you a "sense of coherence and continuity"[16] at any particular moment.

French philosopher Paul Ricoeur gives the label *emplotment* to the process of weaving together multiple stories into a coherent unity by creating a continuous story line across disparate parts of your identity. Emplotment involves organizing the diverse stories "into one meaningful whole" so that the "entire plot can be translated into one 'thought,' which is nothing other than its 'point' or 'theme.'"[17] It synthesizes "heterogeneous elements"—different stories—to transform the multiple stories *"into one* story."[18] You configure a coherent identity by developing a theme that you see running through all of your gender stories. This theme might be, for example, you as a good father, a jock, a gamer, a gay man, or a rebel.

The nature of the process of integrating all of your gender stories into a coherent identity varies according to the nature of your gender stories. If they are largely similar to one another—homogeneous and congruent with one another—you have an easier time developing a theme that gives them coherence than if you crafted some gender stories for yourself that are widely disparate or even irreconcilable. The stories you must integrate as you craft a coherent identity may be (1) homogeneous; (2) different but compatible; or (3) irreconcilable.

INTEGRATING HOMOGENEOUS STORIES

In some cases, the gender stories you have crafted for yourself generally coalesce around a unifying theme, so you don't have to work very hard at constructing some kind of coherent gendered self out of those stories. Most of them have a key element in common, so the narrative you construct to make a coherent identity features that element. If you like to dress in unusual styles, for example, many of your personal gender stories might feature creativity. If you identify as genderqueer, this sense of yourself may infuse all of your gender stories. If your religion is very important to you, your beliefs may guide all of your stories. Your gender identity, then, would include these qualities as primary elements of your stories.

INTEGRATING DIFFERENT BUT COMPATIBLE STORIES

At other times, you discover that you have in your narrative repertoire gender stories that are significantly disparate in how they construct your gender, but they are not incompatible—they don't contradict one another. Although such stories may represent you in dramatically different ways, they are generally not problematic for constructing your larger gender narrative because they simply represent different parts of the gendered person you perceive yourself to be. The process of integrating different stories into a coherent identity requires constructing a theme for your basic identity that transcends the particular stories and enables you to see them as different parts of a larger whole.

Frankie's gender identity contains disparate stories that she integrates in this way. One gender story Frankie has constructed as part of her narrative repertoire is a story that constructs her as feminine, while another constructs her as an athlete. She thus is aligning with one aspect of the binary's norms for femininity but also with a key binary norm for masculinity. She explains: "I first discovered that I could be both a tomboy and feminine when I wore a dress to school for picture day in the sixth grade (because my grandma made me). No one at school was accustomed to seeing me dressed up so nicely, so I received a lot of compliments about how pretty I looked that day. It was then that I realized that even a tomboy could dress up and be girlie every now and then." Frankie is able to integrate two different ways of doing gender into her gender identity without difficulty because she sees them both as elements of a well-rounded, balanced woman. This is the transcendent theme she uses to bring the two gender stories together: Women today have to play many different roles. Being an athlete and feminine are both required for Frankie's definition of self. As Frankie explains: "Now that I am in the middle of being a tomboy and a girlie girl, I am happy. I could never try to just be a tomboy because I love dressing up and going out with my friends. On the other side, I also could never just be a pretty girl and always dress up because I really like working out and playing sports. Both are important ways of enacting balance in my life as a woman."

INTEGRATING IRRECONCILABLE STORIES

When you are trying to integrate diverse gender stories into a coherent gender identity, you sometimes discover that some of the gender stories you have crafted for yourself contradict one another in irreconcilable ways. If you craft your identity using one of the stories, you are directly denying or contradicting another story that you feel represents just as strongly who you are. Men who become disabled sometimes experience this kind of identity contradiction in that "disability and masculinity are conflicting identities because of the contradiction contained in the stereotypical visions of each."[19] Because the binary associates masculinity with physical strength, a weakened body may be perceived as a kind of emasculation.

You also might find that you have irreconcilable stories as part of your identity if you grew up as a fundamentalist Christian or a Catholic and realize that you are gay. The religious narrative has taught you that homosexuality is a sin, but it is contradicted by your sexual orientation. You might see both gender stories—the one that features your religion and the one that includes your sexual orientation—as important to you, and you want to hold onto both stories as key parts of who you are. But the religious story claims that the other story is wrong and even evil and asserts that you cannot be both religious and gay at the same time. When you experience this kind of contradiction with clearly opposing, irreconcilable stories, you typically choose one of several options to manage the contradiction so that you are still able to achieve a coherent identity.

One way to integrate the contradictory stories is by rejecting one of them.[20] You construct a coherent identity by choosing to privilege or feature one gender story and to suppress the other. You simply decide that one story is more important to you than another, as philosopher Howard Kamler explains: "There is a hierarchy of stories for any person. That is, some stories are more all-encompassing for a person than are others. And so conflicts between stories can sometimes be resolved by determining that one is further up in the hierarchy than the other."[21] A paralyzed man might create coherence by emphasizing his heroic effort to overcome the limitations associated with his disability, his perseverance in the face of physical pain, and his competitive spirit. He might affirm qualities of masculinity by joining a wheelchair basketball team, for example, thus downplaying the story of his disability. In the case of a conflict between sexual orientation and religion, you might decide that expressing your sexuality is more important to you than expressing your religion, and you sublimate the story given to you by your religion to the gender story that features your sexuality. Your religion might become less important to you, and you might choose to attend church only on Christmas and Easter or maybe never. You might choose to interpret scripture or your church's teachings in a new way.[22] You suppress or downplay your religion in this case in order to be able to retain your sexual orientation and to create a coherent identity for yourself.

You might choose to manage irreconcilable gender stories you have crafted for yourself by synthesizing or merging the stories into one. You reject neither story, and the two continue to exist to form your gender in a dynamic balance.[23] Using this type of integration, you find or create a framework for the stories that allows the conflicting stories to be synthesized and no longer seen as conflicting. You might say to yourself, "Everything God created is good. God created me gay, so I can't be evil." You may begin to attend a church for gay and lesbian Christians, join the Rainbow Sash Movement for LGBTQ Catholics who want to continue receiving Holy Communion, sing in a gay men's choir, or attend a support group for gays and lesbians who want to retain their faith. You have synthesized elements of the diametrically opposed gender stories to create an identity in which you see yourself as both religious and gay, rejecting neither story.

Another way in which you can create a coherent identity even with irreconcilable stories is by maintaining the two stories in tension with each other without reconciling them.[24] Tali, who is a modern orthodox Jew, provides an example of this method of integration. She became involved with a young man in a sexual relationship when she was in high school, but because her religion forbids premarital sex, Tali kept the relationship secret from her family and her religious community. She continued to dress as a religious woman and identified herself as religious; she simply saw sex as an exception to the religious self she had constructed: "I said—there is religion, there is whatever has to do with religion, and there is being in a relationship with a boy. And that is something else. Like, it's another need. It's a need that I want to fulfill, . . . I want to remain religious, and I never even considered not being religious."[25] She compartmentalized sex and religion into two different spheres that did not overlap, so both stories existed side by side in her identity, with neither one privileged.

Reggie's mother engaged in this same integration process by refusing to acknowledge that a contradiction existed. Reggie explains: "My mother was a single mom until I was a teen, and she ran our household. When she married again, due to their religious beliefs, my mom always said the man is the head of the household. Yet, my mom still ran the house. Neither my mom nor my stepdad ever talked about the fact that he wasn't really the head of the household."

Your experience of yourself as a coherent identity—the result of your integration of various gender stories—does not mean that the identity you construct somehow represents a "true" or a "real" self. Many people think that their sense of a core gender identity is the reason why they want to wear a dress or play football, for example, and they believe that how they act derives naturally from some kind of inner core. As you have seen in this chapter, although your felt gender identity is experienced as inherent and real, it is neither of these. Instead, it is socially constructed through narrative—through all of the stories that others tell you about gender, the stories to which you attend, the stories that you appropriate to draft your own gender stories, and the ways in which you integrate those stories into a coherent identity. Most if not all of what feels internal to you as a gendered self is not internal at all; rather, it is an effect of symbols—of the stories told to you and that you appropriated, drafted, and integrated into a self that feels unified to you.

The particular way in which you choose to synthesize your stories is always changing because you are always adding stories to and dropping stories out of your gender repertoire, which means that your identity is evolving. Because you are constantly inventing and reinventing yourself, your narrative identity is not a static structure but the result of an ongoing integrative dynamic that is "very much in-process and unfinished."[26] As narrative theorist Varpu Löyttyniemi aptly notes: "My identity is never final, every closure is only for now."[27]

Because of the particular gender stories you encounter and the ways in which you integrate them to create a coherent gender identity, your construction of gender is absolutely unique. It can never be identical to how others construct their stories. The particular processes you use to attend to and appropriate fragments from various stories into your gender stories are yours alone. So, too, is the way you integrate them to create the narrative that constitutes your coherent gender identity. No one else can make exactly the same choices you make or use the same set of strategies in all aspects of these processes. You craft your own variations out of all the possibilities available.

Even if your gender stories conform in many ways to a prescribed ideal, you make innumerable choices about your gender identity that cannot help but distinguish you from others. In some cases, your choices are the result of your own desires; in other cases, you feel pressured to configure your gender stories in certain ways and must decide how to respond to that pressure. Jean, for example, is a Mormon wife and mother. She met her husband when they were students at Brigham Young University, she was married in the Temple, she is active in the Relief Society, and she has three sons. All of these choices—conscious and unconscious—have led her to construct what seems to be the conventional gender story of a Mormon wife and mother. But she has made multiple idiosyncratic choices in constructing her gender identity that distinguish her from everyone else with that same identity configuration. She lives in a condo, is a cello player and writer, dresses fashionably, occasionally drinks alcohol, and likes Zumba dancing—choices unlike the choices that others with this same gender identity make. No gender label can contain you, then, because you are always creating a unique way of being gendered by crafting your particular stories and integrating them into the gender identity that contains them.

AGENCY IN CRAFTING GENDER STORIES

The fact that your gender identity is constructed through the process of crafting stories means that you have a great deal of agency. In all of the processes involved, you have many choices about the kinds of actions you take. In chapter 1, we told you that one of our goals for you in this book is for you to feel empowered to make conscious and deliberate choices about how to construct your gender identity. In all of the steps of the process, you have multiple opportunities for deliberate choice making.

Guided by your visions and desires for yourself, you can choose the stories to which you pay attention and that become the resources for crafting your own gender stories. You can be deliberate about which threads or fragments from those stories you want to incorporate into your gender stories and, because these become key features of your personal gender stories, the fragments you pick have much to do with the nature of the stories you develop. You enact agency as you choose how to put your gender stories together in ways that make a coherent self or a gender identity. If some of your stories contradict one another in ways that are uncomfortable for you, you can enact agency by deciding how to integrate them into a coherent identity.

You have another choice as well: You can choose the degree to which your individual gender stories and the narrative that constitutes your gender identity conform to or resist the gender binary. Do you want to be Taylor Swift or Andrej Pejić or someone else entirely? As you learned in chapter 3, the gender binary supplies you with preexisting stories and culturally given plots that retell and reinforce the binary. It has assigned an identity to you and prescribes particular ways of being gendered in line with that assignment. You always negotiate the construction of your own stories in dialogue with this larger cultural system, engaging with that binary and the master narratives it offers. Your selections in terms of crafting your own gender stories are always made within this context.

Because your choices about gender take place against the backdrop of the binary, you can make conscious choices about whether you want to reproduce or repudiate the gender binary. One option is to retell the binary, appropriating stories from the binary and making them your own. The stories offered by the binary often provide comfortable and familiar formulas for crafting your gender identity. In some instances, however, you might decide to challenge those canonical stories. In such cases, you can choose to produce new kinds of stories, generating other possibilities for how to be gendered. Instead of retelling the binary, you revise it, modifying it in some ways, or you rework it, challenging its basic components and creating alternatives. Just as the stories that come to you from your family and friends and popular culture retell, revise, or rework the binary, so, too, the individual gender stories you craft and the ways you integrate them to develop your gender identity have the potential to retell, revise, or rework the binary.

If you have engaged in some of the choice-making processes involved in crafting your gender stories by default or unconsciously, we hope you will become more deliberate in those choices. Reflect on why you might have made some choices without consciously thinking about your decisions, and see if you can determine whether you would have made other choices had you been more conscious of your options in the process of story construction. Make your choices deliberate ones so that the gender stories you craft really are the ones you want to be part of your unique gender identity.

Although the gender stories you create are developed through a social process of interacting with others' stories, they are internal stories. These inner gender stories serve as preparation for your gender performances, where you transform the inner speech of your gender identity into a performance or "social speech" that is "intelligible to others."[28] The next chapter deals with this process by which you translate your internal gender stories into performances for others.

■ NOTES

[1] L. S. Vygotsky, *Thought and Language*, ed. and trans. Eugenia Hanfmann and Gertrude Vakar (Cambridge, MA: M.I.T. Press, 1962), 18, 45–47, 131, 145, and 149.

[2] Jessica Benjamin, "In Defense of Gender Ambiguity," *Gender & Psychoanalysis* 1 (1996): 30.

[3] Margaret Jean Intons-Peterson, *Children's Concepts of Gender* (Norwood, NJ: Ablex, 1988), 53–69.

[4] Sandra Lipsitz Bem, "Gender Schema Theory and Its Implications for Child Development: Raising Gender-Aschematic Children in a Gender-Schematic Society," *Signs: Journal of Women in Culture and Society* 8 (1983): 603.

[5] Mark S. Muldoon, "Ricoeur and Merleau-Ponty on Narrative Identity," *American Catholic Philosophical Quarterly* 71 (1997): 50.

[6] Muldoon, "Ricoeur and Merleau-Ponty on Narrative Identity," 51.

[7] Dieter Teichert, "Narrative, Identity and the Self," *Journal of Consciousness Studies* 11 (2004): 186.

[8] Paul John Eakin, "The Economy of Narrative Identity," *History of Political Economy* 39 (2007) (annual suppl.): 118.

[9] William James, *The Principles of Psychology*, vol. 1 (New York: Dover, 1950), 402.

[10] James, *The Principles of Psychology*, 404.

[11] Ch. Perelman and L. Olbrechts-Tyteca, *The New Rhetoric: A Treatise on Argumentation*, trans. John Wilkinson and Purcell Weaver (Notre Dame, IN: University of Notre Dame Press, 1969), 116–17.

[12] Kenneth Burke, *The Philosophy of Literary Form: Studies in Symbolic Action* (Berkeley: University of California Press, 1973), 293–304.

[13] James E. Marcia, "Development and Validation of Ego-Identity Status," *Journal of Personality and Social Psychology* 3 (1966): 551–58.

[14] Eugene T. Gendlin, *Focusing* (New York: Bantam Dell/Random House, 1978), 11.

[15] Deborah Schiffrin, "Narrative as Self-Portrait: Sociolinguistic Constructions of Identity," *Language in Society* 25 (1996): 168.

[16] Douglas Mason-Schrock, "Transsexuals' Narrative Construction of the 'True Self,'" *Social Psychology Quarterly* 59 (1996): 176.

17 Paul Ricoeur, *Time and Narrative*, vol. 1, trans. Kathleen McLaughlin and David Pellauer (Chicago: University of Chicago Press, 1984), 67.

18 Paul Ricoeur, "Life in Quest of Narrative," in *On Paul Ricoeur: Narrative and Interpretation*, ed. David Wood (New York: Routledge, 1991), 21.

19 Andrew C. Sparkes and Brett Smith, "Sport, Spinal Cord Injury, Embodied Masculinities, and the Dilemmas of Narrative Identity," *Men and Masculinities* 4 (2002): 263–64.

20 Elli P. Schachter, "Identity Configurations: A New Perspective on Identity Formation in Contemporary Society," *Journal of Personality* 72 (2004): 178–80.

21 Howard Kamler, *Communication: Sharing Our Stories of Experience* (Seattle, WA: Psychological Press, 1983), 37.

22 An example of this kind of reinterpretation is provided by John Stackhouse Jr., *Finally Feminist: A Pragmatic Christian Understanding of Gender* (Grand Rapids, MI: Baker Academic, 2005).

23 Schachter, "Identity Configurations," 180–83.

24 Schachter, "Identity Configurations," 183–86.

25 Schachter, "Identity Configurations," 184.

26 Douglas Ezzy, "Theorizing Narrative Identity: Symbolic Interactionism and Hermeneutics," *Sociological Quarterly* 39 (1998): 247.

27 Varpu Löyttyniemi, "Narrative Identity and Sexual Difference," *Narrative Inquiry* 16 (2006): 270.

28 Vygotsky, *Thought and Language*, 145, 148.

seven

PERFORMING

ENACTING GENDER STORIES

Every performance is different. That's the beauty of it.
Van Morrison, Interview

I magine that the classroom in which you are taking this course is a performance space. The large room with identical desks, a whiteboard, and overhead flickering fluorescent lights constitutes the setting or stage. The actors include your professor, other students, and you. Each person has entered this scene in a certain costume—a style of dress and hair, tattoos or earrings, and an array of personal props such as a backpack, laptop, and cell phone. As class begins and the people in the room begin to interact, the professor writes *Gender Stories* on the board, a man takes off his cap and combs his fingers through his hair, and a woman smiles at the student next to her. Each person begins to act a part—the (hopefully) inspiring professor, the man who is trying to be attractive, and the gregarious woman. In acting these parts, all three are performers portraying characters from their own identity stories that fit this particular context. As performers, they are exhibiting parts of their internal senses of who they are to the other people in the room. Each person is also an audience member, watching, experiencing, and evaluating everyone else's performances. The scenes being enacted in your classroom represent a "drama of everyday life."[1]

Among the identities that people in this drama are enacting are their gender identities. That each of the people in this classroom scene is performing a gender story might not be immediately obvious to you, but gender is a key dimension of all daily dramas that occur in the binary. Because the binary system divides all people and all activities into feminine and masculine, dramas of everyday life are almost always interpreted—at least in part—as enactments of gender that fit into one of these two categories. All enacted behaviors—even writing on a board, rearranging one's hair, smiling at someone, or just sitting quietly at a desk waiting for class to begin—can be and usually are assessed by others against normative conceptions of gender that recognize certain attitudes and actions as girlish, boyish, womanly, or manly. In other words, performing gender is constant and unavoidable.[2]

Sociologists Candace West and Don Zimmerman use the term *omnirelevant* to describe gender, highlighting the fact that, in addition to whatever other roles people are enacting in a certain context, they also are doing gender.[3] West and Zimmerman point out that people have multiple social identities—the professor may also be a father and a runner, and each student is a son or a daughter and a friend—but in particular situations, some identities count more than others. That is, an audience takes note of some identities and not others. In class, the identities of professor and student are salient. When the lecture is finished and the students go to their jobs, other identities become more important—partner, parent, server, military officer, and sales associate, for example. In all situations—whether in class, at home, or at work—audiences note and evaluate a person's gender. In a binary culture, people see not only a professor but a *male* or *female* professor and not only a student but a *female* or *male* student. This means that, no matter what else you are doing, other people will see you as performing gender as well.

A gender performance includes appearance, mannerisms, and verbal and nonverbal behaviors. Wearing your hair a certain way, adopting a particular style of clothing, and choosing your accessories are perhaps the most obvious ways you perform your gender stories, but these overt aspects are not the only—and perhaps not even the most important—levels on which other people observe and interpret your gender identity. Everything you say and the tone you use, your posture and gait as you walk or run, the way you use your hands and arms to gesture, and how you smile and laugh are all parts of your gender performance. Even small behavioral details like the angle at which the professor holds the dry-erase marker, how the male student touches his hair, and the particular way the woman student smiles all contribute to distinct gender performances.

This chapter is concerned with how you enact your gender stories when you perform in your own dramas of daily life. In the previous chapter, we discussed how, from all the stories you encounter in your world, you construct your own gender stories. This chapter is designed to help you become more conscious of the ways you share those gender stories with other people. To do that, we explain (1) the functions of gender performances; (2) the elements, stages, and behavioral choices involved in performances; and (3) ways in which you can exercise agency in your own performances of gender.

FUNCTIONS OF GENDER PERFORMANCES

Gender performances involve the way you see yourself, the way other people see you, and how you fit into the larger culture.[4] In other words, gender performances function on individual, social, and cultural levels of human communication. On an individual level, gender performances have a role in constructing your gender, facilitate the development of your internal gender stories, and allow you to share those stories with other people. On a social level, others respond to the behavior you enact, reinforcing or questioning your narrative. On a cultural level, gender performances are the mechanisms through which cultural categories of gender are maintained and continue to develop and evolve.

One function of gender performances is that of constructing an individual's gender. Gender theorist Judith Butler points out that the gendered self does not exist prior to performances of gender—your own gender, then, is only potential until you enact it through performances. This means that when you enact certain "stylized and repeated" performances, you cause particular gender categories to come into existence for yourself.[5] Your repeated performances are not static or constructed in only one form. As you alter your performances over your lifetime, you introduce new elements or change key categories in your gender identity. One of your stylized and repeated performances might involve having short buzzed hair, wearing clothing styled for men, not wearing makeup, and talking in a low register. This configuration of stylized and repeated performances could be the way in which you combine appearances and actions to perform being a masculine woman or a masculine man.

Another stylized and repeated performance might combine lack of body hair, speaking in a higher register, wearing pink and lavender, and holding a cigarette with straight fingers to perform being a feminine woman or a feminine man.

These examples show how, in the binary, routine and habitual performances carry particular meanings—stereotypes of masculinity and femininity—that you and other people use to interpret performances as certain gender constructions. Gender, then, is something you accomplish by repeating certain performances until they become routine and habitual.[6] These repeated performances become your gender, both how you know yourself and how others in the binary interpret who you are. In other words, a person is not inherently male or female, some combination, or none of these. There is no natural body or gender because meanings come into being through communication.[7] You *become* gendered by performing in defined ways—dressing in a certain fashion and speaking and behaving in certain ways—that are culturally associated with one gender or another.

Performing your gender stories is also the way you continue to develop your own sense of who you are as a gendered person. Most people do not sit down and consciously construct a gender. Rather, a personal gender identity comes into being through performances—some repeated and some novel—that contribute new plots and twists to your internal stories. Performing gender in front of other people is how you demonstrate to yourself who you are becoming. For example, one of your usual performances during meetings at work might be to wait to speak up until your boss asks for your opinion. One day, you find yourself compelled to interrupt one of your boss's speeches to interject your own thoughts. Not only is your view respected, but you are almost surprised to discover that you enjoy participating in this new way, so you incorporate more assertive behaviors into your work style. Because being confident and assertive at work is a different gendered behavior than you have performed until now, your behavioral change causes other people to adjust how they experience and treat you. This, in turn, reinforces your new behavior and causes you to modify your internal gender narratives. Thus, your performances spark a recrafted story that includes new information about yourself as well as a modified version of your gender identity.

Your gender identity is sustained and transformed because of your social relationships and interactions.[8] The dynamics of the construction of gender stories that were discussed in the last chapter—working out conflicting internal stories and accommodating different parts of yourself, for example—usually occur while you are performing gender in the presence of other people. One example we gave was how you might work out the internal conflict of being gay and Christian by joining a gay men's church choir. While singing during church services and concerts are obvious gender performances, looking for an inclusive church, talking to the choir director, trying out, and attending rehearsals are also gender performances. These performances contribute to the recrafting of your internal gender story from that of a man with a serious conflict regarding gender identity and religion to that of a man whose religion and gender identity support and nurture one another. Performance is the mechanism through which you craft new stories and develop your gender identity.

In addition to constructing your gender and helping you craft new stories, gender performances are how you share your gender stories with other people. During each performance—each time you interact with other people—you communicate your attitudes, feelings, and beliefs about gender through your words and actions. You translate your personal gender stories—daughter, Navy Seal, cheerleader, friend, lover, father—into a range of verbal and nonverbal behaviors that become performances in different social contexts. Your performances tell other people who you consider yourself to be as a gendered person and provide consistency in how others experience you—a consistency that sets up expectations that you are a person who looks and behaves in certain ways.

In addition to accomplishments on individual and social levels, gender performances function on a cultural level. In the same way that an individual's gender does not exist until it is socially constructed, cultural categories, definitions, and norms of gender also do not exist except as they are socially constructed. In chapter 2, we discussed how gender is a cultural classification system that comes into being through human communication. Gender performances are a type of human communication that socially constructs gendered meanings for bodies by modifying existing definitions or developing new categories in new contexts. Gender categories are not static; they emerge and are altered through communication events—through a process of people performing gender in different social situations.[9] Gender performances continue to construct various cultural definitions.

Much in the same way that the repeated gender performances of individuals create and maintain a stable gender identity, repeated gender performances also function to tell cultural stories and maintain cultural gender categories. The gender binary provides a framework through which members of a culture understand themselves and other people, creating narratives that are internalized and shared.[10] When individuals perform genders that enact these shared narratives, cultural values and beliefs about gender are confirmed and maintained. For example, dating rituals that involve men asking women out, picking them up, and paying for meals and entertainment enact a heterosexual cultural narrative that is replayed and reinforced each time a man and a woman engage in these behaviors. This ritual confirms beliefs that men should be more active than women in initiating relationships and that women should wait to be asked to become involved in a relationship. Likewise, the institution of marriage remains a central cultural narrative because couples—both heterosexual and homosexual—continue to get married. The point is that if no one performed dating or marriage rituals, these narratives would no longer be maintained or continue to function in the culture.

Gender performances also function to change cultural classifications, which are modified as the gender performances of individual people and groups are rejected or accommodated on a cultural level. Because of gender performances, the meanings and values associated with gendered concepts and categories evolve as gender is socially constructed in new forms. For example, the categories *man* and *woman* have carried a variety of social meanings throughout human history. In addition, as people change dating and marriage performances, the cultural narratives of these practices undergo modifications. Marriage once meant a particular kind of union—between a woman and a man. As more gay couples marry and the social construction of marriage itself evolves into having a different, enlarged meaning for many people, the cultural narrative about marriage also changes.

Gender performances socially construct gender categories and norms, maintain some definitions and norms, and make possible an ongoing evolution of definitions and norms. Each time you perform your own gender identity, you continue to develop your own internal stories as you exhibit to others who you think you are as a gendered person. You also contribute to evolving cultural norms and narratives. Thus, there is a dynamic relationship between the gender performances of individual people and cultural gender categories and norms—each exerts influence on the other. We turn now from the functions of gender performances to the key elements involved in such performances.

PERFORMANCE ELEMENTS

Individuals who are presenting who they are to other people in their daily lives are not unlike actors on a stage. Erving Goffman, a social scientist who studied the relational aspects of human behavior, uses the terms *setting, audience,* and *performer* to draw parallels between performance in the theatre and performance in everyday life.[11] Goffman points out that people have habitual ways of acting and that certain situations require certain behaviors, making many performances formulaic and predictable. Nevertheless, an actual performance always has the capacity to be unique because it depends on the specific and complex interactions among a particular setting, a performer, and the other people who are present as the audience. That is, each performance is contextual or, as Van Morrison says in the opening quote of this chapter, each performance is unique because there is never a precise replication of all three elements from one context to the next. Although we discuss the setting, audience, and performer separately in the sections below, all three are intimately connected such that even a relatively minor change in one element inevitably results in a different performance.

SETTING

The setting is the spatial and temporal location of a performance and includes the physical space in which the performer and audience interact, the time and duration of the action, and the objects that are present in the environment. Each of these characteristics of the setting influences the way in which a performance materializes. In addition, the setting of a performance allows audience members to gather information and make inferences about the performer.

Some aspects of setting that affect performance—location, lighting, noise, and temperature, for example—are probably obvious to you. You know from experience that people act differently in church than they do at school and that the norms of behavior in a doctor's office are not the same as those in a sports arena. An intimate conversation conducted in a bedroom two people share does not look or feel like an intimate conversation across a table in a coffee shop. You probably are also cognizant of how dim or bright light, silence or loud noise, and extreme heat or cold can make you feel comfortable and relaxed or uncomfortable and on edge. You know how these physical aspects of environments can cause your behavior to change. When you are uncomfortable, for example, you may be less patient or more inclined to end a performance quickly than when you are comfortable.

Other aspects of setting—familiarity and prior experience, for example—sometimes have a more subtle influence because feelings provoked by particular settings can cause behavioral responses on an unconscious level. Although not universally true, people generally feel more confident of their performances in settings that are familiar to them. Unfamiliar, highly charged environments like emergency rooms, courtrooms, and police stations often make people feel disoriented and unsure of themselves, but there are less dramatic settings that also can impact a performance. For example, if you are accustomed to meeting your supervisor in her office and one day she asks you to meet her in the executive board room, you may experience a sense either of fear or excitement at the change of venue, and either feeling might impact how you act in her presence. Prior positive or negative associations with particular settings can also influence performances. Think about a restaurant, for example, where you had a cozy, romantic meal as compared to one where you had an argument that terminated a close relationship. "Every time I have dinner with my parents," Amanda says, "I fight with my dad about wanting to be a nurse because he wants me to be a lawyer like my sister. I tense up as soon as I pull into my parents' driveway, and I hardly feel like talking to them at all." In this observation of herself as a performer, Amanda illustrates how expectations that a setting will be the scene of a happy or a miserable encounter can contribute to different types of performances.

During most performances, performers interact not only with other people but with objects or props. In the example of your classroom as a performance space, students had backpacks, laptops, and cell phones, and the professor had a dry-erase marker. The objects that are present in a setting directly influence the kinds of performances that are possible—a cook needs a stove, pans, and food; a quarterback needs pads, cleats, and a football; and a rock star needs a guitar, an amplifier, and a microphone. You've probably had the experience of planning a performance that had to be altered because one of your props was missing or didn't function as you had planned—you left the CD you wanted to share with a friend at home or arrived at an important event in damp, rumpled clothing because you were caught in the rain.

Because some physical objects are assigned by the binary as appropriate only for females or males, they have special relevance to gender performances. The objects that a performer carries into a scene—even the color of a backpack or phone cover or the fabric out of which a scarf is made, for example—may cause audience members to make assumptions and judgments about the gender stories the performer is trying to convey. Performers are also judged according to how they interact with the objects that are already present in an environment. In a large department store, for example, there are expectations that only persons who are trying to communicate certain gender stories shop for and try on items that carry strong gendered associations such as evening gowns, bras, and tuxedos. Certainly, anyone can buy bras or tuxes, but these purchases may evoke reactions of curiosity or negativity from an audience if they are purchased by the "wrong" genders. Even seemingly neutral behaviors like which magazine someone chooses in a doctor's waiting room can carry cultural gender expectations because magazines are often marketed to specific gender audiences.

Temporal aspects of a setting involve the day, hour, and duration of a performance. Performances are affected by temporal factors such as a significant date, cultural norms for the use of time, and even whether a performance is during an individual's best or worst time of day. A performance that occurs during the celebration of an anniversary or a birthday is different from a performance that takes place at the remembrance of a death or a tragedy. Fourth of July celebrations elicit performances that include beer drinking, barbeques, and fireworks, for example, while New Yorkers commemorate 9/11 with silence and contemplative gatherings in churches, mosques, and synagogues. In most circumstances, people who are performing gender also conform to accepted cultural guidelines for certain times of day and night. Performances that include drinking alcohol and dancing wildly before noon are rare. Individual daily rhythms—whether a performer is alert and cheerful upon waking or has an afternoon slump in energy, for example—also have an effect on performance behaviors.

In addition to having an effect on specific performances, the particular attributes of a setting allow audience members to gather information about the identity of a performer. For example, if you are invited to someone's house for the first time and find her in a luxury high rise, you know something different about her than if she lived in an old Victorian house that is divided into studio apartments. From the setting, you are likely to make inferences about this woman's finances, standard of living, and taste. If you make an appointment with your college professor and find him in a large corner office with a view of the city skyline instead of in a small interior cubicle, you might infer that he has status—or at least seniority—in his department. In both of these cases, setting reveals information about the participants.

Audience members also make assumptions about performers based on the fact that they are in certain settings, and only certain characters are likely to be found in such settings. When you, as a performer, walk into a classroom carrying books, the other people in the room assume you are a student or an instructor and not a doctor, an electrician, or a housepainter. Because you are on a college campus, you are also assumed to value learning. If you enter a church on a Sunday morning dressed in a suit and tie, the people in the pews assume you are there to participate in the worship service, and they might infer that you are a religious person. Of course, such assumptions are not always true. Austin shares such a misattribution that occurs when he goes out with his gay friends to bars and drag shows: "Because I'm there with gay guys, people think I'm gay—which is understandable, I guess—but I'm not." Likewise, simply because you attend a speech by a political candidate does not mean you are a member of that candidate's party. The point is, even if you are a stranger to your audience, members use their past experience and knowledge to make inferences about aspects of your performance simply by your presence in a setting.

Settings influence performers and audience members on a number of levels. The location of a scene, characteristics of a physical space, and objects in an environment result in modifications to a performer's behaviors. A performer's familiarity and prior associations with a setting can also cause subtle and perhaps unconscious adjustments to be made in a performance. Finally, audiences use settings to gain information about and to evaluate attributes of a performer.

AUDIENCE

The audience consists of all the people who are in a particular location and who are able to observe and interact with a performer. Whenever you are in a group with several other people, you are simultaneously an actor and an audience member for the others; in turn, they are all actors and audience members for you as well. An audience has various impacts on a gender performance before, during, and after a performance. The intentions of audience members and the responses they give to performances will be the subject of the next chapter, but here we focus on how the composition of the audience, the relationship of the performer to audience members, and the power dynamics of those relationships affect gender performances.

When you as a performer come into the presence of an audience, the characteristics of that audience influence how you behave. These characteristics include the size of the assembled group, the social rules of the group, and how alike or different the audience members are from you and from one another. One way to think about these audience qualities is to think about the way you assess other people when you enter a room. You probably immediately notice if there is only one person, five people, or a crowd. The size of the audience is important in terms of performance. Sharing your stories with larger groups, for example, may require such accommodations as a louder voice or larger movements, prompting you to feel more anxious or nervous. On the other hand, you are able to modify your performance—talking more quietly, for example—if your audience consists of only one person. If only a few people are in the room, you can expect them to notice you; if a room is crowded, your presence may go unnoticed unless you make yourself obvious.

The rules and norms constructed by an audience affect performances. In any social group, there are usual and expected performances for various roles. In a classroom, you expect the professor to stand at the front of the room and talk to all of the students. A professor who enters the room and sits in the back row, talking only to one or two students, is in violation of the norms of educational settings. Just as you have expectations of professors, audiences in general expect that you as a performer will perform roles in prescribed ways that they can recognize and understand. The prescriptive nature of social rules and norms means that audience members will judge negatively those performers who violate expectations.[12] On the other hand, performances that follow accepted rules and norms commonly elicit approval from audiences.

As we have discussed throughout this book, the gender binary prescribes one set of behaviors for girls and women and another set of behaviors for boys and men. This means that, in addition to the unique social rules and norms that any specific audience might have constructed, a performer is also expected to perform the role of an appropriately gendered person in the binary. Children who are observed playing with the "wrong" toys—boys who like to dress Barbie dolls or girls who stage war scenes with action figures, for example—are often judged by audiences of parents and peers as playing inappropriately. In a college classroom, a woman who takes out a pocket mirror to apply lipstick and mascara or a man who belches loudly might be judged by their audience to be violating classroom norms because these are not acceptable public behaviors. In the same classroom, if a man takes out a pocket mirror to put on lipstick and eye makeup or a woman belches, the audience's assessment might include not only the judgment that the man and woman are being rude but also that they are doing gender "wrong." In other words, the rules and norms of all audiences are based in part on the binary system.

The homogeneity or diversity of the audience and the degree to which you are like or different from audience members affect your gender performance. Some attributes that you and your audience may share are age, ethnicity, class, educational level, religion, and political affiliation. The more alike the audience members are to you and to each other, even on superficial levels, the more you can assume that people will understand the gender identity you are trying to share. If you walk into a room and the ten people there are all approximately your age, the same ethnicity as you, dressed like you, and listening to music you appreciate, you perform one way. If you enter the same room to find ten senior citizens of various races watching the news on television, you perform differently. Similarly, if you enter a room where there is a diverse group—your classroom, for example—your performance changes again. The confidence with which you approach a performance can depend on your assessment of the audience's ability to identify with and understand your performance.

Another key area of influence that an audience has on a gender performance concerns the relationships between the performer and audience members, both in type and degree. If you consider the range of possible relationships among people, from strangers to intimate partners, you can appreciate how both the kind of relationship and the degree of intensity impact performances. A performance shared with an unfamiliar audience is much different from one with a familiar audience, but familiarity is not the only influential factor. If your audience consists of people you feel uncomfortable around or even dislike, you perform differently than if you are among friends. Jamal provides an example of how relationships affect gender performances when he talks about his job: "We have a new manager at work, and I just can't relate to him. I'm usually pretty laid back, but something about him rubs me the wrong way, and I find myself acting like a jerk around him." Even among friends, there are degrees of familiarity and degrees of affiliation. In other words, you like some friends more than others and love some people more than others, and you perform gender differently in front of a casual friend than you do with your intimate partner. The unique relationships you have with various audiences always influence a gender performance.

The power dynamics between a performer and an audience also have an impact on a gender performance. Power has to do with relative status and is determined by a complex social-political-economic structure that is used to organize relationships and to confer certain privileges.[13] Power is demonstrated through performances of behavior, and those who have power in an interaction often convey their position through their actions. Some of the typical ways people who have more power demonstrate their status is by dominating physically or verbally, touching another person without permission, using less formal means of address than others use with them, asking personal questions that are not reciprocated, and requiring certain behaviors by others in their presence. As a performer, your own behaviors change according to whether you are in a more or less powerful position compared to your audience.

Many social configurations have obvious positions of power. Parent-child, instructor-student, boss-employee, and doctor-patient are all relational dyads in which one person is generally recognized as having more control and influence in a particular context than the other person. The gender performances of more influential people are likely to exhibit the kinds of cues that mark someone with greater power. However, on interpersonal levels, power dynamics are not usually as recognizably stable or overt. You may be part of a group of friends in which one person freely expresses her attitudes and wishes, so the group often tends to do what she wants. You may be in an intimate relationship where power dynamics shift depending on the situation. If one of you knows more about your city's music scene, the two of you tend to go to shows she picks. On the other hand, if you have more skills in dealing with conflict, you tend to dominate and lead discussions when the two of you disagree. As a performer, these subtle shifts in power dynamics cause your behaviors to change.

Audiences have a variety of effects on gender performances as performers adapt their behaviors to respond to the composition and social norms of groups of people. The relationships a performer has with audience members and the power dynamics—whether the performer feels more or less powerful than others—lead to different expressions of gender identity. Performers may accommodate—by behaving similarly to their audience—or behave in more individualistic, nonconforming ways, but an actual performance is always, at least in part, a response to the immediate context of the other people present in a setting.

PERFORMER

A third key element of a gender performance is the performer, who shares internal gender stories by interacting with both a setting and an audience. You know from experience that people perform gender with great variation. As we have noted before, you are surrounded daily by a multitude of gender performances in media, on campus, and among your friends. Gender performances are richly diverse in large part because, although settings and audiences are significant influences on performances, each performer crafts a distinctive gender identity and develops individualized expressions of that identity. Performers bring to each enactment of gender their own behavioral interpretations of cultural expectations, certain habitual and routine ways of performing genders, and unique characteristics such as personality and style.

One way to think of yourself when you perform a gender story in front of other people is as the main character in a play. Like any actor, if you are going to enact an effective performance, you need a costume, a stage, and a script with directions not only for speech but for movements—entrances and exits and forays up and down the stage. Actors on a stage have the benefit of a director to help them understand and perform their scenes, but as a performer in daily dramas of life, you usually have to script and direct yourself. You enter a situation—a scene—having decided what to wear, how to make an entrance, and how to begin your performance. In the context of a given audience and setting, you then have to come up with lines of dialogue, gestures, and meaningful interactions with the people around you so that they understand the particular gender identity you are trying to share.

The scripting of gender performances designed to share the stories you want audiences to experience is something you do all the time. You are aided in this task by the common understandings members of your culture have regarding gender. Goffman considers gender a "socially scripted dramatization of the culture's idealization of feminine and masculine natures, played for an audience that is well-schooled" in this kind of performance.[14] In other words, you as a performer know that any audience living in the binary has definite expectations about how you perform your gender stories and that the audience evaluates you, at least in part, according to cultural norms for femininity and masculinity. You, in turn, as a member of the culture, are also well schooled in how different gender performances—male, female, gay, straight, mother, and father, for example—are generally performed and evaluated. In most situations, you have a preconceived notion of how to script yourself to tell the stories you want to share.

That you and your audiences share a common understanding of performing gender helps you figure out how to express your gender stories. This mutual understanding, however, does not mean that performing your stories is always easy or comfortable for you. Some gender stories that you may want to enact either exist outside of mainstream stories or are not stories that your current audience appreciates. Like Sybil, you may be used to having people respond to your gendered enactments with some degree of negativity. "My traditional grandfather does not like it when I act like a strong, articulate young woman. He complains that I disrespect him." Or, like Trisha, you may be accustomed to hiding parts of your gender identity or modifying aspects of your stories in order to accommodate certain audiences. "I'm not out around my dad," Trisha told us. "It might happen someday, but, for now, he'd flip out if he knew I'm lesbian." As a performer, you depend on your assessments of the setting and audience to craft an appropriate performance, and part of that assessment depends on shared cultural assumptions and values regarding gender.

In many—perhaps most—situations, you script gender performances without consciously thinking about all the factors—costuming, speech, mannerisms, movements, and interactions—that are involved. Your largely unconscious approach to acting out a performance can be understood through a notion that sociologist Pierre Bourdieu calls the *habitus*—those unspoken, taken-for-granted, and invisible ways of doing and being that are acquired through socialization.[15] The *habitus* develops through the habitual repetition of certain behaviors or activities that contribute to a sense of continuity by providing structure and familiarity in everyday routines. Because you have performed some acts so many times—you comb your hair with a center part, wear tight black jeans and T-shirts with band logos, and speak with the particular intonations of the Chinese language you learned as a child—you no longer think about these acts. As you encounter different settings and audiences, you embody and express the *habitus* in your posture and mannerisms, in ingrained habits of behavior, and even in feelings and thoughts. Instead of consciously having to create a unique performance for every setting and audience, for most performances, you rely on your usual or standard presentation of self.

The *habitus* means that you usually assess performance situations almost automatically, reverting to your past knowledge of how similar situations with similar people have occurred and relying on behaviors that you have used in the past to convey your gender stories. Picture yourself entering a friend's house to hang out on a Friday night. You and your friends have habitual ways of greeting one another and of interacting—you play video games, watch movies, or make music together. You talk to each other in patterns that you have worked out in previous encounters to joke, to express support for one another, and to share details of your lives. You have established physical dynamics—how close you sit, how often you touch, and what types of gestures are acceptable. Now imagine that you are meeting your intimate partner for a dinner date. You probably can predict with great accuracy how the evening will proceed, including the types of physical contact and the topics of conversation. For these situations, you have habitual ways of enacting gender that you repeat without thinking about them. Even in unfamiliar situations with people you don't know—during a job interview or when you travel in a foreign country, for example—you often rely on past experiences in similar situations. A large part of any performance is habitual and unconsciously scripted.

Performances are also influenced by factors that are unique to you as a performer—your style or personality, physical state, mood, and state of mind. Think of how you describe your friends: "Brad's funny," "Alima's really outgoing," "Omar is shy." Most people have a usual way of presenting themselves that is carried into each performance—a repertoire of behaviors and a look that constitute an individual style.

In addition, your emotional and physical states affect your performances. If you are depressed, sad, anxious, or angry, your mood most likely becomes part of your performance, perhaps making you less energetic or less talkative than usual. Alternately, if you are happy or excited, you might smile and laugh more during your performance. Your physical state—if you are tired or hungry, are pregnant, or have a broken leg, for example—also influences how you script particular performances. A particular performance is always influenced as well by your state of mind, and even a temporary feeling of optimism or pessimism can have an impact on your performance.

Gender performances are complex interactions among settings, audiences, and performers. In the above discussion, we have treated the setting, audience, and performer as separate entities with their own unique sets of attributes, but in an actual performance, these three elements interact on multiple levels. Alterations in key elements—a power outage in the setting, new members in the audience, or a change in your mood—affect the overall dynamic of the performance. We turn now from how these elements and their complex interactions influence the way you tell your gender stories to the stages of performing gender.

STAGES OF PERFORMANCE

Every performance of gender requires that you consciously or unconsciously devise a means of transforming your internal stories into sharable narratives. A sharable narrative involves creating a range of verbal and nonverbal behaviors that allows others to experience you as a gendered person. Sharing your gender stories—exhibiting them so that the meaning you intend is comprehended by your audience—depends on your ability to adopt an appropriate appearance and range of behaviors.

In other words, you look and act in ways that create a gender performance that will effectively communicate your intended gender story. Of course, you cannot control whether your audience's interpretations match your intended messages—if your audience is unfamiliar with or not receptive to the gender stories you perform, misinterpretation may occur. Nevertheless, sharing your gender stories means enacting performances that effectively express those stories.

There are two steps to performance: (1) anticipation, and (2) enactment. The anticipation stage occurs prior to entering a setting and meeting an audience. You anticipate a gender performance by preparing yourself physically, emotionally, and mentally for your upcoming performance. When a performance is underway, you interact with the setting and audience through a range of nonverbal and verbal behaviors that enable you to develop a performance narrative that communicates messages you want to convey; this is the enactment stage. In this section, we look more closely at both stages to examine the origin and the unfolding of a gender performance.

ANTICIPATION

Even before you enact a gender performance, you already have some notion of what that performance will involve, and you prepare yourself for it. You wake up in the morning, shower, and get dressed for school. You stop by your apartment after classes and change clothes before you go to work. At the end of your shift, you go to the employee restroom and get ready for a date. In each of these situations, you prepare yourself physically by changing clothes, and you prepare yourself mentally and emotionally by considering the scenes you are about to enter. Anticipating a performance usually involves weighing a number of factors, including the cultural and group norms of the setting you are about to encounter, the specific audience, which of your gender stories you want to reveal, and your motivation for the interaction. We consider each of these factors and then illustrate how they interact with a few examples.

In most situations, you can and do rely on your habitual gender performances for conveying the sense of your gendered self you want to share. You possess knowledge about the setting and audience based on conventional expectations and prior information that let you know what to expect. Your knowledge of the binary, previous experiences in particular settings, and prior interactions with certain audiences allow you to assess the situation and, to an initial degree, plan your performance. When you know you will be engaging with familiar settings and audiences, you are able to draw on your usual repertoire of costumes and behaviors to script a performance—like an actor playing a familiar part. Because you have spent a lifetime adapting and crafting your gender performances to depict your gender stories, the anticipation stage for your standard gender performance is relatively rote and stress free.

There are times when you anticipate a setting and audience that are not familiar, when you want to perform a gender story you don't usually perform, or when you want to share a story you usually only perform in certain settings with certain people. There are also situations in which, due to the norms and the expectations of your audience, you may feel that you will not be safe performing a particular gender story. In these cases, you know there may be tension or conflict around your gender performance, and the anticipation stage can be more complex. In these cases, the anticipation stage probably is more conscious as you consider how your appearance and behaviors and your audience's responses to you may affect your upcoming interaction. Anticipation of gender performances is often complicated by the decisions you have to make regarding how you want others to experience your gender—what you want them to know about you—as well as by your motivations for the encounter.

Performances of gender often involve negotiating levels of self-disclosure. Self-disclosure refers to the amount and types of personal information—your history, desires, thoughts, and feelings—that you share with other people.[16] In general, the more familiar and intimate people are with one another, the more freely they share their internal identities. Around people you know well, you may plan to engage a mode of performance that is transparent or that lets your audience see and experience a large portion of your gender identity. But even among people you know well, if you have experienced tension regarding your gender performances, you may anticipate that a transparent performance is not your best strategy. If your gender identity is one that you know from past experience won't be accepted in a certain setting or by a certain audience, you may be hesitant to perform all aspects of a gender story freely and may adopt strategies of performance that involve hiding parts of your gender story. In other words, you might masquerade and only partially reveal who you know yourself to be.

Anticipating a performance also involves acknowledging your level of investment and motivations for the upcoming scene. You enact many performances for which you have a particular conscious motivation—a reason or an impetus for doing something. Among the motivations you might have for a particular performance is the desire to be liked or appreciated, to appear competent or professional, or to be perceived as intelligent or creative. Still other performances might be motivated by a desire to confront someone, to voice your opinion strongly, or to make sure someone knows you are independent and can do what you choose. In most situations, your motivations are plural—in one situation, you might want to be liked, seen as competent, and perceived as independent. In another, you might want to be strong about voicing your views, be appreciated, and appear professional.

Anticipating a performance, then, involves getting ready physically, mentally, and emotionally. Your knowledge of the setting and audience, your level of planned self-disclosure, and your motivation and investment in the upcoming scene inform how you prepare. When Yesenia thinks about going out with a certain group of friends, her anticipation centers on dress and appearance because she feels pressured by her friends to dress and act a certain way: "When I'm getting ready to meet my friends at a club, I feel like I need to fix my hair, wear high heels and a lot of makeup, and dress in a much sexier way than I normally do." Yesenia is voicing her anticipation of a gender performance and is using her past knowledge and experience to assess her audience and setting. This audience is one of close friends, so the type and intensity of the relationship cause them to have a strong influence on her thoughts, feelings, and actions. This group of friends has developed certain rules and norms about their group behavior—dressing up in a sexy fashion to go to clubs.

Even before she meets her friends, Yesenia already has some notion of what her performance might entail and has to make decisions about how she will look and act. Her internal gender stories are somewhat in conflict with her anticipated performance, and she feels tension because she is aware that her usual and preferred gender performance—being modestly dressed and wearing little or no makeup—is not one that meets with her friends' approval. She also is aware that she herself is not comfortable emphasizing the same type of sexuality as her friends. As Yesenia anticipates meeting her friends, she is weighing her preferred enactment of gender against the enactment she feels pressured to perform.

Yesenia's anticipation stage for her upcoming performance involves considering a known audience and a setting, her level of desired self-exposure, and her motivation and investment in the encounter. In other words, she must negotiate her gender. If her primary motivation is to be herself—to be transparent—Yesenia can choose not to dress like her friends. If her primary motivation is to be approved of by her friends, she can dress the way that they do. Yesenia can plan to dress as they want her to; dress in a completely opposite way; or decide on some middle ground by, for example, wearing makeup and heels but not a revealing outfit. She can negotiate the situation—balance her own needs and desires with those of her friends—in a number of ways. In this situation, anticipation involves considering a complex array of factors.

Matthew provides another example of anticipation of a gender performance: "I've lived with my boyfriend Tim for a year now, and we're getting ready to spend the holidays at his parents' house. I've never met them and, although Tim says they are cool with our relationship, his mother doesn't want us to sleep together at their house. I'm afraid there might be tension even around our being affectionate. I don't want to create problems, but I know I'll resent it—I might even resent Tim—if I feel like I can't be myself." Matthew feels ambivalence about his upcoming performance because of a difference between his internal gender stories and what he thinks might be expected of him in this setting and with this audience.

Matthew is anticipating his upcoming performance by consciously weighing several interrelated factors—his internal gender stories, the level of self-disclosure he wants to achieve with Tim's parents, and his motivations for the encounter. Unlike Yesenia's anticipation stage, Matthew is entering an unfamiliar setting and is about to encounter an audience that is largely unknown to him. His own performance of gender is also complicated because it depends somewhat on Tim's performance of gender at his parents' house. Of course, Matthew has options—he and Tim can decide to refrain from being affectionate during their visit; to hug and kiss freely, regardless of who is present; or to stay elsewhere while they visit Tim's parents. The point is that Matthew's anticipation stage is complex and requires him to think consciously about what he wants and what he will do.

Anticipating a performance can be relatively routine when you can rely on your habitual gender performances to prepare. When there are perceived tensions between your internal gender stories and the situation you are entering, however, it can be quite involved. Of course, whatever you anticipate prior to a performance may or may not play out during the actual encounter. Although you have a great deal of control over your own behaviors, you have very little or none over the behaviors of your audience members. The anticipation stage of a performance puts you in the position of having an initial plan for initiating a performance that may—and usually does—have to be modified as you interact with other people.

ENACTMENT

Just as the anticipation stage requires the juggling of several factors, the enactment of a gender performance also involves consideration of multiple factors. The enactment of a gender performance is always con-textual, fluid, and affected by multiple interactions among the setting, audience, and performer. To say that an enactment is contextual means that each performance materializes and develops in response to the par-ticular configuration of these three elements. Consequently, an enactment of gender cannot be precisely replicated in different performances. Enact-ments are always fluid. Whatever you plan during the anticipation stage or whatever your experiences in the past have been, an actual perfor-mance involves adapting and changing your performance to meet the novel dynamics of a particular encounter. Anticipation of a setting, audi-ence, and performer provides a sense of what a performance might look like, but because human behavior—your own and that of other people—is to some degree always spontaneous and unpredictable, you cannot know how a performance will play out until you are in the situation.

Each of your gender performances involves all of your nonverbal and verbal behaviors. *Nonverbal communication* refers to all of the messages that you convey through means other than words. These include behav-iors such as your appearance, facial expressions, and how you use space and touch to communicate with others. *Verbal communication* refers to all of the messages you convey through language. The words you use, how you say or write them, and the meanings you intend as well as those that your audience attributes are all part of verbal communication.

Verbal and nonverbal behaviors have shared cultural meanings that enable people to perform and to interpret gender performances effec-tively, but cultural meanings themselves do not determine how people act. People who don't know each other very well, for example, usually sit and stand farther from one another. Similarly, a smile is considered to be an appropriate expression during a happy or funny occasion and is gener-ally understood to convey pleasure. While behaviors like distance between strangers and smiling have shared cultural meanings, an actual performance involves negotiating between established cultural meanings for behaviors and the contextual interactions among a performer, setting, and audience. This negotiation may result in enactments that do not con-form to cultural norms or that carry additional meanings. Cultural stan-dards dictate that strangers maintain distance between each other, but if you are in a church or a courtroom and want to communicate with some-one you don't know, you have to be quite close in order to speak softly and be heard. In certain situations—when someone makes a comment that embarrasses you, for example—your smile is likely to mean that you are nervous or annoyed and not that you are pleased or happy. These examples illustrate the fact that cultural norms and meanings do not always determine how a behavior plays out during a gender performance.

In this section, we discuss some aspects of nonverbal and verbal behavior to explore how various aspects of communication affect gender performances. The nonverbal behaviors are (1) appearance and artifacts, (2) use of space, (3) use of touch, (4) eye contact and facial expression, and (5) vocal quality. The verbal behaviors are (1) conversational patterns, and (2) language choice. For each behavior, we define cultural norms and illustrate how they might be modified in actual performances. We then provide examples of the contextual and fluid nature of the enactment of gender stories.

NONVERBAL COMMUNICATION

A large part of any gender performance is nonverbal. How you look and act are fundamental ways by which you communicate to other people who you think you are—you share your gender stories by dressing in a particular style, carrying objects that convey something of yourself, and moving—walking, running, and gesturing, for example—in ways that your audience interprets as meaningful expressions of your internal self.

Appearance and Artifact. The most obvious aspect of any gender performance is the nonverbal communication that occurs as a result of your appearance. Your appearance includes your facial and body shape, height and weight, hair and skin color, and perceived attractiveness. Artifacts are those physical objects that you use to express your gender identity such as clothing, purses, backpacks, and hats. In Western cultures, appearance matters a great deal, and there is a common understanding that how you look says something important about you.[17] How you look can cause people to immediately classify you as a certain gender, as a member of certain groups, and as a type of person—artistic, conservative, modest, or flamboyant, for example.

Standards of attractiveness vary from culture to culture, from era to era, and even within different subcultures—ethnic groups and age cohorts, for example—but in any group, there are norms of appearance that define what is attractive and unattractive, acceptable and unacceptable. You know that being attractive to your friends can involve planning a different "look" than being attractive to your grandmother. In all performances, your appearance plays a part in how you tell your gender story. You may assemble different appearances depending on whether you are motivated to conform to an audience's standards of how you should look or whether you want to be perceived as eccentric. Bomba explains his intention to distinguish himself from other members of his group like this: "In the theater department, everyone tries to have a style that's their own. My thing—for now—is my green hair." Both the norms and standards of groups to which you belong and your own motivations with regard to those standards contribute to the appearance you assemble for a performance.

Sometimes, you decide on the appearance you will present during the anticipation stage, and it remains stable during a performance. In the morning before school, you might pull on a pair of jeans, your knee-high boots, and a hoodie; pick up your backpack and cell phone; and be set for the day. When you get ready for work, you might have a standard outfit—perhaps black slacks and a white, button-down shirt—that you do not alter during your shift. Often, however, interactions with a setting or an audience prompt changes in your appearance. If you have to sit for an hour-long lecture in a cold classroom, you might pull a scarf out of your backpack to wrap around your neck and shoulders; if the sun is bright, you might put on sunglasses. If you wake up to unexpected heavy snow on the morning you have to give a major presentation, you might wear snow boots instead of fancy dress shoes—an act that changes your gender appearance. The physical setting, then, can cause a performer to respond by making alterations in appearance through the use of artifacts.

During performances, interactions with audiences often cause performers to change their appearance. In the above example of anticipation, Yesenia finished her story by saying that she decided to get ready to go to the club by dressing like her women friends in heels, low-riding jeans, and a low-cut blouse. In other words, she was motivated during the anticipation stage to fit in with her friends. When she and her friends arrived at the club and sat at a table near the stage, several men approached and asked them to dance. When Yesenia turned down one man's invitation, he pulled up a chair next to her and sat staring at her breasts, making comments about how "fine" and "sexy" she was. "He was a big guy and sexually aggressive toward me—he kept stroking my back. I became very uncomfortable and angry because I think women should be able to look however they want without creeps bothering them. I made him leave—I was pretty forceful—but I also ended up putting on a sweater to cover my chest."

Daniel provides an example of changing appearance in response to a specific audience when he described living in Denver, Colorado, where, he says, people in general wear casual clothing and have widely varying interpretations of being "dressed up." Reflecting the importance that Western binary culture places on enacting a well-groomed gender performance at certain events, Daniel told about showing up at a friend's evening wedding in the mountains wearing a suit, only to find that most guests his age were in fleece jackets and jeans: "I quickly ditched my coat and tie and rolled up my sleeves." Daniel exhibited a common response to entering a scene where the audience causes you to feel overdressed—altering your appearance to fit in.

The examples of Yesenia and Daniel provide illustrations of power dynamics at play in performances. Remember that power differences influence performance behaviors. In Daniel's case, the importance he places on his peers gave his audience temporary power over him. You might not be used to thinking of peer pressure in terms of power, but people whose approval is important to you often have a high degree of influence on how you choose to behave. Yesenia's case involves power dynamics that reflect the social hierarchy of Western culture that privileges men over women. This hierarchy is reinforced by what psychology professor Nancy Henley calls the *micropolitical structure* of everyday life, the routine ways in which social dominance is played out.[18] This social dominance can be seen when, despite clear signals that women don't want to interact with them, men feel empowered to continue to make sexualized advances and comments. In Yesenia's case, these dynamics meant she not only felt bothered by the man who commented on her body but also somewhat intimidated and threatened by his unwanted and sexualized attention.

The Use of Space.   The study of how people use personal space as a means of communication is called *proxemics*. Personal space is that distance around your body that you consider your private sphere; as you move around, this sphere or bubble moves with you. The outer edge of your private sphere is defined by how comfortable you are having other people share this space with you. Think of how close you stand to your best friend or your mother compared to how far away you stand from people you don't know in a near-empty elevator or in a line at a bank. Personal space conveys information about relationships—in general, you stand or sit closer to someone you know well and like than you do to someone who is only an acquaintance. While your personal bubble might vary in any given situation, there are probably distances that make you feel at ease and distances that make you feel somewhat anxious or as though someone were intruding or encroaching on your space.[19]

As with all social behaviors, there are cultural norms guiding the use of space, and certain distances are seen as appropriate and normal for certain kinds of social relationships.[20] Because these norms are socially constructed, they vary from culture to culture. In Western culture, there are quite specific parameters for different social interactions. Intimate distance—the type of distance maintained by people who know each other well—is from zero to eighteen inches. Personal distance—the distance observed between friends and close acquaintances—is eighteen inches to four feet. Social distance—the distance maintained between people who are strangers—is four to twelve feet, and public distance—the distance used between speakers and audiences, for example—is twelve to twenty-five feet.[21] These guidelines, or the *habitus* for space use, may constitute the automatic and default ways you are accustomed to positioning yourself around other people. Your actual use of space also might be different. Priya, who grew up in Bombay and has lived in the US for ten years, says, "In India, people stand much closer together than they do here. So, when I'm at school or work, I observe the norms I've learned, but when I'm at home with my family, we're so close we're touching when we cook, clean, and watch TV." Priya's personal sense of space varies across contexts because of different cultural norms.

Cultural norms also define which people—which characters in a performance—are allowed to make decisions regarding the use of space and how people react to encroachments on their personal territory. In general, those who have more status in or power over a situation—parents, bosses, and the president, for example—have priority when space is allocated in a certain context. In the US, parents may routinely sit in the front seats of a car, while their children sit in back. Even children who are old enough that they don't need to occupy the back seats for safety reasons often sit there because fathers and mothers have more power and thus access to the best spaces in a car. Bosses often have their own offices, while employees often share common space divided into cubicles. There is a radius of space that surrounds the US president, and unless audience members receive signals—the president holds out a hand to shake or gestures to come closer—they are likely to keep a respectful distance. Culture also provides information regarding how people react to the use of space. If a person you don't know enters an elevator and takes a position so that your bodies are almost touching, you probably feel invaded or even sexually threatened. When someone with whom you want to be intimate moves closer—when your date moves next to you on the couch, for example—the act elicits a different type of socialized response.

Cultural norms outline the uses of space that are generally considered appropriate for certain types of gender performances, but the actual use of space always depends on the interactions among the performer, the audience, and the setting. As the following examples show, an actual gender performance is always a negotiation among factors—cultural norms, individual motivation, the relationships among the people involved, and the specific encounter. These factors may require different uses of space from those established by the general rules of a culture.

Imagine that you have scheduled a meeting with your professor to discuss your final paper. Throughout the semester, you have done well in the class, have had several meetings to discuss your class projects, and the two of you are on friendly terms. You anticipate an enjoyable meeting, and you feel comfortable at the prospect of entering her office and asking questions. Your motivation is to maintain your good relationship and to get the information you need to turn in an excellent paper. Because you feel comfortable, you probably do not think about your use of space, and you are likely to adopt the spatial dynamics that the two of you have established in the past—you sit in a chair pulled up to the side of her desk. While the two of you look through your draft, you are considerably closer than the four to twelve feet that is culturally defined as social distance or even the eighteen inches to four feet that is defined as personal distance. Yet, you likely feel at ease and have no sense that your own bubble has been invaded or that you are intruding on her space. The actual circumstances of the setting, your audience, and you as the performer take precedence, in this case, over general cultural norms.

Your use of space in this same situation is likely to change if you have a different anticipation of the performance or if the professor behaves differently. For example, if you have never interacted face to face with your professor, have failed a major exam, have exceeded the number of absences listed as acceptable in the syllabus, and need to write a good paper to be able to pass the class, you might enter her office with less confidence and be hesitant to sit close to her. In contrast to the circumstances described in the previous paragraph, you are likely to have a heightened awareness of your professor's relative status and to be more watchful for her cues as to how you should move about her office. Even if your professor is welcoming, your awareness of the importance of this performance could cause you to stay at the door until invited in, stand until invited to sit, and keep your chair at a social distance from hers. You might even feel more comfortable sitting with the desk between the two of you. If your professor never invites you to come closer, of course, your use of space is likely to reflect the distance she implies by her behavior. The point is that an actual performance—the choices you make about space—are the result of complex personal and social factors.

Space is a particularly clear example of the ways in which gender performances are fluid and depend on a performer's responses to setting and audience. The use of space can and usually does change several times during a single performance, and your knowledge of cultural space rules and a history of using space with certain people must be supplemented with a more immediate ability to evaluate spatial factors. You usually make minor adjustments to space without conscious thought. Ten more people enter the room at a party, for example, and you stand closer to your friends to make room for them. The woman sitting next to you on the bus pulls her coat tighter, and you can tell she feels you are too close, so you shift away. During a conversation, your friend's sudden stiffened posture tells you he is angry, and you step back. If you are in a less accommodating mood, you might refuse to make room for other partiers, the woman on the bus, or your friend's anger. Your own behavioral choices about the use of space are always determined by a combination of your intentions, other people's behavior, and cultural norms.

The Use of Touch. During gender performances, different types of touch convey different messages. Snuggling on the couch with your friend while you watch a movie has a different meaning from sitting in separate chairs. Touching someone on the forearm has a different meaning from touching someone's lips or hair. Like the use of space, different kinds of touch are associated with different relationships. In general, the more familiar and intimate you are with another person, the more freely and often you touch. But because touch is a highly nuanced form of communication, touch expresses more than the nature of your relationship with someone. The same form of touch—rubbing someone's head, for example—can communicate a range of messages from playful to serious, warm to cold, friendly to threatening, and sexual or not. The way you touch someone can communicate power, affection, a desire to comfort, attraction, or even indifference. The study of how people use touch as a means of communication is called *haptics.*

Like the use of space, the cultural norms governing haptics are different in different cultures, and Western culture has adopted specific guidelines to communicate different types of relationships. Love-intimate touch is the type of touch reserved for intimate partners, family members, and very close friends. Friendship touch is the kind of touch that characterizes people in friendships, and although such touch is highly variable, it generally conveys that people are close and feel caring and warm toward one another. Social-polite touch defines ways of touching people with whom you come into contact during routine encounters—shaking hands, touching fingers briefly when handing someone something, or the unavoidable touching that occurs in a crowded elevator or bus. Professional touch is the kind of physical contact made by people whose professions involve touch—physicians and physical therapists, for example. Members of Western cultures are socialized to recognize and maintain boundaries among the types of touches appropriate for various relationships.

Just as with the use of space, cultural norms define who can touch whom in what ways and how people are supposed to react to touch. People who have more power in a situation often feel entitled to touch people who have less power or status. Parents, for example, take a child's hand to cross a street without asking the child's permission or checking to see if the child is comfortable with that touch. A boss might put a hand on an employee's shoulder to communicate approval, and a ballet instructor might hold a student's thigh to illustrate a certain dance position. These forms of touching, based on certain relationships, are socially acceptable. However, if a parent slaps a child in the face, a boss touches an employee on the breast, or a dance teacher aggressively twists a student's foot, norms are violated. Part of socialization is the ability to recognize different types of touch as positive, negative, sexual, friendly, comforting, or abusive and to respond appropriately. Affective or emotional reactions to touch—to someone shaking your hand, touching your shoulder to get your attention, or kissing you to show affection, for example—are such an ingrained part of the *habitus* that, in most situations, people tend to employ cultural standards of touching and responding without thinking about them.

Cultural norms, however, interact with specific performers, audiences, and settings to yield great variation in actual touching behaviors. A particular context, in other words, causes you to conform to, adapt to, or even intentionally to disregard cultural guidelines. You might decide that a situation in which people normally avoid touching—standing in the aisle of a crowded bus, for example—calls for touch as you firmly take the arm of an elderly woman who is having trouble with her balance. While intimate partners usually feel free to touch each other, Jess's description of an experience with her boyfriend on her birthday illustrates how this is not always true: "He totally forgot and didn't get me a present or say anything. He didn't get the message until that evening when he tried to be romantic, and I made it clear that I didn't want to be touched. When he figured out why, he felt terrible." As with any kind of behavioral choices, then, actual touching behavior depends not only on cultural norms but on complex interactions among the performer, audience, and setting.

If you arrive at the airport late at night to meet your romantic partner after his business trip, your anticipatory state depends on a number of factors, including how the two of you related when you were last together, what your usual routine is when greeting each other, and your mood and physical state—whether you feel happy or sad, have had a good or a bad day, and are energetic or tired. Perhaps your customary behavior is to hug and kiss passionately in public, or you may have established a routine of greeting each other with a friendly hug and peck on the cheek. Perhaps you have a bottle of wine chilling in the refrigerator at home and candles ready to light, or you may have had a long, hard day and be slightly resentful that you have had to drive to the airport late at night when your partner could easily have taken a cab. As a performer, you enter the scene with your romantic partner with certain feelings and expectations, and these have a direct effect on your touching behavior. Responding to any of these variables means making slight shifts in your gender performance—shifts that change your gender presentation for yourself and for your audience.

Your own anticipatory state, however, does not completely determine how touch plays out in the actual scene because both the setting and your audience are factors. The airport waiting area may be so crowded that to take up public space to hug and kiss would impede the flow of people trying to get off the concourse. The announcements over the public address system or the people around you might be so noisy that you can't make your warm greeting heard. You could be standing next to an elderly couple or a priest and feel inhibited about passionately touching your partner. Your partner himself also affects your touching behavior. If, when you reach for a hug and kiss, he pulls away, your performance is much different than if he embraces you. Regardless of your planned touching behavior, your actual touching performance is modified as you negotiate both the setting and your audience.

Eye Contact and Facial Expression. The proverb "The eyes are the windows of the soul" is partially true—a person's facial expression can reflect an inner state—but the saying obscures the fact that interpreting thoughts and feelings from a person's face is not always a straightforward process. People can intentionally hide their inner states, as when they adopt a "poker face," for example. Some conditions—like autism or severe depression—cause people to have facial expressions that are not easily translated, and some people simply are not very emotionally expressive. Other people express a great deal on their faces, and audience members can easily tell what they are thinking and feeling, even if they don't want to reveal that information.

The ability to interpret other people's emotions accurately is key to social competence and to success in intimate relationships; family dynamics; and many professions like psychotherapy, police work, politics, and sales.[22] The ability to interpret other people's facial expressions correctly varies from person to person. How expressive your family was, how emotionally intense you yourself tend to be, and your own style of emotional expression are factors that complicate your reading of others' expressions.[23] This means that, during a gender performance, the messages you intend to send through your eyes and facial expression may not be clearly understood by your audience.

Despite the potential for many complications, there are cultural norms for facial expressions that assist the performer in scripting intended performances. Nonverbal communication research indicates that primary emotions like happiness, sadness, anger, surprise, fear, and disgust are probably innate and therefore are fairly easy to interpret even across cultures.[24] Eye contact—how much and how long people should look at each other—definitely varies from culture to culture. Most North Americans make more eye contact than most Chinese, for example. Because most people in Western cultures share common interpretations for facial expressions and eye movements, you can usually ascertain a great deal of information by looking at a person's face. Even a glance usually tells you if someone is interested in, feels ambivalent toward, or feels negatively toward you or the subject you are talking about. You can also tell if someone in your audience is in a good or a bad mood, is receptive or shut down, and is relaxed or tense because you have been socialized to associate certain inner states with certain facial expressions and eye movements.

In most circumstances, shared cultural norms allow you to communicate much of the emotional content and inner state you want to share when you perform gender by using eye movements and facial expressions. You are undoubtedly aware of the many ways in which you can convey information with your face and eyes. In US culture, a common norm is to show interest in your audience by making eye contact and smiling and to show disinterest by refusing to make eye contact and looking bored or adopting a flat, unemotional expression. A smile can communicate that you are approachable and friendly; a scowl can communicate that you want to be left alone. Eyes and a mouth that are wide open show people you are surprised or scared, and a tightly closed mouth can indicate that you are stressed or angry.

Despite shared cultural norms, there are no hard and set rules for the meanings of eye movements and expressions. The complicated nature of eye movements and facial expressions in communicating messages is illustrated by considering one behavior—staring, for example—in different contexts. Although children in Western cultures are often told that staring is impolite, in many situations, staring is a socially appropriate behavior that communicates a variety of messages. Students exhibit their interest in what a professor is saying, in part, by looking directly at her. People who are romantically involved with one another often gaze into each other's eyes as an expression of warmth and, at times, of sexual interest. But staring can also express relational power dynamics, establishing who in a performance feels dominant and in control. In some business situations and sports interactions, for example, staring at another person conveys a sense of relative strength and may be used as a form of coercion or intimidation. Staring at someone on the street or in a bar, for example, can convey a sense of entitlement—that the other person exists as an object available for visual consumption—and may be experienced as sexually threatening. There is not one cultural rule that always applies. Whether you stare or not during a gender performance depends on your setting, audience, and motivation.

In terms of planning your own gender performance, awareness of eye movements and facial expressions can help you convey the story you want to share, but remember that your audience still may misinterpret your performance. Katherine puts it this way: "As a lesbian woman who, because of how I dress and wear my hair, looks fairly straight, I've realized that the way I act around men can sometimes be confusing for them. If a man starts talking to me in a coffee shop and I am interested in what he is saying, I make lots of eye contact, lean toward him, and smile. But because these are usual heterosexual cues of accessibility or openness, he may think I am interested in him. It's an awkward line for me because I want to be friendly, but I don't want to be hit on. I wish that, culturally, we had more subtle cues to convey romantic interest." Katherine's example points out how, as a performer, you cannot control your audience's interpretation of your eye contact and facial expressions.

Lara tells how nonverbal behaviors related to eye movements and facial expressions are having a negative effect on her relationship with her new boyfriend: "I know he cares about me, but half the time, when I'm talking to him, he's looking at his phone or playing some game. I don't know if it's because of differences in how we were raised, but we don't seem to have the same sense of what listening to someone means. When I ask him to listen, I mean I want him to look at me, but he says he *is* listening and repeats exactly what I just said to prove it." In this situation, Lara's boyfriend's performance of eye contact and facial expression is having an effect on an important relationship. According to Lara, her boyfriend is failing to execute a gender performance that conveys warmth and attentiveness—he is not performing according to Lara's expectations for a couple in a romantic relationship. Whether or not his intention is to communicate a lack of interest, this is how Lara interprets his performance.

Vocal Quality. Vocal quality refers to those vocal characteristics that determine the way your voice sounds; it enables you to tell one person's voice from another's. It includes rate of speech, volume, intensity, pitch, inflection, and resonance. Rate of speech is how many words you speak per minute, while volume is how loud or soft your speech is. Intensity refers to choices about which words or sentences you choose to emphasize. Pitch designates how high or low a tone is, and inflection has to do with variations in pitch—whether a voice is singsong or monotone, for example. Resonance relates to how a vocal sound is amplified in the chest, throat, and mouth or how full the sound is.

Vocal qualities have particular cultural associations and contribute in specific ways to gender performance. Different vocal qualities such as rate, pitch, volume, and resonance are culturally linked with different self-presentations and different levels of status or power. Rapid speech, a loud voice, low pitch, and strong resonance are associated in Western cultures with competence; self-confidence; and an authoritative, more powerful presentation. Renowned motivational speakers, for example, often exhibit this performance style. Halting or tentative speech, a soft voice, high pitch, and thin resonance are associated with weakness, insecurity, a lack of self-assurance, and less power.[25] Think about when you are being interviewed for a job, a situation in which you obviously have less power than the people who are interviewing you. In such a situation, you might find yourself adopting this performance style. Because of cultural interpretations of different performance styles, status and power are culturally linked to the confident, authoritative style.

Cultural associations with vocal styles do not universally guide performances or interpretations because actual gender performances depend on the context of a specific setting, audience, and performer. While using a deep, booming voice might be an asset if you are a military officer or in charge of a sports team, there are many performances where a higher and softer voice is necessary in order to achieve social status and success. Psychotherapists who are counseling clients, ministers who are comforting parishioners, and doctors who are discussing sensitive matters with their patients are all successful people with a great deal of social status whose effectiveness in some performances depends on their ability to be sensitive to their audiences and relatively soft spoken as well as self-confident and competent. There are many situations when an authoritative or dominating style simply will not result in social success. Depending on your motivation, then, you will make choices about the vocal qualities and conversational patterns you adopt.

Behruz expressed the complicated nature of vocal style and how a particular performance can violate cultural norms: "My father doesn't approve of my lifestyle in America—specifically, he doesn't like that my girlfriend and I live together or, as he would say, 'in sin.' My father intends to make us split up, so, when Anna and I visit him, he either won't talk to Anna at all, or he talks in a really slow, quiet voice that makes her pay close attention to hear what he's saying. He's very controlling." Behruz is illustrating how the vocal qualities of a slow rate and low volume can be just as dominating as a rapid, loud voice and how someone might try to gain power using such strategies.

Verbal Communication

Most gender performances involve verbal communication or communication that is achieved through the use of words to convey meanings. Sometimes, you perform in settings where you are the only person talking—when you give a demonstration at a training session, act out a monologue on stage, or give a presentation in one of your classes, for example. But most gender performances involve conversations with other people. A large part of how you share your internal gender stories is through conversations where you talk with and listen to your audiences—as when you chat about the weather with the barista who makes your latte, discuss the upcoming elections with your neighbor, or negotiate vacation plans with your partner. In each context, you vary how you communicate verbally—your talk is more or less intimate, and you use different language expressions depending on the setting and audience. In every context, your conversational patterns and word choice are two aspects of verbal communication that impact your gender performance. As with all behaviors, a balance between cultural norms and the actual setting, audience, and performer results in a variety of verbal performances.

Conversational Patterns. Conversational patterns involve your skills at listening to and talking with other people. Such patterns include how much or how little you talk, the degree to which you interrupt or listen, how assertive or unassertive you are, and how direct or indirect you tend to be. Conversational patterns are those aspects of your gender performance that involve talking to other people and knowing "when to speak or be silent, how to speak on each occasion, and how to communicate and interpret respect, seriousness, humor, politeness, and intimacy."[26] In various contexts, your choices in these areas contribute in significant ways to your gender performances.

Western cultural norms attach different meanings to different conversational patterns. Certain conversational patterns carry a meaning of dominance, and other patterns carry a meaning of submissiveness. A dominant conversational pattern involves talking a lot, interrupting, and being assertive and direct. This style often is interpreted as not only powerful but also impolite, unresponsive to the conversational needs of others, and self-centered. A submissive, less powerful conversational pattern often involves listening more than talking, allowing interruptions, and being unassertive and indirect. This style can be seen as polite but also deferential, overly sensitive to the conversational needs of others, and eager to please.

You undoubtedly have had experience with both of these conversational styles during gender performances in different contexts. One example of how context affects a performance is Sonja's friend Frank, who exhibits the dominant style on first dates when he is particularly nervous—he talks nonstop and doesn't ask his date questions. Although he intends to be likable and to make a good impression, he comes across as dominating, uninterested in the other person, and self-centered. Another context generates another kind of conversational performance. You might generally be a talkative, assertive person, but when you are at work, interacting with your boss, you might adopt a more submissive conversational pattern in which you are deferential and do not talk much simply because of the power difference between the two of you. The setting in which you find yourself, your relationship with your audience, and your own motives and desires all influence the adoption of a conversational pattern for a particular gender performance.

Cultural norms might stipulate that a dominant conversational style involves monopolizing conversations, but this pattern does not always hold. Ramón provides an example of how cultural norms for verbal behavior are complicated by specific contexts. Ramón works in a large university library, where he supervises the research librarians. He told us about problems he is having with a new employee: "Sean is extremely well qualified, but he isn't good at relating to people. Helping academicians with their research means you not only have to be able to hear what people are asking for, you have to be able to extrapolate and figure out how our collection fits into their needs. This requires high-level listening skills—you have to listen more than talk. Sean doesn't get that—he interrupts and is directive. I'm not sure he'll work out here." Sean's performance is confident and dominant, but this gender performance is hurting rather than helping his status and success in this setting and with this audience.

In most situations, effective conversational performance involves enacting neither a predetermined dominating nor a submissive style. In most contexts, you choose a mixture of conversational features that produce a performance that cannot be characterized as either dominating or submissive. A simple example is when you go out for coffee with a friend, and you adopt a symmetrical conversational style. You each talk about the same amount, you listen to each other, you refrain from interrupting, and you are both equally assertive and direct. A more complex example is when you are trying to negotiate a better rate for your phone or Internet service with a customer-service representative. In this case, you do not have the power in the situation, so you might be deferential and polite but also direct and assertive. Your conversational patterns are always complicated, then, by various combinations of actual performers, settings, and audiences.

Word Choice.   Language is powerful. Words can be limiting or empowering, toxic or healing, and conducive to desired gender interactions or destructive to those interactions.[27] "I love you," "I hate you," "You rock!" and "Fuck you!" are all phrases that convey important messages that are significant enough to influence and change relationships. Psychologist Mary Crawford points out that talk—like music—constitutes a set of skills and a performing art that are "nuanced and open to many interpretations."[28] An effective gender performance involves crafting verbal messages that your audience can interpret whether you are conversing with your best friend, your mother, or your manager at work. Crafting understandable verbal messages as part of a gender performance involves both word choice and your motivations for an interaction.

Different groups of people react differently to specific words, and choosing to use some words and not others can indicate an intention to be respectful or disrespectful toward certain audiences. An example of this dynamic occurs in Mary's public speaking classes. One of Mary's motivations in the class is to nurture an environment in which students feel they can freely express their ideas, and she starts the term by asking students to jot down words they don't want to hear in the classroom. She turns the words into a list on which to base a discussion about the power of choosing to use certain words and phrases over others. This year, predictable words that showed up on the list were *fag, dyke, cunt, homo, bitch, gay, retarded,* and *you guys.* As usual, the list sparked interesting discussions as students shared their thoughts and feelings. "I use *gay* to describe myself," Terrence said, "but I don't want to hear the word used to describe something that is lame." Ruby said she gets irritated—"I feel entirely ignored and left out"—when she hears the phrase *you guys* used to refer to a group of men and women or to a group composed exclusively of women. Erin explained the word she contributed to the list: "My brother is a special needs child, and I don't appreciate hearing *retarded,* or worse, *retard.*" As these students voiced their desires as audience members not to hear certain words, they also indicated the kinds of performances toward which they would not be receptive.

Other words on the list were not as predictable: *hick, Zionist, terrorist,* and *God.* "I grew up in rural Kansas," Marcus shared, "and I'm tired of people here acting superior just because they live in a city, so that's why I put *hick* on the list." "I know *Zionist* is historically descriptive," Rebecca said, "but it hasn't been used in a non-anti-Semitic way since the 1950s." A discussion of the word *terrorist* revealed students' concerns that Muslims are often characterized in negative ways in the media, and they didn't want to replicate that negativity in the classroom. Stephen's reflection that he is an evangelical Christian who is offended when people take "the Lord's name in vain" explains why the word *God* showed up on the list. "I just ask that you use the name with respect," he said. While a performance always is affected by language use, these examples show that, even if a performer is fairly sensitive to a setting and audience and intends to be respectful, there may be word choices that offend some people.

On the other hand, if a performer's motivation is to offend, knowing which words are likely to insult an audience can facilitate an effective offensive gender performance. If you know your father doesn't like cursing and you do it around him anyway, you may be thoughtless, but you might also be indicating that you are choosing to be disrespectful. If your sister prefers to be called *Ms.* and you refer to her as *Mrs.,* you indicate that you are making a choice to offend her. Likewise, if students in Mary's class, despite knowing which words will trigger negative audience responses, use those words anyway, they display an intention to provoke. Sometimes, offending your audience during a gender performance may occur due to another, more primary or important, motivation—to perform the person you believe yourself to be. "My family is traditional," Gretta explains. "The fact that I kept my last name when I got married is not acceptable to my parents. Whenever I introduce myself as 'Gretta Adler,' they act insulted. I'm sorry they feel bad, but I'm not going to change my name." Gretta shows the complications that can arise when competing motivations—pleasing other people and being yourself, for example—must be negotiated in a gender performance.

Another complicating dynamic regarding word choice in performances involves the kind of talk in which you intend to engage. Do you want to appear relational and focused on the nature of the relationship between you and other people, or do you want to appear focused on content and on the giving and receiving of information? This motivational aspect of verbal style depends on the context. When you are motivated to be relational in a gender performance, you choose words that convey this meaning, which might be as simple as planning to ask questions that allow others to express themselves freely. When you meet someone new at a party or analyze the state of your relationship with a new lover, for example, you engage in a kind of verbal give and take. If your goal during a gender performance is to convey information, you might choose to be less relational, keeping the talk focused through word choice on only certain topics. Giving a lecture, explaining to your parents why you want to move out of a dorm into your own apartment, or advising a buyer on what kind of car to purchase are examples where your word choice likely directs the exchange along certain lines. As with any behavioral aspect of gender performance, your motivation has an impact on your word choice.

Word choice also can indicate power dynamics. Among the ways people who have more power or status in a particular setting exhibit their relative power is by using language that less powerful people do not understand or by adopting a different style from the others who are present. The language of certain professions—medicine, the law, and academia, for example—is full of technical words and jargon that only people in these fields fully comprehend. A lawyer who uses the terms *indemnity, tort,* or *voir dire,* for example, may make people outside of the field feel less capable, intimidated, and less powerful. On the other hand, a lawyer who uses the phrases *a contract to protect you, a civil wrong like malpractice,* or *the questions used to choose jurors* signals a desire to adopt a more symmetrical style by using language that a lay audience can understand.

Louie talks about the power dynamics of casual and formal language when he remembers visiting his girlfriend's parents for the first time. "I'm from Utah, and Francine's parents live in Connecticut. Easterners have the reputation of being stiffer than Westerners, but I knew their behavior was their way of saying they didn't approve of me and didn't want their daughter to marry me. I refused to be cowed, and they came around, but it was a real power play that first visit. They tried to make me feel like a total unsophisticate by using French phrases and talking about the *Hamptons* and the *Vineyard*. I had no idea what they were talking about." Francine's parents adopted a specialized language around Louie in an attempt to intimidate him.

The relationship between context and a performer's motivation for word choice is extremely nuanced. Consider the phrase "I've had a really long day." If you say this to your roommate when you come home from work at midnight, you might simply be describing your day, but if you say this same phrase on a first date at 8:30 in the evening, you likely mean something else—that you aren't having a good time and are ready to go home. Likewise, the phrase "that's interesting" can mean you really are fascinated by what someone is saying, that you disapprove of what is being said, or even that you think what has been expressed is totally ridiculous or stupid. Because the meanings of words depend so highly on specific contexts, an effective performance depends on a performer's ability to match motivation, language choice, and audience.

Word choice is an important aspect of any gender performance. As a performer, the words you choose reflect your motivation for an encounter, your assessment of the audience, and the setting. An effective verbal presentation depends not only on your vocal quality and conversational style but on your word choice. The words you use during a performance have the power to engage or alienate your audience members, show your level of respect for them, and convey your willingness to dominate or share power.

AGENCY IN PERFORMING GENDER STORIES

Although many of your gender performances during dramas of daily life likely occur without conscious thought on your part, we hope the discussion of performance stages and behaviors in this chapter helps you be more aware of the choices you have when you anticipate and enact your gender stories. Just as an effective stage actor approaches each performance as an opportunity to embody a character creatively—by wearing a certain costume, gesturing and moving in ways that bring a character to life and speaking lines an audience will understand—so, too, you can intentionally create and enact the self you want others to experience.

Because effectively communicating with others depends on your ability to assess and respond to your settings and audiences, you can begin by consciously enacting agency during your anticipation of a gender performance. When you anticipate a performance, you can choose to negotiate among your own desires and motivations, the cultural norms for various situations and behaviors, and the specific audience and setting you will encounter. You can be deliberate in deciding whether your best strategy for enacting an effective performance is to be transparent or to hide part of your gender identity. You can think clearly about whether your primary aim for a gender performance is to conform to a group's standards and norms, to present yourself in a unique and individual fashion, or even to challenge your audience. You can consider beforehand whether you want to be respectful or offensive. Of course, when you are anticipating a gender performance, you may have a combination of intentions—to be partly transparent and to conform to some, but not all, of a group's standards, for example. Because performances are interactions with audiences and you cannot predetermine other people's behavior or reactions, there are elements of a performance that are beyond your control. This dynamic will be discussed more fully in chapter 8, but there are always several levels on which you can enact your agency. Such conscious consideration of an upcoming performance puts you in the position of being able to make decisions that contribute to the successful sharing of your gender stories.

You can also become conscious of the potential to craft new or modified gender stories for yourself through performances. Performances are a particularly powerful way to try out new themes and potential plot lines. Mary was reminded of this recently when she entered a women's restroom at a grocery store and struck up a conversation with a woman who was standing at the mirror braiding her hair. The woman told Mary that she was transgender and went on to say: "I'm here trying out some things for myself. I'm figuring out, as a new woman, what works for me and what doesn't in different social situations." This woman was performing new aspects of her gender identity in front of an audience as part of the process of further developing her gender story. This encounter is a reminder that all people, regardless of their internal stories, can test and recraft personal narratives through enacting them in front of other people. When you use gender performances as an exploration—for example, when you wear pink instead of black, sign up for wrestling instead of swimming, or ask your friends to call you *Kit* instead of *Christine*—you consciously choose to expand your sense of self through performances.

Remember that you create and reinforce your own gender identity through performances and that your performances have an effect on cultural norms and categories. You weren't born a certain gender, and you don't have to continue to perform any gender simply because you are accustomed to looking and acting in certain ways or because of cultural norms and expectations regarding femininity and masculinity. If you have a routine and habitual gender performance with which you are comfortable and that truly expresses your internal gender stories, that's great. If, like many people, you sometimes experience tension around gender performances, have parts of yourself you have been hesitant to share, or simply are curious about how it might feel to look and act differently, we encourage you to expand your performance repertoire. You can, in other words, agentically decide to create new habitual and repeated performances that contribute to individual, social, and cultural gender stories.

The most obvious way you can be consciously agentic during any gender performance is by consciously choosing which nonverbal and verbal behaviors to enact and deciding on a combination of behaviors that convey your intended gender stories. You may have adopted certain ways of performing gender because other people expect them or exert pressure on you to stay a certain way. As we discussed in chapter 1, you can change even when change feels difficult or when the people around you are surprised or upset. You may suppress certain aspects of your gender stories because of social pressure or the fear of hostile or even violent responses. Even in these cases, you can maintain personal power by being conscious of the reasons for your choices. You can reframe your decisions as enacting agency to keep yourself safe from psychological or physical harm. The more conscious you are of always having choices about your performances, the more readily available different options become for looking and acting as you desire. By thoughtfully choosing to act and speak in ways that reflect who you think you are—that express the gender identity you want to share—you can be a more effective gender performer in all of your dramas of daily life.

■ NOTES

[1] Erving Goffman, *The Presentation of Self in Everyday Life* (Garden City, NY: Doubleday Anchor, 1959).

[2] Candace West and Don H. Zimmerman, "Doing Gender," *Gender and Society* 1 (1987): 145.

[3] West and Zimmerman, "Doing Gender," 136.

[4] Erica Rosenfeld Halverson, "From One Woman to Everyman: Reportability and Credibility in Publicly Performed Narratives," *Narrative Inquiry* 18 (2008), 31.

[5] Judith Butler, "Performance Acts and Gender Construction: An Essay in Phenomenology and Feminist Theory," in *The Performance Studies Reader*, ed. Henry Bial (New York: Routledge, 2004), 154.

6 West and Zimmerman, "Doing Gender," 126.

7 Peg Birmingham, "Towards an Ethic of Desire: Derrida, Fiction, and the Law of the Feminine," in *Feminist Interpretations of Jacques Derrida,* ed. Nancy J. Holland (University Park: Pennsylvania State University Press, 1997), 133.

8 Douglas Ezzy, "Theorizing Narrative Identity: Symbolic Interactionism and Hermeneutics," *Sociological Quarterly* 39 (1998): 250.

9 West and Zimmerman, "Doing Gender," 126.

10 M. Theodora Pintzuk, "Identity and Cultural Narrative in a Lesbian Relationship," *Journal of Couple and Relationship Therapy* 3 (2004): 28.

11 Goffman, *The Presentation of Self in Everyday Life.*

12 Susan B. Shimanoff, "Rules Theories," in *Encyclopedia of Communication Theory,* vol. 2, ed. Stephen W. Littlejohn and Karen A. Foss (Thousand Oaks, CA: Sage, 2009), 861–65.

13 Nancy M. Henley, *Body Politics: Power, Sex, and Nonverbal Communication* (Englewood Cliffs, NJ: Prentice-Hall, 1977), 2–3.

14 West and Zimmerman, "Doing Gender," 130.

15 Pierre Bourdieu, *The Logic of Practice,* trans. Richard Nice (Stanford, CA: Stanford University Press, 1990).

16 Henley, *Body Politics,* 73.

17 Jess K. Alberts, Thomas K. Nakayama, and Judith N. Martin, *Human Communication in Society,* 2nd ed. (Boston: Allyn & Bacon, 2010), 153.

18 Henley, *Body Politics,* 3.

19 Lea P. Stewart, Pamela J. Cooper, Alan D. Stewart, with Sheryl A. Friedley, *Communication and Gender,* 4th ed. (Boston: Allyn & Bacon, 2003), 41.

20 Alberts, Nakayama, and Martin, *Human Communication in Society,* 150.

21 Alberts, Nakayama, and Martin, *Human Communication in Society,* 149–50.

22 Klaus R. Scherer and Ursula Scherer, "Assessing the Ability to Recognize Facial and Vocal Expressions of Emotion: Construction and Validation of the Emotion Recognition Index," *Journal of Nonverbal Behavior* 35 (2011): 305–06.

23 Amy G. Halberstadt, Paul A. Dennis, and Ursula Hess, "The Influence of Family Expressiveness, Individual's Own Emotionality, and Self-Expressiveness on Perceptions of Others' Facial Expressions," *Journal of Nonverbal Behavior* 35 (2011): 46–49.

24 Alberts, Nakayama, and Martin, *Human Communication in Society,* 146.

25 Charlotte Krøløkke and Anne Scott Sorenson, *Gender Communication Theories and Analyses* (Thousand Oaks, CA: Sage, 2006), 90–91.

26 Stewart, Cooper, Stewart, with Friedley, *Communication and Gender,* 90.

27 Teri Kwal Gamble and Michael W. Gamble, *The Gender Communication Connection* (Boston: Houghton Mifflin, 2003), 59–61.

28 Mary Crawford, *Talking Difference: On Gender and Language* (Thousand Oaks, CA: Sage, 1995), xi.

eight

REWORKING
MANAGING RESPONSES
TO GENDER PERFORMANCES

In a certain sense we are always talking
about ourselves to ourselves if to no one else,
making plans about what we're going to do,
reviewing what we have done and thought and felt.

Paul John Eakin, *Living Autobiographically*

"Y ou aren't going out looking like that, are you?" "Dude, that's awesome!" "Dork!" "Lovely!" "Super cool, man!" "Fag!" "You go, girl!" These are responses to performances of gender. When you take your gender stories out in the world and share them with others, you receive such performance reviews. Your gender identity is either reflected back to you with comments suggesting that your audience likes your performance, or it is challenged and resisted with responses suggesting that your performance isn't appropriate. Once you have received an evaluation of a gender performance, you have the chance to remake and rework your performance in your response. The subject of this chapter is managing responses to gender performances, a process that involves (1) receiving performance reviews, and (2) responding to performance reviews.

Although we discuss the types of reviews others make to your performance and your possible responses to these reviews as a set of sequential steps or acts, the process is not a linear interaction. You don't perform a gender story, receive your audience's response to it, and then react to that response. Rather, you are constantly paying attention to an audience's reaction as you are performing a gender story, making adjustments, and deciding moment by moment whether to modify your performance. The audience, of course, is also responding to your adjustments. All of these things are happening simultaneously in a constantly evolving and interactive process.

RECEIVING PERFORMANCE REVIEWS

As you perform a gender story, audience members respond to it with reviews of your performance. Sometimes, the kind of review you get for a particular performance—whether one of approval or rejection—makes little difference to you. The review comes from someone you don't know, you won't see again, or who doesn't matter to you—the clerk in the check-out line in the grocery store, for example. But at other times, the reviews you receive matter a lot. You pay close attention in such cases because the nature of the reviews you are given affects the kind of relationship you have with someone, whether you fit into a group, the degree of self-confidence you feel in a certain context, and the kinds of actions you see as available to you. If you are harassed on the street by a lewd comment someone yells at you or someone smiles at you flirtatiously on the metro, for example, you might take such reviews seriously either to avoid or to receive similar ones in the future.

If someone important to you responds negatively to one of your gender performances—your manager criticizes your style of speech at meetings as too casual for a professional setting, for example—that negative response can mean you aren't seen to be fitting in very well with your work team, or you may not be meeting your manager's performance criteria; as a result, you may feel less confident about your ability to succeed in the organization. If your romantic partner dislikes a certain gender performance you try out—perhaps growing a goatee—you probably will give that review more careful consideration as well. Some audiences are more important to you than others, and you pay particular attention to the responses to your gender performances from those audiences.

The process of receiving and responding to performance reviews is complicated by the fact that your gender performance is often being witnessed by many different people who may respond in different ways to a gender performance. Certainly, there are many times when you perform gender for a single person, as when you interact with your roommate, a situation in which you can easily monitor that person's reaction and respond to it. But you often enact your gender for a group of people—perhaps the other students in your class, for example. They very well might have diverse responses to your performance, some supporting the gender identity you present and others not. You also might engage in serial gender performances to a number of individuals you encounter in different contexts. If you are coming out as lesbian, for example, you don't come out all at once. You come out multiple times with many different types of performances to many people who have different kinds of relationships with you, different levels of interest and investment in you, and different views on lesbianism. The process of managing and negotiating your gender performances means that you are constantly responding to and adjusting your performances in response to varied performance reviews by multiple audiences, making the process a very complicated one.

Remember that you constitute an audience for your own gender performances as well. As you perform your gender stories for outside audiences, you are also monitoring and evaluating your performances. You are making judgments about them and deciding whether they fit your image of how you want to be in that situation. Tyrone, for example, acknowledges that there are two contexts in particular in which he judges his own gender behavior: "I consciously think about being manly when I'm in the weight room. I feel I have to get bigger to man up. Or if it's a weekend, then I feel like I'm expected to hook up with a woman, or I'm not going to be seen as enough of a man." You are simultaneously playing both the role of performer and critic of your gender performance, a dual role of which Alicia is very aware: "I think about correctly performing my gender identity multiple times every single day, whether it's how to sit in my seat in class or how to walk, dress, and socialize at school or a party. I am aware that I will be judged if I fail to present myself as 'feminine.'"

When you perform a gender story for others, audience members have a continuum of options for responding to you. Their reviews fall into one of three categories, ranging from positive to negative: (1) support for the performance; (2) tolerance of the performance; and (3) rejection of the performance. As your own audience for your gender stories, of course, you have these same options available for responding to your stories.

SUPPORT

In many cases, others accept your gender performance. They are comfortable with or appreciate your performance, think it fits both who you are and the situation, and have no desire to try to get you to change it. When others support your performance, they do so in a number of ways. One type of supportive response is when others try to understand it. They may be initially puzzled by your performance, but they actively work to discover how it makes sense and feels right to you. In this response, others are curious about or fascinated by your performance and would like to respond in a positive way, but they can't fully and enthusiastically support it—at least not yet. Megan's story is a good example. She had worn her hair long since she was a little girl. When she was a sophomore in college, she cut it really short, and her family and friends were surprised by her new look. Her friend Lei expressed the sentiments of her family and friends when she told her, "I think I like it, but it's going to take a while for me to get used to it. I'm curious, though. Why did you decide to cut it?" In this case, the audience members for Megan's performance are mildly supportive of her new style and are interested in learning more about Megan's desire to do gender in a new way.

As a child, Garrett witnessed a gender performance that was puzzling to him. His mother's response modeled an attempt to understand another's performance that he still remembers years later:

> When I was very young, I saw a beautiful young woman in the grocery store with very long dark hair and a flowing summer dress. When I noticed that she had hair on her legs, I was shocked. I asked, "Mom, what's wrong with her?" My mother explained, "Women grow hair on their legs just like men. They just shave it off—most of the time—and it's OK if they prefer not to do that. Shaving is a big pain." Because of my mom's answer, I have always, as an adult, tried to understand others' decisions and preferences instead of judging and dismissing them.

In this type of supportive evaluation, audience members try to see and experience the world as you do and are receptive and open to your gender performance. They suspend judgment for the moment and try to figure out your motive or rationale for the performance you have chosen to enact.

At other times, people may not like your gender performance but may choose to support it nonetheless. In this type of response, audience members typically do not share their misgivings about or displeasure with your performance with you; instead, they communicate support for you as an individual who is capable of making your own choices. When Paco started wearing a purple Mohawk, for example, his parents thought the style was ugly. "With any luck at all, it will go away in a year," they told each other. But they did not articulate their opinions to him, and, in fact, they provided a great deal of nonverbal support for his hair style. They designated certain towels he could use for dyeing his hair, knowing that the dye would ruin them. They bought him gelatin to put in his hair, let him spend fifteen extra minutes in the bathroom every morning to style it, and washed his pillowcase more frequently than usual. His parents worked very hard to communicate their respect and support for his self-chosen performance, even though it was not one they personally liked.

In other instances, the audience for a gender performance accepts and affirms that performance with enthusiasm, as Madeline's story illustrates. She grew up male and was a big, burly teddy bear of a man. At age 40, she chose to have gender-transition surgery to become female and changed her name from *Mark* to *Madeline*. When Madeline wrote a letter to her mother telling her of her decision to have the surgery, she knew that her response might very well be negative. After all, Madeline's mother had given birth to a boy, had raised a male child, and was used to thinking of her child as male. When Madeline called her mother a few days after she knew she would have received the letter, her mother's response was affirming: "Well, I guess I have a daughter!" She has enthusiastically supported and encouraged Madeline's new gender performance, happily shared the news with her friends, and escorted her daughter to a mother-daughter alumni banquet at the university they both attended.

Just as others can affirm your gender performance, you can do that for yourself as well, engaging in the same options of support available to external audience members. You can try, for example, to understand the choices you have made about your own gender performance. Maybe you realize that a particular performance isn't working very well for you anymore or that you're tired of getting flak for something you're performing. You might find yourself analyzing various contexts and thinking to yourself, "What's going on here?" "Why am I doing this?" "Do I really still want to be a part of this group?" or "I don't care if people make fun of me—I like the way I look." Lauren did such reflecting when she was miserable in high school because she didn't fit in with the popular group and didn't dress and act in the ways that those in the group did. As she thought about her situation, she asked herself if she would switch places with the most popular woman in the class if she could. She quickly came to a conclusion that surprised her: "No, I wouldn't switch places with her because I think I'll be OK after I get out of high school, and even though I haven't a clue about how my life will be different, I think it will be more interesting than hers." As you reflect on the choices you have made in your gender performances, you are trying to understand them and, of course, the very act of reflection itself gives you options for the construction of future performances that are more conscious and deliberate.

You also affirm your own gender performance when you thoroughly enjoy and revel in a particular kind of performance. You don't doubt the legitimacy of the performance, you aren't ambivalent about whether you should perform it, and you can't come up with a story you would rather be performing. Singer Lady Gaga, for example, seems to delight in the gender story she tells, and she performs it with enthusiasm and confidence. Whether she is wearing a plastic bubble dress, metal orbs that encircle a silver body suit, or a dress made of slabs of meat, she flaunts and clearly enjoys her gender performances.

TOLERANCE

Another response to your gender performance from an external audience can be tolerance or resigned acceptance. Those who interact with you neither criticize nor affirm your performance; they simply choose to tolerate it. Tolerance implicitly suggests that your audience members are willing to put up with your gender performance, but they disapprove of it and wish it were different.

The response of Alandra's family to her gender performance illustrates tolerance. When Alandra joined the army, her parents and sisters were surprised because they never saw her as someone who would be interested in a military career, and they opposed the wars the United States was fighting at the time. When she came home from serving as a first lieutenant in Afghanistan, Alandra wanted her family to be proud of her, but they asked her very few questions about what Afghanistan had been like or what her duties had been there. One of her sisters asked her about whether she had had any interactions with Afghan women, but when Alandra talked about some of those interactions, her sister didn't really pay much attention. Her family's interaction around her military performance, in other words, was perfunctory and superficial. They didn't try to talk Alandra into leaving the army, but their indifference to and apparent lack of interest in her gender performance as a military officer suggested that they were simply tolerating that performance.

Often, the people in your life tolerate your gender performances because they value their relationship with you and don't want to jeopardize or disrupt it. Rory has tattoos that cover her back, her arms, and her chest, and Rory's mother has chosen to tolerate her gender performance because she wants to maintain a good relationship with her. When Rory was planning her wedding, her mother asked her to select a wedding

dress that covered her tattoos because, although she was willing to tolerate Rory's bodily adornment, she didn't know how other family members
would react. When Rory refused to wear a long-sleeved dress, her mother
sent pictures of Rory's tattoos to the relatives who would be attending the
wedding so that they would not be shocked when they saw her. Another
example of this kind of tolerance is when family members or friends
refuse to attend a gay or lesbian wedding because they disapprove of
same-gender marriage. They continue to have a relationship with the couple and may even be glad that the two people are partners, but by not
attending the ceremony, they are showing that they are only tolerating the
marriage. Tolerance is also the response when parents accept their daughter's lesbianism but don't tell their friends about her sexual orientation.

You yourself can tolerate one of your gender performances just as an
external audience can. When you believe a gender performance can't be
changed, for example and decide just to live with it, you are tolerating
your own performance. A man who is gay and doesn't want to be, for
example, might say to himself, "I wish I weren't this way, but I can't do
anything about it. This is how I am." Isabel has very large breasts and
wishes they were smaller. She tolerates that aspect of her gender performance by telling herself, "I wish they were smaller, but they aren't. I don't
want to have breast-reduction surgery, so I just have to live with them."
Just like an external audience, you can resign yourself to tolerating an
unwanted gender performance.

REJECTION

In some instances, audience members reject one of your gender performances. They communicate to you that they find your gender performance inappropriate, irrational, silly, dangerous, misguided, or evil and
try to make you see why your performance is the wrong one to enact. In
these instances, audience members' rejection assumes one of four forms:
(1) persuasion; (2) harassment; (3) discrimination; or (4) violence.

PERSUASION

The most common means by which people signal their rejection of a
gender performance is to try to talk you out of it. People use various persuasive strategies in an effort to get you to change your mind about your
gender performance and to perform gender differently. Sometimes, such
persuasive efforts involve conquest rhetoric, where the audience's goal is
to have its perspective on gender prevail over yours. If you're not familiar
with how the term *rhetoric* is being used here, it simply means *communica-*

tion; you can think of *rhetoric* as the ancient term for what is now usually called *communication*. In interactions that involve conquest rhetoric, someone wins and someone loses—either someone else's perspective or your perspective on performing gender prevails.

Conquest rhetoric is being used when others see your gender performance as inappropriate and force you to stop performing it. This was the case with Sofia, who remembers that when she would open the car door and start to get out, even as a young child, her father would make her get back in the car and sit and wait until he opened the door for her: "My dad wouldn't let me open my door because a 'man' always opens doors for women." Marie tells a similar story about her mother's effort to persuade her and her sister to engage in appropriate gender behavior: "I remember one time my sister didn't do the dishes. It was 2:00 in the morning! My mother went and woke her up! She said: 'Get up and go do the dishes!' My sister was dead sleeping and she had to get up and do the dishes."[1] Conquest rhetoric showed Sofia and Marie that their parents would not permit them to perform their gender stories. Sofia and Marie were not convinced that the views of gender their parents were promoting were correct, but they had limited say and power in those particular situations and acquiesced to their parents' visions of gender for them.

The Florida legislature got into the business of conquest rhetoric in 2011 when it passed a law that bans sagging pants for male students and low-cut and midriff-exposing tops for female students in high schools. According to the law, repeat violators can be subjected to three days of in-school suspension and up to thirty days of suspension from extracurricular activities.[2] Legislators are not the only ones engaged in conquest rhetoric to register disapproval for such gender performances. Billie Joe Armstrong, singer for the San Francisco pop-punk band Green Day, was kicked off a Southwest Airlines flight because his pants sagged too low. He was searching for a seat after boarding a plane from Oakland to Burbank when a flight attendant asked him to pull up his pants. When he refused, he was asked to leave the plane. He later was allowed to catch another Southwest flight.[3]

Sometimes, people reject your gender performance by trying to convince you of the superiority of their perspective on gender and the inappropriateness of yours. Such efforts constitute conversion rhetoric. In contrast to conquest rhetoric, where you have little choice but to change your behavior, conversion rhetoric is designed to change your view about how you are doing gender by convincing you of the rightness or superiority of another's perspective. You are undoubtedly familiar with these kinds of persuasive efforts. People might use emotion to try to change your mind about how you do gender by appealing, for example, to your pride, your love for them, or your need for security and approval. "If you go out dressed like that, you'll embarrass the family. Don't you love us?" your parents might say, using the persuasion that characterizes conversion rhetoric. Others might try logical arguments to back up their claims about the inappropriateness of your gender performance: "You're not going to get promoted when you talk that way to our clients. You don't see other team members speaking that way, do you?"

A more consequential example of conversion rhetoric designed to change a gender performance is the effort to cure homosexuality. When audience members assume that homosexuality is a mental disorder or a sin, they may try to encourage gay men or lesbians to change their sexual orientations by undergoing conversion or reorientation therapy.[4] Organizations involved in conversion therapy include the National Association for Research & Therapy of Homosexuality, which supports techniques such as psychoanalysis to resolve the unconscious childhood conflicts it considers responsible for homosexuality. Another such organization is Exodus International, a Christian organization that promotes "freedom from homosexuality" through the power of Jesus Christ.[5] Conditioning techniques often recommended for converting homosexual men to heterosexuality include participating in sports activities; avoiding activities such as art museums and opera that are considered of interest to homosexuals; spending more time with heterosexual men to learn to mimic their ways of walking, talking, and interacting; and attending church.

Conversion rhetoric may not always involve discourse; it also may take the form of silence. Others may simply be silent in response to your gender performance, very clearly giving you the message that it is not a suitable way to perform gender. You present your performance, and nothing happens—there's no reaction. Usually, the people who witness your gender performance continue to interact with you and are pleasant enough, but they never say anything about the particular aspect of your performance that they reject. Because they don't acknowledge your gender performance, they implicitly reject or deny it, and the very clear message they are giving you is that it is the wrong kind of performance to be doing. Another kind of conversion rhetoric involves the silent treatment, where someone ignores you completely, even when you are in the same room together. This silence is designed to pressure you into changing your mind about your gender performance. If you change, talk will resume. More drastic forms include banishment or shunning, where individuals are cut off or disowned by their families.

A common situation in which people respond with silence to your performance is when you change your performance so that it is different from the one you have performed for this audience in the past. Because you have violated audience members' expectations for how you are, they are surprised or confused about the change. Your parents are likely to respond to you in this way because they "have both a long, intimate history and an imagined future" with you and are likely to want you to stay the way they have always known you to be.[6] They can refuse to legitimize or sanction your new performance simply by not commenting on it or not engaging with you about it. Maybe you return home from college with a pierced lip, and your parents say nothing about it. You clearly get the message that your new gender performance is not one of which they approve, but they never give you that message directly because they never talk with you about it. When her mother had a face lift and came to visit her, Jordan didn't say anything to her about how she looked. Because she didn't, her mother clearly got the idea that her daughter disapproved of her cosmetic surgery.

Benevolent rhetoric, a third type of persuasive appeal, is communication designed to change you out of a genuine desire on someone's part to make your life easier or better. In this type of communication, your audience seeks to change your ideas about your gender performance out of a concern for your well-being. Benevolent rhetoric usually assumes the form of providing information that you can use. "You might want to put on a little makeup before you head out," your sister might say to you on the morning of your big job interview. She clearly thinks that makeup will enhance your appearance and will give you a better chance at the job. Jenna engaged in benevolent rhetoric with her friend Stacey: "You don't seem to go out much anymore after your wedding, and your husband doesn't seem to let you interact with your old friends. I'm worried about you." Benevolent rhetoric might feel less obnoxious and invasive than conquest and conversion rhetoric, but it still constitutes a rejection of your performance of gender and encourages you to change it in some way.[7]

Many people believe that if they don't like something about you, they have the right to ask or even demand that you change. Changing someone else is very difficult because most people are living their lives in the way that they are for reasons that make sense to them, and they don't respond very positively when someone comes along and suggests they live differently. But many people try, so you will see others' negative reviews or rejection of your gender performance often accompanied by persuasive efforts of various kinds to get you to change.

HARASSMENT

Another way in which others show that they reject your gender performance is through harassment. In harassment, others criticize you, make embarrassing remarks about you, circulate lies about you, call you names, and generally try to diminish your credibility. The strategy is designed to hurt you psychologically and make clear that you are not performing an appropriate gender role. Harassment stigmatizes you, marks you as unacceptable, and makes clear that you do not fit into some group. Harassing actions are usually taken against you in situations in which you have a hard time defending yourself, so they can be powerful means of rejection.

Michael Kimmel, a sociologist whose specialty is masculinity, describes harassment as a frequent response to men who do not perform masculinity according to the expectations of the gender binary:

> What happens if you step outside the definition of masculinity? Consider the words that would be used to describe you. In workshops it generally takes less than a minute to get a list of about twenty terms that are at the tip of everyone's tongues: wimp, faggot, dork, pussy, loser, wuss, nerd, queer, homo, girl, gay, skirt, Mama's boy, pussy-whipped. This list is so effortlessly generated, so consistent, that it composes a national well from which to draw epithets and put-downs.[8]

Harassment in elementary and high schools often takes the form of shaming and bullying by classmates. Darrin remembers one such experience: "At recess, the boys played sports, and the girls played on the swings. The few times I decided to swing instead of joining the boys in a game of kickball (or some other game I was dreadful at), I was called a *girl*." Jesse's experience was far more severe. His classmates decided that Jesse was gay, so they punched him, tripped him in the halls, stuck him to his seat with superglue, and stole his books. One student even pretended to rape him anally.[9] Jesse's harassers engaged in a gender performance of conventional masculinity, policing the borders of acceptable masculinity. Jenny also experienced bullying when she moved to a new town in the seventh grade. The two most popular girls in the school "told everyone Jenny was hooking up with the boys in the woods behind the soccer field"; gave her the nickname of *Harriet the Hairy Whore*; and started a club called *Hate Harriet the Hore Incorporated*, whose members included all of the other girls in the class. They would say "Hhiiiiiiiiiii," laughing, as they walked by Jenny, sounding out the initials of the club, *HHHI*.[10]

Another form of harassment is cyber bullying, where peers send mean messages, threats, rumors, or unflattering or sexually suggestive pictures of someone via their cell phones, Facebook pages, or e-mail. Recent tragic examples have called attention to the powerful impacts and dangers of this kind of harassment. Rutgers University student Tyler Clementi committed suicide in 2010 after his roommate video streamed Tyler kissing a man in his dorm room. In 2011, fourteen-year-old Jamey Rodemeyer killed himself after being relentlessly tormented by classmates for being gay. They had posted on his social networking sites messages such as, "I wouldn't care if you died. No one would. So just do it. It would make everyone WAY more happier!"[11] At a time when you are in the process of trying out various gender performances for yourself and want them to be seen as acceptable to your peers, harassment in the form of bullying, even when less severe than the examples above, can be a very painful response to the gender story you are performing.

Sexual harassment is another type of rejection of the gender story someone performs. This kind of harassment most often takes the form of unwelcome sexual advances by someone who has power over you—requests for sexual favors, touching or fondling in a sexual way, or sexual kidding and innuendo. The gender stories you are trying to perform—stories of competence, professionalism, and expertise—are rejected and ignored as a more powerful person reminds you that you are being perceived first and foremost as a sexual object. In this case, harassment may be occurring because someone—typically a man—is conforming to the patterns of the gender binary. He sees himself as fitting the binary's ideal of a sexual initiator, and he sees the woman being harassed as fitting the binary's expectation that she be sexually available. Elena had such an experience of gender harassment when she was completing her bachelor's degree. When she decided to stay at the same university to pursue her master's degree, one of the professors in the department in which Elena planned to continue her studies told her, "I'm glad you're staying; I like seeing your big tits." Typically, if you don't acquiesce to sexual advances in these situations, you suffer significant repercussions such as a failing grade, refusal to write letters of recommendation, or even loss of a job.

Street harassment is a form of harassment that takes place in public, and it includes verbal and nonverbal behavior usually directed at women by men but also sometimes at gender-ambiguous individuals who do not conform to the ideals of the gender binary. Men working outdoors often assume that all women who walk by are performing a particular gender story—one that says they are looking for men's attention and enjoy comments about their appearance. These men define all women solely as sexual objects who are seen to be valuable only for potential sexual activity, an attitude they communicate through whistles, catcalls, and leers. "I just hate walking by construction sites," complains Jocelyn. "The men whistle and yell at any woman who walks by. They don't know me from anyone, so they don't know if they'd want to have sex with me. I'm not interchangeable with other women. I'm me, and I can tell you that I have no interest." Essentially, the men who engage in street harassment are perceiving only one kind of gender performance from women in their presence—and often this performance is not one the women are choosing. Of course, in many situations of street harassment, men are not allowed to perform gender as they want to, either. If you are a man, you may not want to whistle and yell at the women who pass by your work site, but you may feel pressured to engage in these activities because your coworkers do. In all of these harassing activities, whether you are on the giving or receiving end, the performance of gender is read as exclusively sexual, and any other story you might want to perform is blatantly rejected.

Harassment can happen on a cultural level as well. It can take the form of discourse that circulates in a culture that labels certain gender performances negatively. The discourse around gay men, lesbians, and transgender and bisexual people is an example. Much of the discourse about these kinds of gender performances in movies, comedy, and music asserts that such performances are abnormal or deviant. Comedian Adam Carolla performed this kind of generalized harassment when he suggested that those who identify as lesbian, gay, bisexual, or transgender should "shut up" and use the letters "YUCK" to describe themselves rather than the common acronym of "LGBT."[12] Whether it is targeted at an individual or disseminated more widely through the culture, harassment is a rejection of a gender performance through ridicule or criticism by someone in power or who seeks to enhance a self-perception of power.

DISCRIMINATION

Discrimination—unfair treatment based on some characteristic related to your gender performance—constitutes a form of rejection of a gender performance as well. When discrimination occurs, people with certain kinds of gender performances are told they are inferior and less deserving, while those who perform other kinds of gender stories are considered superior. Lydia, a twenty-six-year-old woman on a work team of men in their forties and fifties, provides an example of a common form of discrimination based on a particular performance of gender. When a new man joined her team, rather than treating her as a professional equal, he acts as if she is his secretary or personal assistant. He gives her his busy work to do and talks down to her. Although all the team members are at the same level in the company, the new hire treats Lydia differently because of her gender performance as a young woman.

Efforts to deprive you of material success and economic security constitute one form of discrimination. Because of their bias against certain kinds of gender performances, some employers may not hire you, may not pay you as much as they pay others, or may let you go first when economic hardships hit the company. In contemporary US society, women tend to encounter pay discrimination more than men: Women, on average, make 79 cents to a man's dollar, a 20-percent pay gap.[13] But men can experience discrimination in the workplace as well. Sergio, for example, who wore his hair long, applied for a job in a cannery one summer, but he was not hired. When he cut his hair and applied again, he was hired three days later. A simple change in his gender performance enabled him to get a job that had not been open to him when his performance of masculinity was different from the norm.

The application of different standards of evaluation can be another discriminatory response to your gender performance. Physician Yvonne Thornton tells of such an experience on her first day of medical school. Dressed in makeup and a miniskirt and one of the few black women in the class, she did not perform the gender story one of her professors, Dr. Luce, expected would be that of a good student. Dr. Luce asked each student to look at the slides in the microscopes lined up on tables around the room and to identify each one in two minutes or less. Thornton volunteered to go first and was through in fifteen minutes, earning a perfect score on the test. She finishes the story: "Dr. Luce called me in and, believing that I had somehow managed to cheat, ordered me to take the test again by myself. Again I identified every slide correctly."[14] Because of the way Thornton was dressed, her professor decided that she could not be a bright student and chose to apply a standard of evaluation to her that was different from the one she applied to other students.

The media coverage of female political candidates provides another example of differential evaluations of gender performances. Women candidates often receive media attention for aspects of their appearance and dress for which male candidates do not. Hillary Rodham Clinton, former First Lady and Democratic presidential candidate and later Secretary of State, has received substantial media attention for aspects of her appearance such as her pantsuits, changing hair style, cleavage, and the butterfly clip she wore in her hair to a meeting of the United Nations General Assembly. Former Republican vice-presidential nominee Sarah Palin was presented in news photos in ways that male candidates never would be. A photograph of Palin addressing a rally in Bethlehem, Pennsylvania, for example, showed a blurred close-up of the back of her legs with the face of a young man framed between them. These examples reveal a double standard in the media coverage of women politicians. Aspects of their physical appearance are noted and seen as relevant to their professional gender performances, while the physical appearance of male politicians is usually not emphasized.

Discrimination also can take the form of silencing particular genders. In this kind of discrimination, you are excluded from certain activities, you might not be invited to important meetings or social events, and others don't pay attention to your opinions. James often found himself in this position in an organization in which the founder and all of the top administrators shared an intense interest in baseball, which was not something that interested him. When James sought to influence policies or to contribute to decision making in the organization, no one paid attention, or if his contributions were briefly acknowledged, no action was taken to follow up on them. He decided to leave the organization, knowing he would not be promoted simply because of the expectation that all senior managers should share an interest in baseball.

Overly polite behaviors or excessive deference and respect are sometimes used to discriminate against some gender performances and to privilege others. Those who treat you in this way act as though they are particularly interested in helping you or watching out for you, but their efforts are really rejections of a particular gender performance. Such efforts are designed to keep you from gaining access to important information and resources and to protect you from negative evaluations that might help you improve your performance. An overly courteous man, for example, might speak differently in the presence of women, beg their forgiveness after using a swear word, and withhold certain information from them because "women shouldn't worry about such things." Sometimes, those who are the targets of excessive helping behavior are given less demanding assignments, a practice that can harm their effectiveness on the job. Tony tells of such a case at the restaurant where he works:

> At my job at a restaurant, if you're a woman, you immediately go to the registers if you are new. If you're a man, you immediately go to bussing. Bussing can be a pretty dirty job, and I think the managers don't want women to have to do that. This policy isn't beneficial for the restaurant, though, because it has a lot of employees who don't know how to bus, and if the guys who are supposed to bus don't

show up, the women don't know what to do. The women also aren't learning all the inside details about how the restaurant works that you learn when you bus.

In this case, regardless of whether job applicants are heavily muscled or weak, they are assigned jobs according to stereotype rather than to individual capacity, which can harm the women employees who want to move up in the restaurant.

Discrimination, then, assumes many forms. In all of them, your gender performance is rejected or devalued, while another's performance is privileged. As a result, you are accorded fewer resources and benefits than those whose gender performances meet norms and expectations.

VIOLENCE

The most extreme form of rejection of a performance of gender is violence or physical harm. Efforts to harm another are often used as a way to reject another's gender performance and to gain a sense of power over the person and the gender story being presented. Unfortunately, violence is a common response to the gender performances of others, particularly in intimate relationships: Each year, nearly 3 in 10 women and 1 in 10 men in the US experience rape, physical violence, or stalking by an intimate partner, and because many victims fail to report such violence, these numbers underestimate the problem.[15] Some of the violent acts are incidents of situational couple violence, which arises in a single argument in which a partner physically lashes out at the other. Others are acts of intimate terrorism, in which someone (statistically most often a man) engages in a general and sustained pattern of control through physical or psychological violence. When you are the target of one of these forms of physical violence or harm, the message being transmitted to you from the perpetrator is that real women or real men engage in gender in a certain way, and because you aren't performing gender that way, you should be punished. Regardless of whether your gender performance is conscious or unconscious, your intimate partner judges it to be wrong.

The media and popular culture are full of examples of people trying to harm intimate partners because they reject the nature of their gender performances. Singer Rihanna was battered by Chris Brown, her then boyfriend, and golfer Tiger Woods was attacked by his wife after she found text messages on his phone from another woman. These are just two of many celebrity examples of domestic violence. Fantasy violence also pervades the media, seemingly sanctioning intimate violence as a way to respond to the gender performances that others choose to enact. In

"Love the Way You Lie," rapper Eminem sings (along with Rihanna) of a physically abusive relationship: "Now you're in each other's face spewing venom in your words when you spit 'em. You push, pull each other's hair, scratch, claw, bite 'em. Throw 'em down, pin 'em, so lost in the moments when you're in 'em." He threatens violence with the promise, "If she ever tries to fuckin' leave again, I'm a tie her to the bed and set this house on fire." The video shows a couple alternately hitting and kissing one another and ends with the woman lying lifeless on the bed while the house burns around her. In the song "Kim," Eminem continues to fantasize about violence, imagining himself killing his ex-wife by slitting her throat, dragging her body through the grass, and putting it in the trunk of his car. Such fantasies involve the use of violence as a punishment for not performing gender in a particular way—leaving a relationship instead of staying as long as a partner would like, for example.

The rejection of a gender performance by means of violence doesn't just happen in intimate relationships. It also occurs between strangers. The story of 21-year-old Matthew Shepard, a gay college student who encountered Russell Henderson and Aaron McKinney in a bar in Laramie, Wyoming, in 1998, is a notorious example of the violence done to those whose gender performances are perceived as unacceptable. Henderson and McKinney robbed, pistol whipped, and tortured Shepard and tied him to a fence, where he was discovered eighteen hours later. He died without regaining consciousness. Unfortunately, such violence happens regularly. When friends Bryce and Trevor were walking home following dinner at a restaurant a few blocks away, they were attacked and beaten so badly that they were hospitalized for several days. Their attackers kept yelling *faggots* as they were beating them. Neither Bryce nor Trevor is gay, but men who disapproved of gay gender stories chose to respond with violence to a gender presentation that involved thin body builds and long hair.

SELF-REJECTION

When others reject your gender performance and try to get you to change it, they use strategies such as persuasion, harassment, discrimination, and violence. Because you are your own audience for your gender performances, you also have available a number of options for rejecting and trying to change a performance of your own. One is to ignore it and pretend you aren't really performing that story or identity. This type of response is often what happens with individuals who believe they were born with a body that doesn't match their felt gender identity. Internally, they construct a gender performance of themselves as the woman or man they would like to be, but they often deny this performance, even to themselves. Ben is gay but doesn't want to be and, for several years, he convinced himself he wasn't gay by dating women. Ben was rejecting a gender story he didn't want to perform and was trying to convince himself that he could perform a story he saw as more acceptable.

Self-talk is another way to substitute a new story for one you no longer want to perform. Using this strategy, you reject a particular interpretation of one of your gender performances. Sometimes, you need the help of a counselor or therapist in order to engage in a new form of self-talk, but in other instances, the process is something you can do on your own. Most people have inner dialogues about who they want to be and who they think they should be, and you can consciously reframe your talk in these inner dialogues to engage in what is for you a new kind of gender performance. In this instance, you have a different interpretation of a performance than you previously did.

Aiden provides an example of the use of self-talk to change a perception of a gender performance. In high school, he was berated for being short by the jocks with whom he hung out. They all had girlfriends and said he couldn't get a girlfriend because of his height. For a while, their abuse made him feel bad about himself, and he thought he was doomed to be unsuccessful in love. But then he decided he didn't have to accept his friends' interpretation of the situation. "There are many men who are short who have girlfriends and wives—the president of France, for example," he told himself. "Plus, there's nothing I can do about my height, so obsessing about it doesn't do any good." He engaged in self-talk to change his interpretation of his height and to change how he viewed a characteristic he and others saw as a key part of his gender performances.

You can reject a gender performance by substituting another story that works better for you. You might try to physically change some aspects of yourself if that physical characteristic dominates a gender performance you no longer want. If your weight or your focus on your weight has kept you from performing your desired gender story, you might diet to achieve your goal or decide to stop dieting and focus on other elements of your gender story. You might buy new clothes or cut your hair in a different way to perform gender differently. In these cases, you take some action to change a gender story that no longer works for you and replace it with a new performance.

Cosmetic procedures such as facial reconstruction or cosmetic surgery are other examples of changing your body in order to change an unwanted gender performance. Such procedures can include the injection of Botox to treat frown lines or implants of gore-text to plump up the lips. Surgical face-lifts, eyelid surgery, tummy tucks, liposuction, stomach stapling, and breast augmentation and reduction are also options for radically altering a gender performance. Fox's TV show *The Swan* showed the extent to which some women go to alter their gender performances and to create a gender performance they prefer. On the show, women who hated their bodies subjected themselves to a team of plastic and cosmetic surgeons and endured a three-month makeover involving various surgical procedures. Although women undergo the majority of cosmetic procedures, many men are now opting to change their gender performances through cosmetic surgery as well—typically nose surgery, eyelid surgery and the removal of excess skin. Physically changing your body is a way of enacting a new and different gender performance, often one more in line with the gender binary.

Choosing to undergo gender-transition surgery is another means of rejecting a socially assigned performance of gender and replacing it with another. Although the process is complicated, lengthy, and costly, changing an unwanted gender performance in this way is very important to many individuals. When you perceive that your biological features tell a gender story at odds with your real gender, you might believe that the only way for you to perform gender the way you want to is to change your physical body. The gender-transition process for transgender or trans women (male to female) may involve multiple surgeries and cosmetic procedures, including breast augmentation, the surgical construction of a vagina, the shaving off of the Adam's apple, and electrolysis to remove facial hair. For trans men (female to male), the procedure may involve a hysterectomy, removal of the female breasts, chest reconstruction to shape a male-contoured chest, nipple grafts, and sometimes construction of a penis. The process typically involves counseling to prepare for a new life; speech therapy to alter voice pitch; and a great deal of practice learning how to walk, sit, and act in ways considered appropriate for the new gender.

Sometimes, rejection of a gender performance assumes the form of harming your own body in some way. You might become so obsessed about diet and weight that you develop an eating disorder such as anorexia or bulimia. Other forms of self-injury include cutting yourself or pulling out your hair, eyebrows, and eyelashes—coping mechanisms that may provide temporary relief from feelings of anxiety, depression, abnormality, or self-loathing but that do not end up remediating your negative feelings about a particular gender performance. Drug and alcohol abuse are other strategies sometimes used to try to diminish uncomfortable feelings about gender performances. Francesca engaged in violence of this type when she was in middle school and hair started to grow all over her body, including a mass of fine hair on her abdomen. When Francesca wore a bathing suit, the hair was visible on her stomach, and her friends teased her about it. In response, she plucked out every hair individually and spent middle school with a raw but bare abdomen.

Rape is a form of violence also designed to reject your own gender performance. You might think of rape as something violent done to someone else, which, of course, it is. It often is used to try to control the gender performance of the person being raped. But it also can be a means by which (usually) a man rejects his own gender performance of a story in which he perceives himself as powerless and uses rape as a means to transform his self-perception. Instead of seeing himself as lacking control and agency, he is able to perceive himself as a powerful person in control of those around him. Dave's explanation illustrates this link between feelings of powerlessness and rape: Women "have all the power. They have the big power—the power to say no. I want them, I want sex with them, and they're the ones who decide whether it'll happen or not. Some bitch decides whether or not I get laid. I don't decide, she does."[16] More than 18 percent of men say they have engaged in heterosexual intercourse— sometimes through rape, if necessary—simply because they "did not want to appear to be shy, afraid, or unmasculine."[17] Rape alters the gender performance of the perpetrator, then, by rejecting his gender performance of powerlessness.

Once you take your gender stories out into different contexts and perform them for various audiences, you receive reviews for your performances. Some may support your performance reluctantly or enthusiastically, some may tolerate your performance, and some may reject it and communicate that rejection in various ways. As soon as you register a response from an audience member, you begin to react in various ways. We now turn to the process involved in responding to the performance reviews you receive and the options available to you.

RESPONDING TO PERFORMANCE REVIEWS

If others (or you yourself) respond to one of your gender performances by trying to understand it, accepting it, or enthusiastically supporting it, there's nothing for you to do but to continue to perform it with delight and enjoyment. The reviews are great, so you can revel in your performance of one of the gender stories you have crafted for yourself. But if you find that others (or you yourself) respond negatively to a gender performance you are offering, you must reflect on and somehow deal with the negative responses. Three options are available to you for responding: (1) acquiescing; (2) adapting; and (3) maintaining. Of course, you may find yourself alternating among all three options in any one gender performance because your performance and your audience's responses are constantly changing as you monitor and adjust to one another.

ACQUIESCING

When others' reactions to one of your gender performances are negative, you might choose to adjust or rework your performance so that it conforms more closely to their beliefs and preferences. You acquiesce, give in, or submit to their view of how you should perform gender. In responding this way, you essentially accept someone else's performance preferences for you over your own.

There are a number of reasons why you might acquiesce to someone's demands to perform gender differently. If a person has power over you, you may perceive that challenging that person could cause you further difficulties, and you don't want to make your relationship even more problematic. Caitlin chose to adhere to someone else's gender script for her in order to avoid negative repercussions: "When I was in the fifth grade, all the girls played on the monkey bars and jungle gym, twirling ourselves around on one leg and swinging from one rung to the next on the parallel bars. One day, a teacher came over to us at recess and said it wasn't ladylike for girls to play on this equipment, so we stopped. I was probably stronger and more physically confident at that time than I've ever been since, but I was forced to stop that kind of physical activity." Because the teacher had power, Caitlin and her friends acquiesced to her vision of an appropriate gender performance for them.

If you are in a relationship that is very important to you, you might acquiesce in order to be able to maintain that relationship. When Nora was twenty-five, she realized she was lesbian, and she began to bring a partner, Lois, with her to family gatherings. Her mother and sisters made snide, hurtful comments about Lois always being around, and Nora realized that lesbianism would not be tolerated by the family. Because her relationship with her family was very important to her, she broke up with Lois, moved back home with her mother, stopped spending time with her women friends, and did not seek an intimate relationship again. Her reaction was drastic, but she acquiesced to the gender story her family wanted her to perform because her relationships with her mother and sisters were primary for her. In some situations, you may choose to accommodate someone else's preferences for your gender performance because of the importance of the relationship for you.

Sometimes, a particular gender performance isn't central or very important to you and doesn't matter much, so you have no trouble giving it up and acquiescing to someone else's view of how you should do gender. Sarah bought a fun lime-green miniskirt and wore it to school one day. Stopped by the assistant principal, she was told that students were not allowed to wear skirts that short to school and that she either had to change clothes or be suspended. Sarah chose to stop wearing the skirt to school. The skirt wasn't that important to Sarah—she had just seen it in the store and thought it was cute—so she had no problem acquiescing to the assistant principal's rules about appropriate dress.

You may acquiesce just because you want to get along with others and make things easy for yourself. This is the case with Malik, who adjusts his gender performance when he's with his father because he doesn't want to be hassled by him: "I'm a really emotional guy, and sometimes I cry. My dad can't stand it. He thinks I'm not a man when I cry, so I don't cry around him." Ryan also chooses not to perform a gender story he would like to perform because of the negative reactions he knows he would get from friends and family: "I have long hair, and I like when people wear hair wraps. I wouldn't get one, though, because mostly women wear them, and I know I would be teased." Ryan finds life easier if he doesn't enact a gender performance he would like to try and adheres instead to others' preferences. Sometimes, this kind of acquiescence means submitting to someone's preferences for your gender story so that you don't stand out and attract unwanted attention. After a mastectomy, Laurel wore a prosthetic breast even though she would have preferred not to. She didn't want to be subjected to unwanted attention because she only had one breast.

You might acquiesce when a performance is negatively received because doing so will help you achieve a goal that is important to you. Jade, for example, met a man who asked her to marry him; getting married and having children had been her goal since she was a little girl. This man was very religious and insisted that she attend church with him and stop drinking alcohol. Jade wasn't religious and enjoyed wine now and again, but she agreed to join his church and to stop drinking in order to achieve her goal of marriage and children. She regarded church attendance and abstinence from alcohol—two somewhat substantial changes to her gender performance—to be acceptable trade-offs for achieving her long-time goal of marriage and motherhood.

When you acquiesce, you engage in audience analysis and rework a gender story that you believe audience members will prefer. Whether this kind of adjustment is substantial or means very little to you, it can be an appropriate response in many contexts to someone's negative reaction to your gender performance.

ADAPTING

Adapting is a second response to a negative evaluation of your chosen gender performance. When you adapt, you accommodate another's preferences by modifying or editing some parts of your gender performance. The key pieces of your preferred performance remain in place, but you alter some details to make the performance more acceptable to others. In this type of adaptation, you are "passing" by presenting a gender performance that hides some aspects of who you are and highlights only those parts of the performance that meet with the approval of the audience. Nina provides an example of this kind of adaptation. She has a nose ring, but she knows that her grandmother hates it. Nina loves her grandmother and doesn't want her to be disappointed in or angry with her. When she is with her grandmother, Nina flips the ring inside her nostril so that her grandmother can't see it because she is willing to edit her performance in order to maintain their good relationship.

Another way in which you might adapt a gender performance is by enacting a certain performance in one context and not in another. To present a self-image that is acceptable to a particular group or individual, you bracket out or screen off aspects of your identity that you believe would be seen as inappropriate. Consequently, there are aspects of a gender performance that some of your family, friends, or coworkers never see and have no idea that you perform. Hallie provides an example of this form of adaptation: "There's a divergence between my professional and private life. In my private life, I feel comfortable expressing my gender in many different ways. Professionally, I feel pulled to express myself as a 'woman.' I have part of my head shaved, and at work, I hide it with hair. After work, I pull my hair back to show off the shaved spot." Talah similarly adapts her gender performance in the presence of a certain audience: "My Arab father-in-law is very traditional, and when I know I am going to see him, I dress a little more modestly than I normally would. My behavior is altered even more when my father-in-law has his Arab family over. They are very traditional, and I dress even more modestly. I help cook, I help clean, and I bring the men tea. It is a small sacrifice. These events do not happen very often, and they keep my husband's father satisfied." When you use this strategy of adaptation, you maintain your preferred performance in one context, but you perform gender differently in another context.

When you adapt to others' responses to a gender performance, you modify that performance in some ways. You conceal some aspects of yourself and reveal others as you perform one gender story or parts of a story to one audience but not to another audience. You thus are able to maintain key gender stories by performing them only when you know they will be received positively or at least tolerated by an audience.

MAINTAINING

You do not always want to accommodate or adapt to someone else's vision of how you should do gender. In some cases, your response to a negative review is to maintain your gender performance exactly as it is. You express your gender as you choose and keep intact the gender stories you have crafted for yourself, perhaps strengthening your commitment to your story.

In many cases, maintaining assumes the form of simply dismissing or ignoring others' coercive responses. You simply stick with your performance of a story, regardless of what others think about it. If they object to it, you are likely to say something like "Leave me alone," "Just shut up about it," "It's my hair!" or "I like it this way." You continue to perform your gender as you choose, which is the kind of response Stella offered in middle school to negative responses to her gender performance: "When I was in middle school, everyone around me started to care about their outward appearance except for me. I didn't understand why they were so concerned about this, so I didn't change. My soccer T-shirt and sweats were always mocked by the popular crowd, but I didn't care." Similarly, Chang ignored a comment made by someone about his weight-lifting style in the gym: "I was once told that I lift weights like a girl, but I just ignored it." Natalie provides an example of a situation in which she maintained her performance, even in the face of substantial pressure to change it:

> I never fit in in high school, and I was dorky, shy, and self-conscious. But I didn't do some things that would have helped me fit in because they didn't match my perception of myself. All of the girls in high

> school who weren't cheerleaders were in the Pep Club, and every Friday, they all wore burgundy uniforms to school. I was one of only three girls in the whole school who didn't join the Pep Club. Athletic competitions made no sense to me, and I certainly didn't want to spend evenings cheering for some silly team. So I was one of three girls not dressed in the uniform every Friday. I wanted to fit in, but I would only go so far to conform.

In her case, maintenance of her gender performance took considerable courage for Natalie, but it was something she was willing to do despite pressures to change that performance.

You can also maintain your gender performance by making jokes, laughing off or trivializing negative comments, or distracting others from focusing so much on what they don't like about your gender performance. Marco tells how he responds when he feels negatively judged by a group of guys in his neighborhood who enjoy boxing with each other. He doesn't like boxing because, as he explains, "It's very odd and almost overdoes the 'man' role." He responds using humor: "I generally make witty comments to the person who feels boxing is absolutely necessary." Gerard uses humor as well to get out of a situation in which others are criticizing him for his gender performance: "I often do things that others think are feminine. Once, several guys saw me vacuuming and asked, 'There are three girls here; why aren't they doing it?' To that I replied, 'This is the most manly thing I have ever done!' Then I smiled." Responding with humor or irony enables you to maintain your performance without directly challenging the person who is criticizing you.

Sometimes, when you maintain a gender performance, you are proud of it and not only want to display it, but you want to help others understand your choices. Hallie, the woman with the shaved spot on her head, is pleased to offer an explanation of her gender performance when she is asked about it: "The first time I shaved my head, a little boy asked me, 'Are you a girl who turned into a boy?' I responded, 'I'm still a girl. I just like to cut my hair because it makes me happy.'" Dannisha also has an explanation she uses with those who question her gender performance: "I'm lesbian, but I present as a straight woman. At times, I've been told I need to be more 'butch' or more 'obviously gay.' I respond, 'We're all just trying to be ourselves. The fact that I look straight has no bearing on how much I love my girlfriend.'" She explains her own perspective to help others understand. Mike also tries to explain one of his gender performances to other men: "When other guys try to push me into hooking up at a party, I explain I'm not really interested in sleeping with just any woman. I must say, though, that my explanation is rarely satisfactory. Some men are at a total loss when I tell them this."

You also can maintain your gender performance by enlisting allies or joining forces with others to bolster your performance. In response to your parents' objections to your tattoos, for example, you might argue that tattoos are simply a new form of body adornment and point to respected people like professors, doctors, lawyers, athletes, and politicians who also have them. If the person who is reacting negatively to your gender performance is a big fan of football player Tim Tebow, you can mention something he said or did as support for the legitimacy of the gender story you are performing. Or maybe you can enlist friends or relatives to talk about your gender performance positively—perhaps getting your aunt who adores you to reassure your mother that there's nothing wrong with the style of clothing you choose to wear.

Another option is to bond with others who are performing a similar gender story to yours by joining support groups or simply developing friendships with these people. You might search for websites, books, music, or films that reinforce your gender performance. If you are a mother who often feels judged by other mothers for not parenting correctly, you might find an online chat room in which mothers exchange ideas about mothering and pride themselves on being people rather than perfect mothers. Finn is someone who has found support for his gender performances in such groups: "I am part of a book club and a men's club, where five guys and I meet and talk about our lives. Some men tease me about these groups, but I don't care. I like them and find them helpful."

Cruz used a similar strategy in high school. He had been friends with the same guys since grade school, and he liked many things about them. But they never let up on him about his lack of athletic ability and could be quite cruel about it at times: "I finally joined the staff of the yearbook so I wouldn't be available to play sports after school and found a whole new group of awesome friends." You might also choose to join groups or movements that celebrate particular gender performances, such as a Christian youth group, a feminist group, a mothers' group, or an LGBTQ alliance. In various ways, then, you can get support for maintaining your gender performance from others whose gender performances are similar to yours.

Exaggeration of a gender performance is yet another available response to negative reviews. You magnify your performance and may even flaunt it, usually becoming more firmly committed to your identity in the process. Needling or irritating your audience in this way may be the only power you perceive you have in such situations. "My parents were always on my case about the streak of bright red I put in the front of my hair," says Tynice. "I got so tired of them nagging me about it that I dyed all my hair that same bright red. To put it mildly, they didn't respond well, but there was really nothing they could do about it." Children can also make decisions to exaggerate or overstate a particular gender performance. If a little girl is often told by her parents that she shouldn't buy into the princess culture, she may decide she's only going to wear dresses, and, furthermore, only pink dresses, therefore exaggerating the very gender performance her parents oppose. You also may choose to exaggerate a gender performance because you enjoy the story you are performing. You might wear a short skirt that emphasizes or exaggerates a conventionally feminine gender story, for example, just because you like the skirt and feel good when you are wearing it.

If you choose to maintain the gender story you are performing, despite a negative response from an audience, you simply continue to perform your story, ignoring negative comments about it, trivializing their comments, explaining to them the rationale for your story, finding allies to support your performance, or perhaps exaggerating it. The use of any of these strategies is likely to reinforce your commitment to that particular gender performance.

AGENCY IN REWORKING GENDER PERFORMANCES

When you perform a gender story for others, they can respond to it in various ways. They may support it, tolerate it, or reject it, and, of course, you can do all of these, too, because you are functioning as your own audience for your performances. As individuals react in different ways to a gender story you are performing, you have choices about how to respond to their evaluation. You can acquiesce to their preferences regarding your performance, adapt by suppressing or editing aspects of your performance, or simply maintain that performance as is.

As you are making your choices about how to respond to others' assessments of a gender performance, you also are negotiating your relationship to the matrix of the gender binary. If you acquiesce to someone else's vision for a proper gender performance, you might very well find yourself acquiescing to the binary's norms for gender in a particular context. Maybe you and your partner want to get married in a simple ceremony in your back yard, but your father wants you to have a big, fancy traditional wedding. Acquiescing to his wishes for your gender performance in this context would mean performing in ways that align with the binary's expectations. But acquiescing also could mean that you rework a gender performance in ways that would challenge binary norms. If you want a lavish wedding and your parents are encouraging you to use the money they would spend on a wedding to go to graduate school instead, you must decide how much you are willing to deviate from the expectations established by the binary for women and weddings. In other words, the same types of choices arise if you decide to revise your gender performance in some way or maintain it. You still must decide how to negotiate the norms of the binary and whether you want to align with or deviate from them.

You have considerable agency about how you respond to others' evaluations of your gender performances. You might want others to respond positively to a gender story you are performing, but, of course, you have no control over how they actually do respond—they get to respond as they choose. What you *do* have control over is how you respond to their assessments. While your responses to others' evaluations until now may have been unconscious or habitual, you can make more deliberate choices now that you know you have a choice in terms of your response. Regardless of how you feel about the reviews, you can choose how to respond. You can decide to see the reviews, for example, as useful because they provide feedback about how others are responding to you, as a means of helping you understand someone better, and as a way to encourage you to discover your level of commitment to a gender performance. In the next chapter, we turn from the process you use to create and perform your own gender stories to the process of interacting with the gender stories of others.

■ NOTES

[1] Nancy Lopez, "Homegrown: How the Family Does Gender," in *Gender through the Prism of Difference*, ed. Maxine Baca Zinn, Pierrette Hondagneu-Sotelo, and Michael A. Messner, 3rd ed. (New York: Oxford University Press, 2005), 471.

[2] Barbara Liston, "Florida Lawmaker Hands Out Belts Under Saggy Pants Ban," August 30, 2011, http://www.reuters.com/article/2011/08/30/us-florida-saggypants-idUSTRE77T60Y20110830

[3] Marc Hogan, "Billie Joe Armstrong Kicked Off Airplane," September 6, 2011, http://www.spin.com/articles/billie-joe-armstrong-kicked-airplane

[4] Chuck Bright, "Deconstructing Reparative Therapy: An Examination of the Processes Involved When Attempting to Change Sexual Orientation," *Clinical Social Work Journal* 32 (2004): 471–73.

[5] Exodus International, "Help for Leaving Homosexuality," http://exodusinternational.org/find-help/leaving-homosexuality/

[6] Monisha Pasupathi and Trisha L. Weeks, "Integrating Self and Experience in Narrative as a Route to Adolescent Identity Construction," *New Directions for Child and Adolescent Development* 131 (2010): 40.

[7] For more information on these and other types of rhetoric, see Sonja K. Foss and Karen A. Foss, *Inviting Transformation: Presentational Speaking for a Changing World*, 3rd ed. (Long Grove, IL: Waveland, 2012), 4–6.

[8] Michael Kimmel, *Guyland: The Perilous World Where Boys Become Men* (New York: Harper, 2008), 48.

[9] Kimmel, *Guyland*, 77.

[10] Rachel Simmons, *Odd Girl Out: The Hidden Culture of Aggression in Girls* (Orlando, FL: Harcourt, 2002), 26.

[11] Olivia Katrandjian, "Jamey Rodemeyer Suicide: Lady Gaga Plays Tribute to Bullying Victim," September 25, 2011, http://abcnews.go.com/blogs/entertainment/2011/09/jamey-rodemeyer-suicide-lady-gaga-pays-tribute-to-bullying-victim

[12] "Adam Carolla Rants about Transgender, Gay Issues; GLAAD Reacts," August 17, 2001, http://www.metroweekly.com/news/last_word/2011/08/cranky-comic-adam-carolla-rant.html

[13] Ruth Mantell, "Salary Gap Between Men and Women Narrows, But It Hasn't Been Erased, Report Shows," April 21, 2010, http://www.cleveland.com/business/index.ssf/2010/04/salary_gap_between_men_and_wom.html

[14] Yvonne S. Thornton, as told to Jo Coudert, *The Ditchdigger's Daughters: A Black Family's Astonishing Success Story* (Secaucus, NJ: Birch Lane/Carol, 1996), 152–53.

[15] Centers for Disease Control and Prevention, Injury Center: Violence Prevention, "Understanding Intimate Partner Violence," http://www.cdc.gov/ViolencePrevention/intimatepartnerviolence/index.html

[16] Kimmel, *Guyland*, 227.

[17] Kimmel, *Guyland*, 225.

nine

THE NEXT CHAPTER
CONSTRUCTING GENDERED WORLDS

You'll find your own strategies, invent your own solutions.
Which is as it should be. Does one self-consistent
fragment tell another what to do? Too wise for that,
they only dance alongside each other in a
vision emerging as they share it.

Robin Morgan, *The Anatomy of Freedom*

At the beginning of this book, we set three goals that we hoped you might achieve in your journey through *Gender Stories*. We hoped that you would (1) participate in a spirited discussion about gender; (2) become more conscious of how you construct and perform gender; and (3) respect other people's gender stories. We selected these goals because we had in mind certain experiences that we wanted you to have and insights that we hoped you would gain about how gender is constructed and performed in the world around you. We wanted you to be in conversation with people who have a variety of different gender stories so that you could appreciate the multiplicity of forms that gender takes in people's lives. We wanted you to become more conscious of how you construct and perform gender so that you would be able to embody and communicate the genders that are important to you and feel most right for you. In addition, we wanted you to understand the gender stories of other people so that you could contribute to a more civil and humane world where all genders are treated with respect. Because we believe that gender multiplicity, the ability to live any gendered life you choose, and respecting others are fundamentally important to creating this world, we don't want these goals to end when you finish this course. In fact, we sincerely hope that you will make the pursuit of these three goals a lifelong endeavor.

We want to stress that each of these three goals has larger implications than just your own opinions about gender and your own stories and performances of gender. Your decisions and actions have important consequences for the nature of the world in which you live because you are a cocreator of that world. According to the theory of social construction, reality—the world in which you live—is not something natural and eternal but something that comes into being through communication. Your communication can create either a world of singularity and restriction or a world of multiplicity and abundance as you engage with others in conversations about gender. Your communication likewise creates a shared gendered reality as you and the people around you talk about gender, enact gender stories, and respond to one another's performances, constructing a world of support for, questioning of, or challenge to the gender binary. Your interactions with other people impact the world in which you live. Whether you acknowledge, try to understand, and respect the gender stories of others or isolate yourself from or reject them, you are contributing to the construction of a particular kind of world.

In this chapter, we review our three goals for you and encourage you to reflect on the consequences of your communication regarding gender for the ways in which it produces greater appreciation for multiplicity; contributes to the cultural system of gender categories, norms, and attitudes; and creates a more civil and humane world. Because we know that you live in a world that does not always make it easy to appreciate multiple views, to be yourself, or to interact with people who are different from you, we discuss how certain characteristics of Western culture function to discourage you from engaging in these activities. For each goal, we offer you some perspectives and tools that can help you achieve it despite these obstacles. We end the chapter with a discussion of invitational rhetoric, a strategy for living with and appreciating difference that is useful for achieving all three goals and that captures the kind of participant we hope you will be in the world we are creating together.

PARTICIPATING IN A SPIRITED DISCUSSION

Our first goal for you is to participate in spirited discussions about gender. Making a decision to continue participating in spirited discussions about gender is one way that you can contribute to constructing a world in which multiplicity is valued. We set this goal so that you have the opportunity to hear many different gender stories and gain an appreciation for the multiplicity that exists in terms of gender stories and performances. When we based this book on the different gender stories that real people create and perform, we did so because these stories provide multiple perspectives on gender. This multiplicity—and especially conflicting perspectives—enhances everyone's knowledge and understanding about gender. We wanted you to experience how your knowledge of life expands and is enriched when you deliberately interact with multiple perspectives.

Because we hope you will participate in a lifelong spirited conversation about gender, we want you to see the value in choosing to interact with perspectives and stories that are different from your own. We hope you see that these perspectives represent resources because they provide you with new ways of looking at and understanding the world and yourself. Participation in a spirited conversation about gender is not just about having a conversation that is engaging and lively. Neither does *spirited* mean having a traditional debate. Instead, its hallmark is an engagement with multiple perspectives.

Understanding gender requires engaging with multiple views because your view of anything—including gender—is necessarily limited by your own experiences and by your ability to interpret and make sense of those experiences. When you observe or experience something, you understand only part of it, and other people see and experience something entirely different. Each one of these understandings is incomplete, but when you connect your pieces of reality with the pieces of others who see things differently, you end up having a much fuller and richer understanding of a bigger reality. The more individuals who contribute to the process and the more diverse their unique interpretations are, the greater the understanding that results for everyone.[1] When you and other people participate in spirited conversations about gender, you contribute to the construction of a world in which a more complete knowledge about everyone's gender choices, stories, and performances is valued as worthy of attention and effort.

HEGEMONIC RESTRICTIONS ON MULTIPLICITY

Although spirited discussions about gender with people who have different beliefs and lifestyles contribute to a richer shared understanding of gender and to a greater cultural value of multiplicity, you may not be accustomed to engaging in such discussions outside of a classroom. You might think that because different patterns of belief and ways of doing things exist in your culture—because multiplicity exists—that there would be a cultural value placed on acknowledging many ways of seeing and living. Instead, just the opposite is the case. Instead of valuing multiplicity, there are cultural dynamics that function to make some beliefs and behaviors more evident, prominent, powerful, and influential than others.

Hegemony refers to the privileging of one ideology over other ideologies. A hegemonic ideology, then, is "a belief that is pervasive" or dominant in a culture[2] and that invites and persuades individuals "to understand the world in certain ways, but not in others."[3] While people in a culture do not have one uniform belief system, dominant perspectives mask difference so that hegemonic positions come to seem natural and provide a sense that the way things are is the way they should be.[4] They establish what is normal, encourage you to acknowledge only some perspectives as valid, and brand alternative perspectives as abnormal or even as wrong. Institutions such as schools, religions, families, the media, governmental agencies, the legal system, and popular culture perpetuate dominant ideologies and, by excluding other views, persuade members of a culture to accept normative attitudes and behaviors and to discourage alternatives.

Hegemonic ideologies infuse almost every aspect of life in US culture. You are well aware by now that the gender binary constitutes a dominant ideology in Western culture. Because the binary is the hegemonic system, other ways of believing about and living gender—being asexual, uninterested in parenting, or invested in maintaining an androgynous body or wardrobe—are considered peripheral and not normal or mainstream. There are similar hegemonic ideologies in other areas—education, health care, and religion, for example. Even if you personally believe that a college education isn't absolutely necessary for success and that other kinds of experience are equally valuable, the dominant—or hegemonic—ideology concerning education in the US is that a college education is beneficial and almost crucial for life success. Similarly, although there are many different religions and spiritual practices in the United States, the Christian religion has become hegemonic, and, as a result, for public events to open with a Christian prayer or an appeal to a Christian God seems perfectly natural to many people. There are many practicing Muslims and many atheists in the US, for example, but to begin a banquet with a Muslim prayer—or to forgo any prayer—would seem strange to many people. The point is that there are multiple views or perspectives on all subjects, but those multiple views tend to lose value and visibility as one ideology becomes dominant. Multiplicity can be difficult to see and appreciate because the hegemonic order positions dominant beliefs and practices in the foreground while repressing other beliefs and practices.

All hegemonic ideologies offer only a partial view of the world because they represent only the experiences and perspectives of some people—usually the most powerful groups of people in the culture. Because of the existence of hegemonic ideologies in a culture, multiplicity is often invisible, and you might not think about all the different ways there are to approach and perceive any subject. You aren't encouraged to seek out and value alternative perspectives. When you develop alternative perspectives or lifestyles, you may feel insecure or question yourself because you are aware that you are thinking and behaving outside of the norm. You may be frustrated because you feel like you are the only one who appreciates how a norm dominates and excludes other perspectives. If you decide that you don't want to endorse the dominant perspective, you might be reluctant to voice your dissent because your performance is likely to be seen as strange.

In a similar way, instead of seeing enactments of alternative views as resources for you on how you understand and perform gender, you might see them as abnormal. In hegemonic contexts, even when you are excited to find other people who affirm your perspectives and experiences, you may fear that the group will be misunderstood and suffer discrimination. Because hegemonic ideologies persuade members of a culture that only one perspective is valid, devaluing alternative perspectives becomes routine. When you venture out into the world from your classroom, then, you might feel discouraged from continuing to have spirited discussions about gender with people who are different from you.

COCREATING MULTIPLICITY

For those of us who live in cultures with hegemonic ideologies, there is a tension between wanting to benefit and grow from exposure to different perspectives and the cultural pull to ignore or denigrate different perspectives as unimportant and invalid. In order to benefit from multiple perspectives, you have to intentionally expose yourself to different views, or—as our goal states—you need to have spirited discussions with people who are not like you. This means listening to others instead of debating them or trying to prove that their beliefs are wrong. Even if you want to learn from other people, you may not have had very much experience with being open and respectful toward difference because you live in a culture that acknowledges only dominant views. Staying open to and respectful of perspectives that are unlike and perhaps opposed to your own may require you to adopt new strategies of engagement with others.

Political scientist Wendy Brown provides a metaphor of counterpoint for the process of accommodating different perspectives to achieve greater understanding. *Counterpoint* is a musical term that describes the texture that results from combining different musical lines; when different lines are juxtaposed, an entirely new melody is possible. Counterpoint allows for several beliefs—or truths—to be enriched by coming together and playing off of one another. Brown says that using this musical concept involves a deliberate practice of multiplicity in which oppositions are not ignored but are considered together in all of their complexity. This complexity doesn't always add up to a harmonious whole, but it does produce greater opportunities for insights because of the multiple and sometimes conflicting perspectives that are brought together.[5] Different views are not drowned out or discouraged but are valued for what they can offer in terms of new knowledge and experience.

In order for the spirited conversation we imagine for you to produce comprehensive knowledge about gender, it must be characterized by a "respectful openness to other perspectives."[6] Such openness requires that you embrace the differences that people embody and even celebrate and delight in people who do not think as you do or behave like you. In chapter 1, we introduced you to Kate Bornstein and Joseph Nicolosi—Bornstein is a lecturer and gender theorist who believes gender is fluid and takes many forms, and Nicolosi is a psychologist who believes that the only genders are male and female. If Bornstein and Nicolosi were to enter a conversation with each other using a stance of respectful openness, they would listen to one another not to change each other's minds but to understand very different viewpoints and experiences in the world. They probably would end their conversation holding the same views that they had at the beginning, but they could also gain a broader perspective on gender by listening with respect to one another. If they were able to be open to each other's perspective, they would gain resources for greater understanding. Engaging with perspectives very different from their own would provide opportunities to encounter previously unknown ideas, to use those resources to reflect on personal worldviews, and to think new thoughts.

Respectful openness means that you try to see the world from another person's viewpoint and that you suspend your own beliefs long enough to give credence to that viewpoint as a valid perspective on life. It means that you see others as people whose perspectives on life make sense from the vantage points of their own experiences. The stance you take as you listen to others is that you come to the conversation empty—not empty of "experience or history—but empty of the belief" that your "experience or history defines the limits of possible meaning and experience."[7] You suspend your assumption that your way of thinking about life and living is the only right way.

Philosopher Martha Nussbaum's idea of narrative imagination is a useful tool for entering another person's story without thinking that your own story is superior. Narrative imagination is a stance toward another person that involves the "ability to think what it might be like to be in the shoes of a person different from oneself, to be an intelligent reader of that person's story, and to understand the emotions and wishes and desires that someone so placed might have."[8] Miller's Law provides another way to think about the same concept. Psychologist George Miller proposed this stance toward the perspectives of other people: "In order to understand what another person is saying, you must assume it is true and try to imagine what it could be true of."[9] Miller's Law suggests that you suspend judgment about what others are communicating so you can see the world from their point of view without imbuing their messages with your own interpretation. Respectful openness requires, in other words, imagining how other people have come to be who they are as they share their unique stories with you.

Notice that to be respectfully open to others does not require that you give up your own perspective or acquiesce to the preferences of others. You do not need to blindly accept the views that others offer you about gender. You also do not need to agree that the lifestyles or behaviors of others should be a social norm that guides all of society. You do not need to accept any particular ideology. You may participate in a spirited conversation, be open to the perspectives of others and learn from them, and decide that you still prefer your own views. But participating in a spirited conversation does mean that you adopt behaviors that make such a discussion possible and that you recognize that sharing gender stories is much easier for people who have hegemonic views and lives than for people who have nondominant views and lives. By engaging in spirited discussions regarding gender as an open and respectful listener, you will continue to develop new understandings of gender even if you choose to retain your original perspective. By engaging in spirited discussions, willingly sharing your gendered life, and making it possible for other people to share theirs with you, you will contribute to a world in which people have a wider and richer understanding of gender.

CONSCIOUSLY CREATING AND PERFORMING GENDER

Our second goal is for you to construct and perform your own gender stories consciously. Throughout this book, we have encouraged you to be more conscious about all of the ways in which you communicate gender. We have repeatedly reminded you that you can have agency about who you are as a gendered person and about how you share your gender stories with others. While you cannot avoid being surrounded by a constant barrage of gender stories from other people and the media, when crafting your stories, you can choose the stories to which you will pay attention, seek out new stories, and be deliberate about which fragments you want to incorporate in your own gender stories. You can consciously negotiate the parts of your gender stories that cause you tension as you develop your gender identity.

When performing your gender stories, you can choose how to negotiate among your desires and motivations, the cultural norms for various contexts, and the specific audiences and settings you encounter. You can use your performances to try out new themes and plot lines in your stories and intentionally script your nonverbal and verbal behaviors. When responding to other people's reactions to your gender performances, you can consciously decide to acquiesce to their preferences regarding your performance, adapt by suppressing or editing aspects of your performance, or maintain your chosen gender story and continue to perform it. We hope that you will continue to consciously construct and perform the gender stories that are important to you so that you can fully develop the stories and performances that have value for you and that allow you to feel fulfilled as a gendered person.

In this class, you have focused on reading about and discussing gender. We hope we have made clear, however, that communicating gender is much more than reading a book and talking to other students. You and the people around you continually give and receive symbolic gender messages in your interactions with others. When you smile at a stranger on the bus, buy your girlfriend coffee, or walk by groups of other students on campus, you are communicating gender messages. You and everyone around you communicate gender all day, every day, through your appearances and all of your verbal and nonverbal behaviors. Everything you do and say in different contexts—at home, in school, at work, and when you are out with friends—on some level not only communicates gender but also contributes to the social construction of your culture's gendered reality.

How you construct and perform such gender stories has an important effect on the social construction of the gender binary. In chapter 7, we pointed out that when you craft and enact your own gender performances, you have an effect on the matrix or the cultural narrative that is the gender binary. In the same way that an individual's gender does not exist until it is socially constructed, cultural categories, definitions, and norms of gender also do not exist except as they are socially constructed. Gender performances function to reinforce or change existing cultural classifications, which are modified as the gender performances of individual people and groups are rejected or accommodated on a cultural level. In a direct way, then, your own consciously crafted and performed gender stories have the capacity to affect the binary system in which you live. Your stories and performances are forms of communication that can sustain the binary, modify existing gender definitions, or even develop new categories in new contexts.[10]

Although your contribution constitutes only one of the many threads in the ongoing collective creation of gendered reality, the way you have constructed your gender is a unique enactment of body and meaning. In other words, the meaning you assign to your own body through your gender stories and performances provides a lens on gender that no one else is able to provide in quite the same way. Consequently, the contribution you can make to the collective cocreation of gender cannot be made by anyone else; your intentional involvement, therefore, can have an effect on cultural categories, norms, and attitudes that no one else can offer.

BINARY RESTRICTIONS ON GENDER

The ability you have to affect the cultural gender binary by freely constructing and performing gender stories exists in tension with the binary matrix that functions to restrict and confine your choices regarding gender. Just as having spirited discussions about gender is easier in a classroom where you are studying gender, performing different forms of gender is also easier to do in an environment where you feel free to reflect on and even experiment with your gendered self. Such freedom of expression and experimentation, however, typically is not prevalent in the outside world.

The binary master narrative or matrix—the hegemonic ideology of gender—makes freely constructing and performing gender very difficult.

As we have discussed throughout this book, the binary gives you clear and strong messages in virtually all areas of your life about how you should be as a woman or a man. Although the pull of the binary is waning in some communities, it continues to affect not only how you behave but also how you think about your behavior and the responses of others to you. When you leave your classroom and try to construct and perform your gender stories consciously and deliberately, you may find that negotiating your gender is difficult because of the strong impact of the binary on your own behavior and on others' responses to your gender constructions.

Because of the strong and ubiquitous nature of the binary, you might find that you have difficulty performing gender in nonnormative ways and that you believe that you alone cannot have an impact on it. The dominant gender binary discourages you from thinking that you have an important role in how cultural norms, categories, and standards about gender are constructed. Not only are you provided a script for how to be a gendered person, you are also, to a large degree, taught to think that there is not much you can do about this script beyond choosing to think or live differently in your own private sphere. You have been taught that your options for changing public gendered life are restricted to voicing your opinion, criticizing others, and expressing your preferences by voting. Your culture does not highlight the ways you can exercise agency that we discussed in chapter 1—actively making changes yourself, influencing others to help you make changes, or reframing situations you want to alter. Few of us are taught that how we create ourselves as gendered people and perform our genders actually has a profound effect on the cultural gender system. In fact, whenever you perform gender—however you perform it—you are contributing to cultural gender communication and having an effect on the gender system in which everyone around you lives.

COCREATING GENDER SYSTEMS

That you play a role in constructing the cultural gender system in which you live means that you have an ongoing opportunity to have an effect on that system. Your conscious choices can sustain, modify, or create new systems. If you perform the binary's current construction of reality—if you believe in and are comfortable with the guidelines the binary system prescribes for being masculine and feminine—then you perpetuate the definitions, categories, and norms of that construction. Geoff, for example, grew up in a fundamentalist Christian household and is engaged to be married: "My fiancé and I plan to join a Bible study group for newly married Christians. We believe that God designed marriage to be a loving, holy institution, and we want to make sure that we are prepared to live out the Biblical promises that we will be making to each other on our wedding day. I want to learn how to be the head of my family; my fiancé wants to learn how to obey and support me." Geoff is expressing his comfort with and belief in one interpretation of the binary's master narrative. When he is married and performs his gender by taking on the responsibility of being the moral leader in his household, Geoff will be perpetuating and maintaining a certain interpretation of the binary—that of a Christian, married man. By performing his gender in a fashion consistent with this interpretation, Geoff will be socially constructing reality by cocreating the continuation of a binary world.

Perhaps you find yourself in a somewhat ambivalent position with respect to binary ideals, norms, and institutions. If you believe in some of what the binary tells you about being male or female but find some of the prescriptions unrealistic or confining, you can help modify the overall system by changing your gender performances. Perhaps you value your roles as a wife and a mother and find fulfillment in creating a comfortable and emotionally safe home for your husband and children. But perhaps you are also a college student who intends to have a successful career as a professor. The traditional binary script for you accommodates part but not all of what you want for yourself. You find yourself in the position of wanting to modify the binary prescriptions for wife and mother so that you can continue to nurture your family while pursuing your own growth as a scholar.

Another example of choosing to modify the binary is making the decision to get married if you are lesbian. The binary prescribes ideal forms of masculinity and femininity that come together to form a stable unit with the purpose of bearing and raising children—maintaining culture through the institution of family. You might decide to follow this prescription by getting married and having children, but you've modified the prescription by being a lesbian couple. By being a wife and mother who also pursues her education and career or by choosing to marry your lesbian partner, your performances contribute to ongoing cultural gender communication. This communication results in modifications of socially constructed gender reality—a reality that includes not only scripts that follow the binary's ideals but scripts that modify them as well.

If you find yourself outside of the binary master narrative—if the binary simply does not accommodate who you believe yourself to be or how you want the world to be—you can help cause a different world to come into existence by performing something different from the binary. Brigid has deliberately chosen to perform ambiguously in terms of gender: "I don't like being categorized in a certain way in terms of my gender, and I certainly am not about to dress in any frilly, feminine ways. But I also don't want to look male. I want to be something in between, so I deliberately choose clothing that doesn't mark me as one gender or the other. I wear my hair short and in a style that people don't see as either male or female." Because they innovate in the binary and present an alternative way of being gendered, Brigid's gender performances are altering the binary, opening up possibilities for ways to be that do not follow its expectations and norms.

The significance of your own gender performances to the cultural gender system cannot be overstated, which is why it is important that you think carefully and deliberately about the choices you make. You have the capacity to contribute to the nature of gender in the world in which you live whether your preference is for maintaining, modifying, or changing the gender binary. You are creating your gendered world and the kinds of norms and expectations that characterize it through the gender stories you craft and perform. We want you to realize that your own constructions and performances of gender are powerful mechanisms through which you cocreate the gendered world you share with others.

RESPECTING OTHER PEOPLE'S GENDER STORIES

Our third goal is for you to understand the gender stories and performances of other people and to reflect this understanding in respectful interactions with them. We want you to be aware that the way you interact with others has the ability to help create a certain kind of world—a world that is tolerant, welcoming, civil, and humane or one that is judgmental, hostile, and violent. Although we have focused on you as a performer of gender during most of this book, now we want to suggest that you also communicate gender in two other ways—as a character in other people's gender stories and as an audience for their performances. Whenever you interact with others, you become part of their ongoing narratives, and you serve as an audience for their performances. You are an integral part of other people's gender stories whenever you interact with them—when you borrow a pencil from the man who sits next to you in class, for example, applaud the performance of your favorite local band, or invite your new intimate partner to meet your mother. As a character in and audience member for others' gender performances, you have the opportunity to have a greater impact on gender than you might have imagined.

Each time you are a participant in the gender stories of others, you have the opportunity to contribute to their gender development in ways that are respectful and that display your willingness to understand stories that are not like your own. Likewise, each time you interact with someone else's gender story, you have the choice to disregard and reject that story. This means that what matters is not simply that you are a character or an audience member; what matters is what kind of character or audience member you choose to be. How you interact with others becomes a part of other individuals' personal stories and, as a result, may be incorporated into their future gender performances and their gender identities.

You have influence on how other people see themselves as gendered people and create their ongoing gender stories. How you exercise this influence, in turn, socially constructs a certain kind of world. When individuals interact with respect and regard, the world that they create collectively is one that is civil and humane. A civil world is one in which people treat one another with courtesy, politeness, and esteem. A humane world is one in which people value one another's humanity and are compassionate toward each other. A civil and humane world is one in which all people are accorded immanent or inherent value and are accorded respect.

CULTURAL RESTRICTIONS ON CIVIL INTERACTIONS

The desire to contribute to a civil and humane world exists in tension with the reality of practices in Western society. Many of the models for interaction that you see around you—in popular culture, politics, government, and the legal system, for example—are not based on respect and regard. People often are not trying to understand the choices and lifestyles of others; rather, the tendency is to disregard and discredit stories that do not match preferred narratives. The adversarial model teaches you to view your way of life and your system of beliefs as superior to the lifestyles and beliefs of other people and to work to keep your views dominant. You are encouraged, as a result, to turn away from the opportunities in your life to engage respectfully with people who live differently from how you live.

There are a number of common ways in which society encourages you to distance yourself from and even reject people who are different from you. One way is by isolating and insulating yourself from perspectives and lifestyles that are different so that you can protect your beliefs and ways of living from challenges. The most immediate way to do this is to surround yourself with people who are pretty much like you. Most people do this to some extent—your closest friends are probably people who share most of your beliefs and whose lifestyles are somewhat similar to yours. But there are many mechanisms and institutions in society that encourage or facilitate this behavior. Technology, for example, allows you to isolate yourself by participating only in blogs or with media that address topics and opinions you already know about and accept as valid. You might watch only *Fox News* or *The Daily Show with Jon Stewart*, for example, in order to confirm and bolster your own belief system and lifestyle.

Some churches suggest very specific behaviors and beliefs for their congregants and develop close-knit communities around those beliefs and lifestyles—churches, for example, that advise young adults to maintain their virginity until marriage. These churches advise spending time only with other young adults who have taken vows of abstinence because having a community of like-minded friends will reduce the temptation to have sex. Isolating yourself, then, is encouraged in various ways in US society. As a result, you may have little motivation for trying to understand or even encounter gender stories and performances that differ from your own.

The cultural view that criticism is an appropriate and acceptable response to those who think and act differently also restricts the effort to understand multiple perspectives. When individuals engage in criticism, they judge the people who hold different perspectives as bad, stupid, incorrect, or immoral. This kind of response is a very common way in which some politicians, comedians, and church leaders, to name a few, respond to perspectives and lifestyles that are different from theirs. They often blame others—often certain genders—for what they perceive as societal problems. When people blame gay people who want to get married for the instability of modern marriages, they are engaging in this response to diversity. Stereotyping and scapegoating are other forms that criticism can assume, attributing a certain characteristic to a group. When people talk about the harm caused to society by feminists or by mothers who work when their children are small, they are stereotyping large groups of people and using them as scapegoats for society's ills. Criticizing is a practice rampant in Western society; adopting it as a mode of response to difference is very easy to do. Once this becomes your dominant mode of response to difference, your own belief system and way of living may feel safe and unchallenged, but you have little motivation to interact respectfully with people who do not behave and believe as you do.

Probably the most common response to encountering difference is trying to change others so that they conform to your preferences. In chapter 8, we discussed ways people might try to change you—by rejecting you, discriminating against you, harassing you, or even being violent toward you. In Western culture, attempting to change others through various forms of persuasion is a key dynamic of the political and legal systems. Trying to change other people as the response to difference can be seen, for example, when people try to pass laws that make whatever is different illegal or when they ridicule people who look and act differently from them. Advertising, marketing, sales, religion, politics, friendships, and family are all arenas in which efforts are made to persuade others to adopt certain ideas, values, and behaviors. Attempting to change others happens at the interpersonal level as well. Howard, for example, is trying to persuade his girlfriend to change: "She's content to live apart—she says she needs her own space—but I think we're at the stage of our relationship where we should make more of a commitment. I'm trying to convince her to live with me." Like isolating and criticizing, the effort to make others change is so common in US society that it seems like a natural way to respond to difference. Such tactics may protect you from fully engaging with ideas that could affect you and your beliefs. They also make it less likely that you will embrace opportunities for understanding and possibly being transformed by other people's perspectives.[11]

Remember that you are creating your reality through your communicative choices and that the type of communication you use creates the particular kind of world in which you live. If your usual approach to people who think and behave differently from you is to criticize or try to change them, you may contribute to an adversarial, hostile, and contentious world marked by "a pervasive warlike atmosphere."[12] You might also contribute to a homogenous world in which everyone's thoughts and actions are similar to one another's. Isolating, criticizing, and trying to change others can produce negative emotions such as feelings of inadequacy, humiliation, guilt, and anger. Linguist Suzette Haden Elgin describes the world that is created through these kinds of responses to difference in this way: "Everybody bickering and badmouthing and putting each other down."[13] When you refuse to interact openly and respectfully with people who are different from you, you forego the opportunity to help construct a more civil and humane world.

COCREATING A CIVIL AND HUMANE WORLD

The desire to help socially construct a more civil and humane world exists in tension, then, with societal norms for encountering people whose gender stories and performances are different from your own. Isolating yourself, criticizing others, and trying to change others are cultural norms, but there are other approaches you can take that will help socially construct a more civil and human world. You have choices about the kind of influence you want to have as a character in other people's gender stories and as an audience member for their performances. Being a character or an audience member in gender stories that you appreciate and with which you agree is uncomplicated. In these cases, you simply provide support. If you find yourself a character or audience member for a gender story with which you disagree or with which you are uncomfortable, the situation is more difficult.

Chapter 8 reviewed a number of options in such situations—rejecting the performance through responses such as persuasion, harassment, discrimination, and violence. Because the binary gender system and the hegemony in which you live have reinforced the sense that one way must be right/moral/superior and the other wrong/immoral/inferior, you are likely to position yourself—at least in some areas of your life—in opposition to those who differ from you and to adopt some of these strategies. Although these approaches might make you feel safe and self-assured, you may actively harm others. Another problem with these approaches is that you miss out on opportunities to be influenced and maybe even transformed by other people and their stories—to cocreate a civil and humane world that acknowledges and respects different beliefs and lifestyles.

An alternate approach that you can take to encountering difference—when you find yourself confronted with a gender performance that is offensive to or uncomfortable for you—is to stay open to and welcome the difference. This response does not require that you support or affirm a particular gender story or performance but only that you try to understand and respect it. English professor Susan Stanford Friedman offers the metaphor of the "good traveler" as a way to position yourself when you come across someone or something that seems odd and different to you.[14] Being a good traveler means admitting your ignorance of the other person and staying aware of your own biases. When you travel to a foreign country, you look forward to seeing unfamiliar sights and people, and you are open to learning from newness. Friedman says this is how you can approach people who look or act in ways that are unfamiliar to you—you can respect them and try to understand how and why they present themselves as they do.

Every time you interact around a gender story or performance, you are choosing a certain kind of world by the nature of your communicative choices. How you perform gender and how you respond to the gender choices of others helps to create the kind of world in which you live. When you choose to communicate in ways that are respectful and open to the different choices of others, you create a reality of multiplicity and respect and compassion for difference. In this world, the gender stories that you craft and perform are appreciated, and you value the performances of others as well.

INVITING A NEW WORLD

Participating in spirited conversations about gender, consciously creating and performing gender, and trying to understand other people's stories all require an ability to deal with difference. A tool that we find useful and that we encourage you to use to accomplish all three goals is invitational rhetoric.[15] This perspective for approaching difference constitutes an invitation to the audience to enter the world of another and to see it as that person does.

To be invitational with others means to invite them to show you a perspective or vision—one that may be very different from your own. At the same time, of course, you are offering other people an invitation to understand your perspective. As psychotherapist Carl R. Rogers explains this idea, "to be with another in this way means that for the time being, you lay aside your own views and values in order to enter another's world without prejudice."[16] When you try to understand someone's performance of gender that is disturbing or disconcerting, you "venture outside the walls that normally protect" you from "things that don't fit" your worldview. You make room for another point of view.[17]

Because of hegemonic power dynamics—some views and lifestyles are considered more valid than others—taking an invitational stance is different for different people. If you are a person with a normative or hegemonic view of gender who has been or is prejudiced against people who have other views and lifestyles, being invitational means trying to understand not only the beliefs of people who are different from you but also making an effort to understand your own biases and assumptions. In other words, you make the effort to understand yourself, too. On the other hand, if you are a person with views or lifestyles that do not conform to hegemonic positions, being invitational may mean trying to understand how people prejudiced against you think and feel. These two forms of invitation—being open to exploring your own prejudices and trying to understand people who deny the validity of your beliefs and lifestyle—obviously require different efforts. You might ask: Why should I try to understand someone who is prejudiced against me? The reason is that the effort helps you contribute to the creation of a world where people acknowledge and listen to one another and in which you create the opportunity for greater understanding.

A key feature of invitational rhetoric is that you enter an interaction open to the possibility that your perspective might change. As Rogers notes, "if you are willing to enter [another's] private world and see the way life appears to him . . . you run the risk of being changed yourself."[18] When you openly contemplate different ways of doing gender without being judgmental, you could encounter a fragment that changes some aspect of what you believe and how you yourself perform gender. Note that a willingness to change is not the same thing as being required to change. We have not changed our position that you are able to do gender and believe about gender however you please. Invitational rhetoric simply asks that when you encounter beliefs about gender and gender performances that are different, you engage them fully, which can mean that there is a possibility you will decide to change.

This willingness to change, of course, can be very uncomfortable and even scary. Some of the things you know to be true and right about gender might very well be challenged by someone's gender performance. You may be asked to call into question some ideas about gender that are very important to you. As consultant and author Annette Simmons points out, "There is always a risk when you engage in the process of learning. Even though you can be assured that this mental redesign will incorporate a higher level of understanding than you have right now, the potential disruption is daunting. Like renovating a house, it can be inconvenient to add that new wing."[19]

Invitational rhetoric involves adopting a few key communication behaviors as you respond to difference. As a performer, you adopt verbal and nonverbal behaviors that convey your willingness to encounter and be transformed by difference. One such behavior is that you use communication in a way that encourages others to share their stories with you. If you are going to understand someone's gender story, that person must be willing to share it with you—both nonverbally, as people always do when they express gender—and through verbal explanation of thoughts, feelings, motivations, and desires around the performance. There are some things to keep in mind as you communicate with others around their gender stories to let them know that you are willing to have them perform their gender stories for you. In addition, you are willing for them to share their perspectives on those performances with you. One way to prompt such sharing is to create particular external conditions—safety and freedom—in the interaction. When these conditions are present in an interaction, the possibility increases that others will feel free to share their stories with you in gender performances.

The condition of safety is the condition of feeling free from danger or risk. When you create safety through your communication, other people trust you, are not fearful of interacting with you, and feel you are working with and not against them. If participants in an interaction do not feel secure physically, emotionally, and intellectually, they will be reluctant to share their ideas about gender or to enact certain kinds of gender performances. If others are afraid you will harm them, for example, they will not feel safe. Safety concerns the degree to which those with whom you are interacting feel they can perform certain ways of being gendered without being harmed in some way. In other words, safety concerns the sense other people have about whether their performances will be treated with respect and care. To grant safety to others means, of course, that you do not physically harm them, but it also means that you do not dismiss ideas about gender with which you do not agree; ridicule others; or judge another person as silly, stupid, or ignorant for choosing to perform gender as they do. You can exhibit safety by refraining from some behaviors, but you can also show your willingness to experience other people's gender stories by making positive comments and by affirming them with your nonverbal behaviors.

A second condition to create in your interactions with the gender performances of others is freedom, which is the power to choose or decide. When you allow freedom to others, they are able to make decisions about what to believe about gender, the stories they want to construct, and how to perform those stories. When freedom is present in an interaction, you do not exert pressure on the other person to make the same choices that you do. Freedom also is created when you do not place restrictions on the nature of another's gender performance. If another person's performance challenges assumptions you consider sacred, you don't discontinue your interaction with the person but continue to engage with the gender performance. Allowing other people the freedom to be who they are might mean that you deliberately interact in contexts that make you uncomfortable, choosing to value their freedom to enact gender as they choose over your own sense of comfort.

Probably the most important means by which you can create the external condition of freedom is to communicate to others that they do not have to perform gender in the way that you prefer. You convey to them that they can choose not to accept your viewpoint about appropriate gender stories and performances without fear of reprisal, ridicule, punishment, or humiliation. You communicate to them that your relationship with them does not depend on their performing gender in ways that align with your preferences. You allow them self-determination, recognizing that they are the authorities on their own lives. You accord respect to their capacity and right to construct their gender stories and performances as they choose. As feminist theorist Sonia Johnson explains, you trust that others are doing the best they can at the moment and simply need "to be unconditionally accepted as the experts on their own lives."[20]

Responding to the gender performances of others from an invitational perspective involves certain kinds of communication. If you have created the conditions of safety and freedom in the interaction so that others are willing to perform gender as they choose in their interactions with you and perhaps to engage in discussion with you about their performances, you want to respond to their performances and their disclosures with openness. This openness involves letting go of your ideas about how others should do gender and genuinely letting them inform your thinking. You might think of this open stance as "a hosting. This hosting of other is as a guest, as a not-me."[21] As communication theorist Lisbeth Lipari explains this stance, "What I do need to do is to stand . . . with you, right next to you, and to belong to you, fully present to the ongoing expression of you. Letting go of my ideas about who you are, who I am, what 'should' be. I let all that go, and stay present, attending, aware."[22]

When you react invitationally, you try to make others' perspectives vivid in your own mind. You don't argue mentally with their display of gender, you pay close attention to the performance instead of focusing on formulating a good comeback or an argument against their performance, and you encourage them to perform their preferred gender as fully as they can, giving their gender stories as complete an expression as possible. You ask questions, if possible, to test your understanding of their gender performance. As you listen to, observe, and reflect on the gender performances of others, you are asking yourself questions such as: "How attentive am I to this person and to this gender performance?" and "What gender story is this person trying to share with me through this performance?" "How are my experiences and values affecting what I am observing?"[23] "What could I say or do to show I understand?"

Invitational rhetoric is an approach to difference that can help all of us communicate gender in ways that will bring about the world in which we want to live. When we open ourselves to other people with a genuine intent to understand their perspectives, we invite the construction of a world of multiplicity. When we craft and perform our gender stories with the intent to share our genuine selves, we invite the construction of a world that includes our perspectives and lifestyles in cultural systems of gender. When we respond to the gender stories and performances of other people with openness and respect, we invite the construction of a civil and humane world where we feel safe to be ourselves, free to perform whatever gendered stories we choose.

YOUR NEXT CHAPTER

Our intent throughout this book has been to engage with you about gender stories in order to increase your awareness of how you construct and perform your own stories and to expose you to how other people construct and perform their stories. When you engage in discussions with people who have different beliefs about gender, you honor multiple gender stories. While you are negotiating your own gender, other people are, too. Each of us is attempting to live out the gendered selves that we find valuable and appropriate. When you enact being a gendered person, you affect the cultural system of categories, norms, and attitudes regarding gender. How you act toward other people's gender stories influences how their stories develop. All of these activities communicate gender and contribute to the social construction of a certain kind of gendered world—one in which differences are treated with respect or not.

We hope this book has provided you with useful ways for you to think about gender as you continue participating in the cultural conversation and head into your future as a gendered person. We trust that your unique contribution to your world will be insightful and valuable. Just as you are crafting and will continue to craft the gender stories that make sense for your life, you will come up with your own answers for how to respond to the gender stories of others. In the end, we know that, indeed, you will "find your own strategies, invent your own solutions. Which is as it should be."[24]

■ NOTES

[1] Margaret J. Wheatley, *Leadership and the New Science: Discovering Order in a Chaotic World*, 2nd ed. (San Francisco: Berrett-Koehler, 1999), 67.

[2] Karen E. Rosenblum and Toni-Michelle C. Travis, "The Meaning of Difference: Framework Essay," in *The Meaning of Difference: American Constructions of Race, Sex*

and Gender, Social Class, and Sexual Orientation, ed. Karen E. Rosenblum and Toni-Michelle C. Travis, 3rd ed. (Boston: McGraw-Hill, 2003), 323.

³ Alan O'Connor, "Culture and Communication," in *Questioning the Media: A Critical Introduction*, ed. John Downing, Ali Mohammadi, and Annabelle Sreberny-Mohammadi (Newbury Park, CA: Sage, 1990), 36.

⁴ Victoria Pruin DeFrancisco and Catherine Helen Palczewski, *Communicating Gender Diversity: A Critical Approach* (Los Angeles: Sage, 2007), 23.

⁵ Wendy Brown, "Gender in Counterpoint," *Feminist Theory* 4 (2003): 367.

⁶ Pat Arneson, "Provocation: An Ethic of Listening in/and Social Change," *International Journal of Listening* 24 (2010): 167–68.

⁷ Lisbeth Lipari, "Listening, Thinking, Being," *Communication Theory* 20 (2010): 355.

⁸ Martha C. Nussbaum, *Cultivating Humanity: A Classical Defense of Reform in Liberal Education* (Cambridge, MA: Harvard University Press, 1997), 10–11.

⁹ Suzette Haden Elgin, *The Last Word on the Gentle Art of Verbal Self-Defense* (New York: Prentice-Hall, 1987), 24.

¹⁰ Peg Birmingham, "Toward an Ethic of Desire: Derrida, Fiction, and the Law of the Feminine," in *Feminist Perspectives on Jacques Derrida*, ed. Nancy J. Holland (University Park: Pennsylvania State University Press, 1997), 133.

¹¹ This discussion of various possible responses to difference is summarized from Sonja K. Foss and Karen A. Foss, *Inviting Transformation: Presentational Speaking for a Changing World*, 3rd ed. (Long Grove, IL: Waveland, 2012), 3–9.

¹² Deborah Tannen, *The Argument Culture: Stopping America's War of Words* (New York: Ballantine, 1998), 3.

¹³ Suzette Haden Elgin, "Peacetalk 101," 2000, preface, www.forloving-kindness.org/peacetalk2.html

¹⁴ Susan Stanford Friedman, "Academic Feminism and Interdisciplinarity," *Feminist Studies* 27 (2001): 3.

¹⁵ Invitational rhetoric was created and theorized by Sonja K. Foss and Cindy L. Griffin, "Beyond Persuasion: A Proposal for an Invitational Rhetoric," *Communication Monographs* 62 (1995): 2–18. For further development of the theory of invitational rhetoric, see: Foss and Foss, *Inviting Transformation*; and Jennifer Emerling Bone, Cindy L. Griffin, and T. M. Linda Scholz, "Beyond Traditional Conceptualizations of Rhetoric: Invitational Rhetoric and a Move Toward Civility," *Western Journal of Communication* 72 (2008): 434–62. Much of the summary of invitational rhetoric in this section is from Foss and Foss, *Inviting Transformation*, 9–19.

¹⁶ Carl R. Rogers, *A Way of Being* (Boston: Houghton Mifflin, 1980), 143.

¹⁷ Annette Simmons, *A Safe Place for Dangerous Truths: Using Dialogue to Overcome Fear & Distrust at Work* (New York: American Management Association, 1999), 99.

¹⁸ Carl R. Rogers, *On Becoming a Person: A Therapist's View of Psychotherapy* (Boston: Houghton Mifflin, 1961), 333.

¹⁹ Simmons, *A Safe Place for Dangerous Truths*, 45.

²⁰ Sonia Johnson, *The Ship That Sailed Into the Living Room: Sex and Intimacy Reconsidered* (Estancia, NM: Wildfire, 1991), 162.

²¹ Lipari, "Listening, Thinking, Being," 350.

²² Lipari, "Listening, Thinking, Being," 350–51.

²³ "Improving Listening Skills," www.livestrong.com/article/14657-improving-listening-skills/

²⁴ Robin Morgan, *The Anatomy of Freedom: Feminism in Four Dimensions* (New York: W. W. Norton, 1994), 329.

INDEX